ABOUT ISLAND PRESS

Island Press, a nonprofit organization, publishes, markets, and distributes the most advanced thinking on the conservation of our natural resources—books about soil, land, water, forests, wildlife, and hazardous and toxic wastes. These books are practical tools used by public officials, business and industry leaders, natural resource managers, and concerned citizens working to solve both local and global resource problems.

Founded in 1978, Island Press reorganized in 1984 to meet the increasing demand for substantive books on all resource-related issues. Island Press publishes and distributes under its own imprint and offers these services to other nonprofit organizations.

Support for Island Press is provided by Apple Computer, Inc., Mary Reynolds Babcock Foundation, Geraldine R. Dodge Foundation, The Energy Foundation, The Charles Engelhard Foundation, The Ford Foundation, Glen Eagles Foundation, The George Gund Foundation, William and Flora Hewlett Foundation, The Joyce Foundation, The John D. and Catherine T. MacArthur Foundation, The Andrew W. Mellon Foundation, The Joyce Mertz-Gilmore Foundation, The New-Land Foundation, The J. N. Pew, Jr. Charitable Trust, Alida Rockefeller, The Rockefeller Brothers Fund, The Florence and John Schumann Foundation, The Tides Foundation, and individual donors.

RURAL
ENVIRONMENTAL
PLANNING
FOR SUSTAINABLE
COMMUNITIES

RURAL ENVIRONMENTAL PLANNING FOR SUSTAINABLE COMMUNITIES

Frederic O. Sargent

Paul Lusk

José A. Rivera

María Varela

ISLAND PRESS

Washington, D.C. ☐ *Covelo, California*

Portions of this publication were adapted from *Rural Environmental Planning,* Vervana Publishers, 1976, and *Rural Water Planning,* Vervana Publishers, 1979.

Illustrations by C. Kinsman Design

Library of Congress Cataloging-in-Publication Data

Rural environmental planning for sustainable communities / Frederic O. Sargent . . . [et al.].
    p. cm.
    Rev. ed. of: Rural environmental planning / Frederic O. Sargent. 1976.
    Includes index.
    ISBN 1-55963-025-6 (alk. paper).—ISBN 1-55963-024-8 (pbk.: alk. paper)
    1. Regional planning—United States—Citizen participation.
2. Environmental policy—United States—Citizen participation.
3. Rural development projects—New Mexico—Case studies. 4. Rural development projects—Vermont—Case studies. 5. Environmental policy—New Mexico—Citizen participation—Case studies. 6. Environmental policy—Vermont—Citizen participation—Case studies. 7. Land use, Rural—New Mexico—Planning—Case studies. 8. Land use, Rural—Vermont—Planning—Case studies. I. Sargent, Frederic O. II. Sargent, Frederic O. Rural environmental planning.
HT392.N47 1991
363. 7'058'0973—dc20   91–2620
                                                                     CIP

Printed on recycled, acid-free paper

Manufactured in the United States of America
10 9 8 7 6 5 4 3

Contents

Part II
THE COMPONENTS OF RURAL ENVIRONMENTAL PLANNING

Preface

RURAL ENVIRONMENTAL PLANNING (REP) is a method used by citizens in small towns and rural areas to plan their own future. The area covered by a rural environmental plan ranges from a village of a few hundred people to a town with a population of up to ten thousand. The area may also be defined by a geographic feature—a watershed, part of a river basin, a mountain valley, or some other place where people share an interest in the sustainable use of natural and other resources for the betterment of their community. REP assumes that the primary social value of rural people is to enhance a community's long-term viability by respecting the carrying capacity of the natural environment.

REP derives its strength from the direct participation of those people affected by a plan: they determine its goals, shape its content, and implement its components. REP reduces the cost of planning by drawing on the expertise of state universities, public agencies, not-for-profit organizations, volunteer-professionals from the private sector, and increasingly, graduates of rural planning programs—all vital resources available to rural people when they plan for their future.

Rural Environmental Planning for Sustainable Communities is intended as a guide for rural citizens, planning commissioners, small town and rural planners, and others seeking practical information on how to manage local resources and improve their community's quality of life. It is also designed as a manual for planning professionals, state and local government officials, agency managers, and community organizers, and as a methods text for rural planning students.

The first edition of *Rural Environmental Planning*, by Frederic O. Sargent, professor and former director of the rural planning graduate program at the University of Vermont, was published in 1976 and reprinted in 1977 and 1980 in response to growing demand. This revised and enlarged edition is coauthored by Paul Lusk,

xi

associate professor of architecture and planning in the community and regional planning program at the University of New Mexico; José A. Rivera, associate professor of public administration and director of the Southwest Hispanic Research Institute at the University of New Mexico; María Varela, rural development specialist and adjunct professor at the School of Architecture and Planning, University of New Mexico, and professor Frederic O. Sargent.

There have been many changes in rural communities, in the forces that affect them, in opportunities to control their future, and in the tools available to them since the original publication of *Rural Environmental Planning* in 1976. This updated, enlarged text draws from over a decade of additional experience with REP in New Mexico, New England, and other regions of North America. The book retains case studies from the first edition and adds new ones from the Southwest and other areas of the United States. Two chapters have been included on planning for sustainable economic development. The text confirms the interregional nature of REP's basic principles and practices as well as REP's potential breadth of application and multicultural relevance.

Contributions, case studies, and results from others involved in REP are welcome. This text will be updated in accordance with changing conditions and project results. Case studies and other materials that demonstrate REP principles can be shared with the team of authors and with other interested persons by writing to one of the following addresses:

REP Exchange
Professors Lusk, Rivera & Varela
School of Architecture & Planning
University of New Mexico
Albuquerque, New Mexico 87131

REP Exchange
Professor Frederic O. Sargent
Dept. of Resource Economics
University of Vermont
Burlington, Vermont 05401

Acknowledgments

THE AUTHORS WISH to acknowledge and thank the many students who contributed to the development of rural environmental plans at the Universities of Vermont and New Mexico. Gratitude also is extended to various academics, practitioners, and professionals who provided information for the case studies and examples featured in this text. Special recognition goes to the Southwest Hispanic Research Institute at the University of New Mexico, particularly Frances Rico and Rosemarie Romero, for seeing the manuscript through many drafts. José A. Rivera, director of the Institute, served as managing editor of the manuscript from inception.

PART I

The Basis of Rural
Environmental Planning

1

The Scope of Rural Environmental Planning

RURAL ENVIRONMENTAL PLANNING (REP) is a community process to determine, develop, and implement creative plans for small communities and rural
areas. The goal of the REP process is to establish sustainable rural communities by balancing economic development and environmental protection in
accord with the carrying capacity of the land. REP treats conservation of the
natural environment and development of the human community as equally
important. REP develops people to plan and develops plans for people.

Rural, in this context, means open or sparsely populated areas as well as
villages, small towns, Indian pueblos, and other tribal communities. *Environmental* is used here in its broadest sense, meaning all the surroundings,
including social, cultural, physical, and economic. *Planning* involves people
in the process of assessing needs, inventorying resources, formulating goals,
drafting and testing a plan, and then adjusting that plan over time. The written plan is the map, not the destination. The intent of REP is to develop the
ability of rural residents to manage a sustainable environment, a viable community economy, and other aspects that make up the rural ecosystem.

This book considers the rural community as the center, the providers of
planning and development services as a supporting ring. Local citizens determine community goals; educational institutions lend the services of environmental planners and student assistants to coordinate REP; selective teams
from public and volunteer agencies contribute technical data, analysis, and
preliminary recommendations.

REP is a partnership among three participants: the client, the planner, and
the technical team. The client can be a single unincorporated community, a

political jurisdiction such as a village, town, or county, or an Indian pueblo or tribe. It also can be a multiple-jurisdiction area such as a watershed, a cluster of mountain villages, or any other geographic area where people have a common interest in the sustainable use of shared resources. The planner is the organizer, coordinator, and facilitator of REP. The role of rural environmental planner may be filled by a faculty member, a graduate student, a recent graduate of rural planning at a state university, a rural-planning specialist with a state planning or economic development agency, or a qualified professional engaged by residents of the community.

Technical teams are people who have the expertise to assist the community during various stages of inventorying, planning, and implementation. Team members supply data, analysis, and preliminary recommendations. These technically skilled experts may come from a state university, state or federal agencies, not-for-profit organizations, or professionals from the private sector. What is important to the REP process is that the technical team and the

STATE UNIVERSITIES
Rural Planners,
Natural Scientists,
Libraries, Data Banks

FEDERAL AGENCIES
U.S. Department
of Agriculture:
SCS, FmHA, REA

STATE AGENCIES
Natural Resources,
Economic Development
and Tourism Departments

THE RURAL COMMUNITY
Citizen Volunteers
Planning Commission
Town Officials

COUNTY AGENCIES
Extension Agent,
County Managers,
Planning Boards

REGIONAL AGENCIES
Councils of Government,
Soil and Water
Conservation Districts,
RC&D Areas

NOT-FOR-PROFIT ORGANIZATIONS
Foundations, Churches,
Community Development Corporations

FIGURE 1.1. The Rural Environmental Planning Process: Sources of Planning and Development Assistance

rural residents form a partnership of mutual learning. In the transfer of knowledge and skills, each learns from the other. REP allows for the time it takes for this relationship to grow. The confidence that develops from successful interaction between community members and the technical team cannot be reproduced by one or two meetings, workshops, or information sessions. Rather, confidence is built over time by successes that result from the REP process.

Some critics of REP say the approach is value-loaded and biased. Nothing could be closer to the truth. The assumptions and values behind REP are as follows:

1. Rural people place a high value on self-reliance and self-determination. They have experience with techniques for cultural and economic survival. They can make decisions regarding their long-term interests, design and carry out programs, evaluate the results of their work, and make necessary adjustments.

2. Rural people value cooperation as a guide to problem-solving. This attitude has evolved from generations of experience in rural living, where cooperation is a major tool of survival and community maintenance.

3. Long-term sustainability of a rural environment is achieved when citizens guide economic development according to the "physical carrying capacities" of the ecosystem. Land ownership is valued not just for its market value but also for sustaining a way of life. Consideration of the ecosystem's physical carrying capacity assumes that, although efficiency of use can vary, physical and natural resources are finite and can bear only so much use.

4. Increasing the self-reliance of citizens in rural communities can be the basis for sustainability. A self-reliant community possesses the knowledge, skills, resources, and vision to identify changing conditions, locate appropriate technical assistance, and initiate actions in a manner that conserves the rural environment and distributes benefits in an equitable manner.

In planning for rural self-reliance, human, animal, and plant ecologies are understood as *the* prime interdependent system. The rural community is seen as the conservator of its own resources, habitat, and culture. Local citizens are directly involved in the control of community assets as they plan for the retention, enrichment, and equitable use of those assets for present and future generations.

Conventional large-scale urban planning assumes that growth is inevitable and desirable, that increasing the tax base is a prime concern, and that authorities setting public goals are the planners and municipal administrators. REP employs a more democratic method of determining public goals: people are asked what they want. REP helps people to evaluate what they have, to envision choices for the future, and then to realize that they have the competence *and* the responsibility to act on those choices. REP results in new and sometimes alternative public goals, often very different from traditional goals.

REP is an open planning process. This means it involves as many citizens as possible in each step of planning and decision-making. As described in chapter 3, citizens define goals and make choices, take field trips to study existing conditions and land uses, hold public meetings to determine preferences and priorities for resource access, development, and protection, and so on. The involvement of local citizens in an open and democratic planning process helps to shape a plan in their minds as well as on paper and thus enhances the prospect that the plan will be implemented.

REP should not be confused with regional planning. Regional planning— a long-established subdiscipline of planning—addresses regions with urban centers or very large geographical land areas such as whole river basins or clusters of counties within a state. In traditional large-scale urban planning, the first step is often a projection of population growth, proposed commercial and industrial growth, jobs needed, housing needed, and the public facilities and transportation networks to serve all this. Land-use maps are prepared and colored yellow, red, blue, purple, and gray to allocate these projected needs. Land left over is colored green and labeled "open space." Open space may include cemeteries, wasteland, or other land that cannot be developed. In REP, the approach is the opposite. First, lands to support agriculture, recreation, wildlife, and soil and water conservation, as well as natural areas such as mountains, mesas, river valleys, and wetlands, are identified, classified, and mapped in multiple shades and patterns of green. Lands left over are colored red or yellow and designated for intensive uses: residential, commercial, and industrial.

REP also differs from conventional urban planning in the methods it employs for determining and developing public goals, in projecting future land-use needs, in the concepts and techniques it uses for implementation, and in the relevance it has to citizens of rural communities. This book, in fact, is intended for use by citizens in rural areas as well as by professional planners and technicians.

COMPONENTS OF REP

Rural Environmental Planning is defined by listing its significant components. The first three chapters in REP, Part I, describe the basis for planning rural environments and how this process differs from, yet complements, urban and regional planning. The basic concepts and the scope of *Rural Environmental Planning* are defined in chapter 1. The history of planning for rural settlements and an update on recent perspectives are described in chapter 2. How to get started, the role of jurisdictions, and steps in creating and implementing a plan are discussed in chapter 3.

Eight components of REP are defined in Part II. The discovery and development of community goals are discussed in chapter 4. The purpose and process of inventorying resources are detailed in chapter 5. Methods of classifying and protecting natural areas are described in chapter 6, while chapter 7 lists ways and gives examples of keeping land in agriculture. Chapters 8 and 9 present methods and examples of planning lake and river basins. How to plan for rural character, recreation, and historic preservation are described in chapter 10. Chapter 11 expresses the concern for equity and plan evaluation.

Part III focuses on guiding the process of rural development. Ways to assess economic options and examples of growth management are described in chapter 12. Elements, examples, and a case study of sustainable economic development are presented in chapters 13 and 14. The legal framework of planning and relevant case examples are presented in chapter 15.

The chapters that follow provide detailed methods and examples of REP. Because of their special importance, several issues taken up in detail later are emphasized here: economic development using local resources, diversity and equity as the basis for sustainable growth, the protection of natural areas and the preservation of wildlife habitats, the maintenance of agricultural land, conservation zoning, public access to public waters, water-quality improvement, provision for rural recreation, and planning for "rural quality."

In REP, economic development using local resources is the foundation for guiding growth. Development should be consistent with land capacities and community goals. A rural environmental plan requires the protection of natural cycles if economic growth is to be sustained. For instance, instead of draining and filling a marsh for an industrial site, the marsh is evaluated as a flood reduction sponge or wildlife habitat. The industry is located not on the cheapest land but where long-term costs for the entire community are the lowest.

In REP, economic growth can be a major goal only when it is compatible with environmental well being. REP is based on the assumption that if the quality of the environment is maintained, land values will actually increase. The most profitable use of the land can be developed in concert with the best environmental and social uses. In chapter 2 the history and evolution of these concepts and new dimensions are described. The definition of the elements of sustainable economic development and their application are presented in chapter 13. Chapter 14 then describes an expanded case study incorporating each of the elements.

The notion of diversity and equity as the basis for economic growth recognizes that increasing the number and variety of income sources can help rural residents to guide economic growth in balance with environmental objectives. From the outset, a rural environmental plan identifies and incorporates the public interest. Growth is permitted in accordance with the ability of the local jurisdiction to supply public services, to build and maintain roads and schools, to retain the rural character, and to protect historic sites and cultural resources. In the REP process we assume that the whole public, not just a favored few, should participate in planning and have access to the quality environment that is its end. Methods to achieve a more sustainable, resilient, and equitable economy are discussed in chapters 11, 12, 13, and 14.

The protection of natural areas and the preservation of wildlife habitats are readily appreciated by rural residents. A natural area is any area that concerned citizens (those affected) say should be protected and maintained in its natural state for present and future public use. This definition is vague because each area is unique. Examples of natural areas include mountain summits, caves, mesas, waterfalls, river floodways and marshes, virgin timber stands, habitats for unusual species, unique or representative geological formulations, and other natural phenomena with ecological significance. In REP, wildlife habitats are identified, located, and evaluated. Their protection is especially appropriate in areas that are unsuitable for development because of water conditions or topography. Techniques for identifying and inventorying these unique resources are presented in chapter 5. Techniques for protecting these areas and enhancing their performance are described in chapter 6.

The maintenance of agricultural land and the reduction of pressure for changing these lands to intensive urban use are mutually supportive goals in REP. Specific methods of accomplishing these goals—without depriving landowners of legal rights, without reducing the value of land accumulated or inherited over generations, and without significant cost to the community—are detailed in Chapter 7 and illustrated with case studies.

The concept of conservation, that is, the prudent and sustainable use of natural resources, is generally accepted as desirable by town officials, residents, and landowners in rural jurisdictions. Protecting these resources through conservation zoning, however, may encounter resistance from some rural residents. This book will propose strategies for identifying and conserving areas in order to protect water quality, prevent soil erosion, and achieve other community objectives. Such areas include steep slopes, stream banks, floodplains, arroyos, groundwater recharge areas, wetlands, and high elevations. Conservation designations or zones, when applied to areas unsuitable for development, do not have to deprive rural landowners of inherent land rights. In fact, conservation zones may enhance land values by guaranteeing wise land use in the area. Knowledgeable landowners understand this potential. Principles and examples of conservation zoning are described in chapters 5, 6, 7, and 10.

Public access to public waters is another concept important to people in rural areas. Typically, rural areas or towns with extensive frontage on public rivers, streams, or lakes have little or no public access. While exploring public goals, participants can promote awareness of the notion that public waters are owned by the community, that the public has a right to multipurpose access, and that such access is both feasible and appropriate. Methods for providing significant access to public lakes, streams, and rivers are described in chapters 8 and 9.

Water-quality improvement is a major thrust of REP in both humid and arid environments. Bodies of water including underground springs have often been used as dumping places for sewage and toxic waste. When people became concerned about water quality, they delegated the task of improving it to a state or federal agency. In REP, water supply and quality are looked upon as *the* prime public health, recreation, aesthetic, and economic resource of a rural area or town. Chapter 9 describes methods and examples of water quality planning.

Provision for recreation is indispensable for a quality rural environment. Traditionally, residents in rural New England could go anywhere in the jurisdiction of their town to hunt, fish, study nature, collect, think, hike, walk, climb, ski, or just sit. If the resident came across a No Trespassing sign, he or she knew it did not apply to local folk. This freedom of movement is being lost as rural areas undergo incremental urbanization with its attendant posting of trespassing signs. With the growth of metropolitan areas and the expansion of communication and transportation networks in all parts of the United States and Canada, the open countryside has largely fallen into private hands, resulting in limited public access. As an example, for many centuries in the Southwest, large parcels of open land were held in common by Indian, Spanish and Mexican settlers. Land grants were not deeded for private land until the application of English law and custom in the mid-1880s. To counter these trends and recapture freedom of movement outdoors, it is necessary to address the subject of common lands directly in a rural plan. Specific techniques to address rural recreation, trail networks, conservation zones, and related issues are detailed in Chapter 10.

Planning for rural quality is a conceptual and functional breakthrough of REP. People often say, "You can't plan aesthetics." However, there has been sufficient general agreement concerning aesthetic value to make planning for the character and quality of a rural community the least controversial section of most rural environmental plans. Most people concur that unscreened auto graveyards and billboards are ugly, and that trees, grass, flowers, and mountain views are beautiful. A plan may include landscaped areas in commercial zones, scenic overlooks or picnic areas, rigorous sign control, tree-cutting controls, and reforestation programs. It also may include the identification and preservation of "sacred places" such as the town plaza, a historic building, or a mountaintop. Chapter 10 describes approaches to and gives examples of planning for rural character, a sense of place and historic preservation.

CASE: CHAMA, NEW MEXICO

REP is applicable to diverse physical and cultural settings. For example, in 1980 a rural environmental plan was developed by the citizens of the village of Chama, New Mexico (1980 population 1,090), and its surrounding area (population 2,022).[1] The plan addressed areawide resource use and economic development to complement a 1973 master plan defining village services and capital improvements. While the REP process was supported by a grant from the Farmers Home Administration under the sponsorship of the Chama village council, and while rural planning students from the University of New Mexico contributed much of the technical work, it was mostly volunteer and nonprofit community organizations that implemented the plan's key components. Sections of the plan calling for valleywide coordination of health and social services were implemented by the community-owned and operated La Clinica del Pueblo. Sections calling for economic development based on agricultural and human resources were implemented by an agro-economic development corporation, Ganados del Valle. Inventorying human resources in the Chama Plan is described more fully in Chapter 5; economic development aspects are presented in Chapter 14.

CASE: SAN YSIDRO, NEW MEXICO

Then there is the example of the village of San Ysidro de los Dolores, New Mexico (population 198), which initiated a rural environmental plan in 1985. This predominantly Hispanic village has existed for almost two hundred years. The recent impact of increasing traffic flow, highway widening, and population growth prompted the citizens to seek help in identifying their resources and defining their goals. With the assistance of graduate students in the community and regional planning program at the University of New Mexico, a survey of every village household brought forth a clear idea of what the community wanted for the future. The survey helped to identify goals regarding local employment opportunities, outmigration, travel outside the valley, water quantity and quality, and growth.[2] The process of surveying goals in San Ysidro is described in chapter 4.

CASE: ESSEX, VERMONT

The following example is presented in greater detail because it illustrates well the initiation, evolution, and implementation of a rural environmental plan. It also shows how such a plan, developed by the people of an area rather than for them, can continue to affect community decisions for many years. In 1970 the village of Essex Junction, Vermont, and the surrounding town of Essex faced unprecedented growth. An IBM plant had been located in the village in 1957 and had undergone expansion in 1965. Recognizing the need for planning, and taking advantage of a federal "701" planning-assistance grant, the village and town engaged a planning firm active in the region to provide a comprehensive plan. The town plan, completed in 1967, was a typical municipal plan. It primarily addressed the built-up areas and those areas slated for development in the near future. It designated some areas of the town as open space and stressed the importance of preserving them but provided few details concerning their future use or management. The comprehensive plan was updated by the same firm in 1970.

During this period, the IBM expansion had brought many new residents to the area. They became concerned about the problems resulting from poorly planned growth and started to look into ways of improving prospects for future development. At planning commission meetings, they learned that the principle means of maintaining open space was large-lot zoning. Clustering and other methods familiar to some of the newer residents were not being considered.

At this time the University of Vermont, with the assistance of the Department of Agriculture's Soil Conservation Service (SCS), had designated REP technical teams to assist towns upon request. One of the new residents, Ann Harroun, and her colleagues called upon a technical team for assistance. A meeting held with the team resulted in the appointment by the Essex and Essex Junction planning commissions of a joint village-town natural resources subcommittee of twenty residents. The subcommittee was assisted by the Chittenden County technical team. This team consisted of six members: an SCS representative, the county forester, a University of Vermont rural planner, a university extension-area development specialist, a cartographer from the Chittenden County Regional Planning Commission, and a university resource economist. They in turn were assisted by three experts from the state departments of water resources, recreation, and forests and parks.

The village and town REP committee met again with the technical team to organize subcommittees and divide the workload. The technical team wrote reports on geology, soils, water resources, and wildlife. The subcommittees, with technical assistance, conducted inventories and wrote reports on historic sites, conservation and recreation areas, neighborhood parks, trail systems, and scenic vistas.

A few months and many meetings and field trips later, the subcommittees and technical team produced a document entitled "Proposal for a Quality Environment, Essex, Vt."[3] It carried seventy-six recommendations, eighteen maps, and an appendix reporting the results of a survey of local attitudes. The proposed plan was presented to the village and town select board and planning commissions as a draft for use in preparing a "quality-environment supplement to their master plan." Copies were supplied to libraries and to participants. The planning commissions were pleased with the plan, but they did not recommend to the select board that it be adopted. Members of the select board did not adopt the plan; they did, however, together with the planning commissions, consider its recommendations. These were gradually implemented in the course of revising zoning and subdivision regulations, approving developments, and so forth.

THE INDIAN BROOK RESERVOIR

Communitywide activities such as the development of a rural environmental plan usually have a continuing impact on the whole community. One or more proposed projects may capture the imagination of REP participants, projects that continue to shape and influence community actions for a long time. When the quality-environment plan for Essex was completed in 1972, a number of REP committee members led by Ann Harroun turned their attention to a major recommendation of the Essex plan: the acquisition and improvement of the Indian Brook Reservoir.

Indian Brook is a 450-acre hilly and wooded tract containing a 50-acre reservoir behind an old reinforced-concrete dam. The reservoir was located in Essex town but was owned and used for water by Essex Junction. While the REP plan was being developed, Essex Junction was in the process of joining the Champlain water district; in the future the village would get its water from Lake Champlain, not the reservoir. Seizing on this opportunity, the REP committee and the technical team identified the Indian Brook area as having the highest potential for public recreation. It could be used, the plan stated, for "boating, fishing, picnicking, camping, nature trails and scenic overlooks." Abandoned roads could provide access.

The citizen committee tried but failed to get the town to obtain a direct grant from the Bureau of Outdoor Recreation (BOR) for 50 percent of the cost. Next they turned to the Winooski Valley Park District (WVPD) for assistance (see chapter 9) and just missed a deadline for joint purchase using BOR and WVPD funds. Then the Essex Village Board of Trustees changed their objective from preservation to development and sold the parcel to a consortium of developers—the only party to submit a bid. The bid price was adjusted downward to compensate for a flaw in the title.

Deterred but not defeated, the supporters launched phase two of their campaign, the creation of a support group, the Friends of Indian Brook Reservoir (FIBR). This group enlisted community support for public purchase of the Indian Brook property. The expanded support group pursued the following tactics:

1. *Creation of a card file of supporters/members.* With the permission of the new owners, a sign was posted on the property: "Technically, you are trespassing. If you would like to help protect this property from private development and turn it into a public park, please call FIBR, at [telephone number]." With these signs, and by talking to recreational users at the site, workers gathered names for the card file. Three membership categories were drawn up: active members, persons available for occasional special projects such as fund raisers, and those who would cast favorable votes when the time came. Many teens joined FIBR. They worked hard in all of the activities, brought their parents

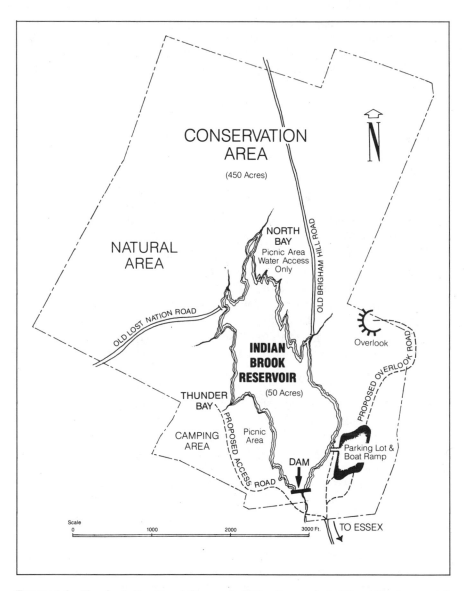

FIGURE 1.2. Plan for Indian Brook Reservoir: Major Component of Essex Environmental Plan

into the fold, and exerted peer pressure to keep the place clean and reduce vandalism.

2. *Policing the area to make a good impression.* Volunteers regularly cleaned the area of trash and broken glass. Trash barrels painted with the FIBR logo were set out. Returnable cans and bottles were collected and cashed in to buy trashbags. Volunteers with pickup trucks hauled trash to the dump.

3. *Publicity.* Open houses, tours, and canoe rides were held with the public and press invited. Slide shows were presented to private groups and at the polls. Coffee and baked goods were sold at the slide shows. A newsletter was mailed to members. A history of Indian Brook and proposed development plans were circulated and published.

4. *Surveys.* Volunteers conducted surveys at the site to demonstrate the extent of its use and discover preferences for limited development.

5. *Planning for the area.* Harroun, by then on the select board, persuaded the town manager to prepare a development plan reflecting user preferences and an estimate of the costs of that plan.

6. *Petitions.* Two petitions were circulated door to door in the town and the village, one in favor of acquisition and one opposed, in order to demonstrate public opinion to the select board. Accompanying the petitions were color photographs of the site, its history, results of the user survey, plans and costs of development, and its effect on the tax rate. The petitions showed support for acquisition exceeding 90 percent.

This campaign won a lot of members for FIBR (over two hundred), but it did not buy the land. Political pressure had to be applied. Over a period of time, members and supporters of the Indian Brook project gained positions on public commissions and boards. One member, Noah Thompson, University of Vermont extension development specialist, became the chairperson of the Essex Town planning commission. Ann Harroun was also elected to the planning commission, as well as to the select board and later to the state legislature. During the tenure of these two, Essex town adopted and enforced strict subdivision regulations requiring developers to provide water, sewer, paved roads, dual access, and storm drainage in all subdivisions. This made private development of the Indian Brook parcel more expensive and difficult.

In 1987, with private development unlikely, the select board authorized a bond vote for the acquisition and development of Indian Brook Reservoir. The proposal passed overwhelmingly. Unfortunately, there was one more hitch. The positive vote sent the asking price up. The town board rejected the increased price; the members of FIBR held their breath and supported the board. This standoff was resolved when Congress passed the 1987 tax reform act, which eliminated the benefits of capital gains. On December 31, 1987, the eve of the new law's effective date, the town and the would-be developers signed an agreement for sale.

Indian Brook Park, as it is now called, has a repaired dam, improved access roads, better parking, a new launch ramp for nonmotorized boats, and picnic tables. The park is extensively used by citizens for swimming, canoeing, fishing, hiking, picnicking, skating, bird watching, and cross-country skiing.

While FIBR focused on one project, the rest of the quality-environment plan had not been forgotten. By 1989, twenty-six of the plan's seventy-six specific recommendations had been implemented. Major accomplishments included floodplain zoning and a subsurface sewage-disposal ordinance, easements for nonmotorized public access over roads in Saxon Forest, increased use of town school buildings and grounds, pedestrian trails in town subdivisions, bicycle lanes along Maple Street, a nature trail at the town's middle school, a scenic overlook in Winooski Valley, a pool, and four public parks.[4]

In 1991 another benefit flowed from the 1972 plan. Essex town and village won a Vermont Agency of Transportation grant of $288,090 for construction of a "transportation path." This award, which came from Federal Highway Administration funds, was made to three towns selected from twenty-four applicants. The 2.8-mile bike/pedestrian path will connect important points of traffic origin and destination within the town and village. Dawn Francis, former planner and now community development director of Essex town, states that the 1972 rural environmental plan with a chapter devoted to trail systems was a major reason for winning the award.

CONCLUSION

In each of these and other examples of REP, planners followed four basic guidelines:

1. Public goals were discovered by survey and public discussion.
2. Resource inventories were prepared through the cooperative efforts of local citizens, technical experts, and the rural environmental planner.
3. Each plan was designed to be environmentally sound, politically acceptable, and financially feasible.
4. Objectives included the protection of the natural environment, di-

versification of economic opportunities, and preservation of cultural values.

Completion to date of over thirty rural environmental plans has led to a pattern of results that permit general conclusions about REP as a creative planning process. The costs of planning in rural areas can be reduced by using the expertise of public, private, and volunteer professionals together with specialists from state universities and, increasingly, graduates of rural-planning programs. This expertise is combined with the extensive knowledge of local citizens to produce a unique plan for a rural community or area. REP uses planning concepts that are relevant to contemporary rural society. REP serves client groups not addressed by conventional urban planning; it protects community values and promotes public access to a quality environment; and it develops a plan in accord with public goals. Because a rural environmental plan evolves through the direct participation of local citizens, it is more likely to be adopted and implemented.

REP can serve as a model for state universities and state planning offices to guide rural communities in local planning. It is a tool for unlocking thousands of dollars' worth of planning expertise in state and federal agencies, state colleges, and the private sector and for applying this knowledge and skill to local planning problems. The initiative to undertake REP, however, must come from the community. Sources for such an initiative can be diverse: local civic leaders, citizens ad hoc committees, community development corporations, individuals with leadership and organizational skills, and local agencies established to work in one or more sectors of community development.

2

Rural Environmental Planning in Perspective

HUMAN SETTLEMENT WITHIN the present boundaries of the United States did not begin with small towns on the eastern seaboard. Centuries before the establishment of Williamsburg and Jamestown, Virginia, the Hohokam, the Anasazi, and other Pueblo Indian cultures of the arid Southwest designed and built agricultural communities sustained by water-control systems and small farms. Canals, ditches, headgates, diversion dams, contour terraces, and contiguous-grid bordered gardens supported permanent settlements and a sedentary way of life.[1] Archaeological remains indicate that these prehistoric peoples used design technology for long-term occupation: thermally efficient pithouses and kivas constructed from twigs and mud, pits and cisterns for storage, as well as outdoor hearths and roasting ovens.[2]

EARLY SETTLEMENT PATTERNS

Village size and town layouts varied considerably during the early periods of settlement. In many cases planning was haphazard, resulting in informal arrangements of houses and other structures. However, some societies developed complex village, town, and regional systems of planned settlement, most notably the Anasazi of Chaco Canyon:

> In the tenth century a distinctive organization developed within Chaco Canyon. Although probably localized at first, the system eventually incorporated an area of about 53,107 km² of the San Juan Basin and adjacent uplands [parts of New

18

Mexico, Arizona, Utah, and Colorado]. The Chaco Phenomenon is characterized by construction of large planned towns, the presence of contemporaneous unplanned villages, roads, water-control features, . . . and construction of the Chacoan outliers.[3]

During its period of peak population, around A.D. 1100, the Chaco region included some two to four hundred villages connected by an intricate road network of more than 400 miles to outlying sites. Village designs incorporated major apartment units and ground plans for D-, E- and L-shaped pueblos, curved walls, multifloor apartments of masonry construction (sandstone and decorative veneer walls), open plazas, kivas, and other structures sited and designed for passive solar heating.[4] Portions of these village structures still stand and are open for public viewing at the Chaco Culture National Historical Park in Northwestern New Mexico, near Crownpoint.

Some five centuries after the decline of Chacoan culture, Spanish explorers and land-grant petitioners established villages and towns on the northern frontiers of New Spain, diversifying the region's already-established forms of settlement. Guided by city-planning ordinances embodied in the Laws of the Indies, the Spanish introduced a gridiron system of square blocks and paid careful attention to the layout of plaza, church, streets, and merchant portals; plans provided for the location of house plots and common land for livestock.

The Laws of the Indies, issued by King Philip II in 1573, contained 148 separate ordinances. Prior to settlement, sites had to be selected in proximity to water for domestic and agricultural use. They "should be in fertile areas with an abundance of fruits and fields, of good land to plant and harvest, of grasslands to grow livestock, of mountains and forests for wood and building materials for homes and edifices, and of good and plentiful water supply for drinking and irrigation."[5] Application of the Laws of the Indies varied from one location to another, depending on topography, natural resources, climate, the requirements for social and political organization, and many other factors. Ordinances requiring square or rectangular plazas and governing land use and town layout, however, left a permanent imprint on the landscape of the West and Southwest, as exemplified in early Spanish cities as diverse as Santa Fe, St. Louis, and Los Angeles.[6] The criterion of proximity to water is best observed in the hundreds of villages and towns scattered throughout the valley of the Rio Grande and its tributaries in New Mexico and southern Colorado. Some thousand *acequias* (irrigation ditches) continue to nurture and support village agriculture on a small scale, particularly in the sierras of north-central New Mexico.

EVOLVING RURAL PATTERNS

The rural landscape in other parts of the United States, meanwhile, took shape according to influences contributed by other cultures. The colonists who settled Williamsburg, Jamestown, and Washington, D.C., also built carefully planned towns. In each case the site was surveyed and marked, and all building conformed to a master plan. The eventual opening up of the continent to pioneers, though, did not see widespread application of this orderly procedure. Land-hungry frontiersmen rushed to claim, clear, and settle land without attending to the formalities of surveying or planning.

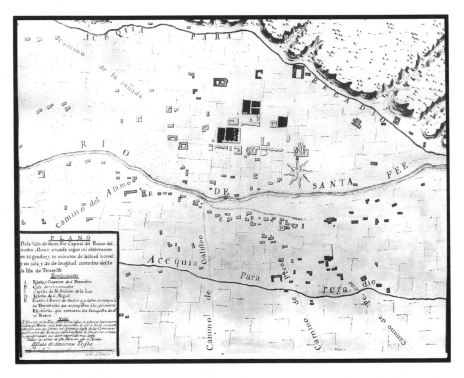

FIGURE 2.1. Villa de Santa Fe. *Drawn c. 1766–68, when Santa Fe was still a village, this map by José de Urrutia depicts the Rio de Santa Fe with two* acequias *constructed by Hispanic settlers to irrigate crop fields and common land as required by the Laws of the Indies. Hundreds of towns and villages in the region continue to reflect colonial ordinance requirements pertaining to town layout and land use.* (Courtesy of the Museum of New Mexico.)

The New England states were generally settled according to the frontier pattern. Land in Vermont was granted on paper by New York and New Hampshire governors and settled by woodsmen, squatters, grantees, speculators, and in some cases, draft avoiders. Adventurers of all types cleared and fought for homesteads and speculative acreage. The governments they established were minimal, local, informal, and primarily concerned with maintaining independence from New York and New Hampshire. Individual landowners or small corporations determined land use. Public planning was limited to laying out military highways. This system of a weak state government, strong local authority, and negligible town planning persisted until the 1930s, when the Great Depression together with natural catastrophes forced the national government into concerted action.

From the mid-1930s until well after World War II, federal agencies planned rivers and watersheds for navigation, hydroelectric power, flood protection, and commercialized agriculture. They also constructed dams and planned scenic parkways, national forests, and parks. The states, at this time politically and financially weak, were content to let the federal government take financial responsibility and, with it, responsibility for planning and decision-making.

CONCEPTUAL BASIS OF REP

While the tactics and procedures of REP developed more recently, its basic values and theoretical concepts can be traced back to the utopian experiments of Robert Owen and others, as set out in Ebenezar Howard's *Garden Cities,* as well as to large-scale projects in regional water-resource planning such as the Tennessee Valley Authority. As regionalism took shape in America, planners grew more interested in environmental quality, public involvement, and equity.

In the early 1920s, concern over uncontrolled growth in industrial centers as well as aggressive mining and logging in rural regions caused a group of urban planners to form the Regional Planning Association of America (RPAA). The city, they believed, "could only survive in organic balance with the totality of its regional environment."[7] That is, it could survive as a cultural and civic repository for civilization's achievements only if it existed in harmony with its rural surroundings. The RPAA saw regions not only as geographic areas but also as entities that combined geographic, economic, and cultural elements in distinctive configurations. The challenge was to create balance within a region and between rural regions and metropolitan centers.[8]

This concept established the foundation for a view of regional planning articulated by Benton MacKaye, a forester and one of the founders of the RPAA:

> Cultural man needs land and developed natural resources as the tangible source of bodily existence; he needs the flow of commodities to make that source effective; but first of all he needs a harmonious and related environment as the source of his true living. These three needs of cultured man make three corresponding problems: (a) the conservation of natural resources, (b) the control of commodity-flow, (3) the development of environment. *The visualization of the potential workings of these three processes constitutes the new exploration—and regional planning.*[9]

Another prime mover in the RPAA, Lewis Mumford, combined the concept of regional planning with the idea of communal education. Mumford also redefined the planning process, normally undertaken solely by professionals, to include community participation. "Regional plans are instruments of communal education; and without that education they can look forward to only partial achievement."[10]

These two ingredients of regionalism, ecological balance and community education, were taken up by Southern regionalists concerned about the problems of endemic poverty, underdevelopment, cultural disintegration, and the ravaging of Southern natural resources by Northern investors. Regionalism became for them a symbol of self-determination.

One of the most important advocates of regionalism was Howard Odum, a Southern sociologist with populist inclinations. In Odum's words, "regionalism . . . represents the philosophy and technique of self help, self development and initiative in which each areal unit is not only aided, but . . . committed to the full development of its own resources and capacities."[11] Regionalist thinking as expressed by Odum and others had evolved from the search for an urban-rural environmental balance to the search for an economic and cultural balance within and between regions.

> The heart of the problem [of balance] is found in search for equal opportunity for all the people through the conservation, development, and use of their resources in the places where they live, adequately adjusted to the interregional culture and economy of the other regions of the Nation. The goal is, therefore, clearly one of balanced culture as well as economy, in which equality of opportunity in education, in public health and welfare, in the range of occupational outlook, and in

the elimination of handicapping differentials between and among different groups of people and levels of culture may be achieved.[12]

Regional planning as envisioned by the early planners of the RPAA—that is, planning as a holistic discipline that would create balanced regions, conserve cultures, equitably distribute wealth and opportunity, and develop environmentally sound growth models—was never implemented. Rather, it was eclipsed by the military and economic mobilization of World War II and the ensuing postwar economic explosion, which occurred as wartime industries retooled to meet pent-up consumer demand. According to John Friedmann and Clyde Weaver, "Growth would become a substitute for distribution. . . .With economic growth, the labour force would be fully employed. . . . In a growth economy, everyone was bound to share in the general prosperity. . . . Re-distribution could then be either avoided altogether or more easily resolved than under the conditions of stagnation."[13]

RECENT RURAL PLANNING

The contemporary period in rural planning was ushered in and stimulated by the expansion of environmental consciousness in the mid-1960s. From that time to the early 1980s, in a climate of increasing public concern over rural poverty, state and regional planning intensified along with rural community planning. Encouraged by federal policy, citizen participation expanded to support and guide local governments and community-based organizations as they took on the new role of planning. Threatened by multiple environmental crises, states adopted new planning goals and various means of achieving them. It was during this period that a number of state universities—the University of Vermont, Appalachian State University in Boone, North Carolina, and the University of New Mexico, among others—began to address the needs of small communities in their planning programs.[14]

A succession of federal programs between 1965 and the early 1970s stimulated and supported community development planning at the state and local levels. In 1972 Congress passed the Rural Development Act, which designated the U.S. Department of Agriculture (USDA) to oversee federal involvement in rural development. For the first time, an assistant secretary position was created to coordinate various USDA-sponsored agencies such as the Farmers Home Administration (FmHA), the Rural Electrification Administration (REA), and the Rural Development Service (RDS).

The Rural Development Act also provided grants to finance the process of planning for area development. These "section 111 planning grants" were intended to encourage and underwrite comprehensive planning for rural communities. Grants were obtained by states, substate districts, local governments, and community-based organizations to design housing, economic-development, water and sewer, and energy projects. More than any other single source, however, the categorical programs, which originated in President Johnson's War on Poverty during the mid-1960s, fueled and financed thousands of rural projects in health, education, job training, economic opportunity, social services, housing, community centers and other local infrastructure.

After more than a decade of substantial federal intervention, the Carter administration capitalized on the growing perception of the need to coordinate federal rural policy with local and state implementation. Between 1976 and 1980, the federal executive departments undertook collaborative projects through a series of interagency joint agreements. Various departments (labor; health, education and welfare; agriculture; housing and urban development; energy; and transportation), the Economic Development Administration, EPA, ACTION/VISTA, and the Community Services Administration pooled grant dollars in order to finance local initiatives in such areas as rural housing, health, water and sewer, education, social services, job training and employment, economic development, energy, transportation, communication, and natural resources. The aim of the Carter policy was to stimulate comprehensive planning on the state level by setting an example at the top executive levels of government.

In September 1980, the rural planning legislation of 1972 was amended by passage of the Rural Development Policy Act. This act reiterated the role of the USDA in providing leadership throughout the executive branch. It also mandated that federally sponsored rural development programs coordinate efforts with state and local governments. Annual authorizations for FmHA section 111 planning grants were increased from $10 to $15 million.

In 1981 the Reagan administration took office. By then, the Rural Development Policy Act required the submission of updated reports on a "national strategy" for rural development. Successive reports from the Reagan administration, however, deemphasized the leadership role of the federal government and instead called for a deregulated and decentralized approach to rural development. Greater involvement by and partnerships among state and local governments, the private sector, volunteers, and the farming community were strongly advocated by the Reagan administration.[15] Many of the categorical programs that had earlier financed interagency agreements were eliminated, cut back, or consolidated into block grants to the fifty states. The executive branch chose to pursue a macro-policy of economic growth that it contended would trickle down to all of America, including the rural sector.

During both the Carter and the Reagan administrations, there was mounting evidence, however, that neither federal intervention nor trickle-down economic development strategies were benefiting chronically poor rural areas. The gap between less developed rural regions in the South, Southwest, and West and more developed regions was growing. Using per capita income, unemployment rates, and other economic indices, the USDA tracked counties where poverty persisted. Between 1949 and 1979, nearly one-fifth of the rural counties in the United States remained "persistent low income counties," and one-quarter of rural counties or parts of rural counties fluctuated between persistent poverty and less-persistent poverty during this period.

Industrial recruitment strategies underwent a reevaluation in the 1980s. In 1985 the USDA's Economic Research Service released a series of studies done in clusters of counties in Georgia and Kentucky where manufacturing plants had located and in the Ozarks where resort tourism combined with manufacturing to create new economic growth. The aim of these studies was to determine who had benefited from the economic growth between 1974 and 1979. The following quote from the Kentucky study typifies their findings:

> Overall employment growth in rural areas will probably not benefit all households or residents in that area. In a nine-county area of south-central Kentucky, rapid employment growth between 1974 and 1979 did create new job opportunities. However, only 18 percent of the households had members who took advantage of new jobs. The employment growth also did not reduce the area's overall poverty level.[16]

The Reagan administration did not address conditions of persistent poverty; instead it responded to the farm crisis by supporting legislation that would diversify rural economies by making available loan capital to finance development in nonagricultural sectors such as tourism and small business. In addition, the Reagan White House endorsed new legislation at the federal level to establish "enterprise zones" which, combined with state and local commitments, would provide tax, financial, regulatory relief and various incentives to businesses willing to locate in distressed rural and urban areas.

In 1988, after numerous false starts, Congress passed "Title VII: Enterprise Zone Development" as part of the Housing and Community Development Act of 1987. This legislation called for the federal designation of one hundred enterprise zones, at least one-third of which had to be rural areas. Indian reservations were also mentioned as eligible sites. Meanwhile, by

1989, thirty-seven states had enacted their own enterprise-zone legislation.[17] Subsequently, designated projects were reported in over two thousand local jurisdictions, urban and rural. The decade of the 1980s closed with continued emphasis on local solutions to the problems of persistent rural poverty. This shift in policy brought greater sensitivity to the diversity and complexity of rural America and the major postindustrial forces shaping emerging and future needs.[18]

NEW DIMENSIONS FOR RURAL PLANNING

Rural Environmental Planning asks people to define their own goals. All rural settings are different, of course, and the conditions of each produce unique insights. Many rural communities do, however, share the same general goals. For example, enhancing the quality of life, improving economic opportunity, and protecting the natural environment are aspirations of the majority of people in REP communities.

SELF-RELIANCE

Throughout the 1980s the authors of this study noted new dimensions emerging in the formulation of community goals, in particular, an emphasis on increased self-reliance, reduced economic dependency, and a diversified economic base. Regarding the first, self-reliance, it should be noted that the term is used here with some caution. Self-reliance has become part of the development lexicon, in particular with reference to less-industrialized or nonaligned countries. It has almost as many meanings as authors who write about it. It has been utilized in conjunction with both autonomous utopian communities and practical strategies for feeding people.

Much of the current interest in self-reliance results from dissatisfaction with past development strategies formulated by agencies and institutions in the industrialized world and applied to the so-called third world. Strategies emphasizing rapid industrialization, capital-intensive tourism, or the commercialization of agriculture often created single-product economies lacking adequate infrastructures. As these economies grew more and more dependent on, say, single-crop harvesting or single-product mining, or manufacturing, planners and economists noticed that the economic gap between rich and poor was actually widening. The resulting system could not generate its own investment base to create a diverse and balanced economy because the profit was exported and did not enrich the local economy.[19]

Similarly, until very recently, rural communities in the United States were encouraged to join the mainstream economy by courting industry, luring capital-intensive tourism development, and industrializing the agricultural sector, and welcoming extraction industries—all with little sense of what it would mean to lose local control over community resources. This approach resulted in rural economies skewed to support a single product or subject to a boom and bust cycle that left them open to chronic depression and dependency.

Self-reliance does not mean that a community is isolated from the mainstream economy. Self-reliance is used here to mean the regeneration of the community through community-controlled development of its own resources (natural, human, and cultural). This includes the determination of the manner in which resources relate to both the community's internal economy and the mainstream economy. Regeneration involves the separation of unhealthy social and economic dependencies by diversifying the sources of local income, increasing the net flow of money into the local economy, developing a self-investment capability, and improving local productivity.

Planning for self-reliance requires broad citizen participation; the process determines the product. Self-reliance and top-down planning are mutually exclusive concepts. Self-reliance cannot be achieved in a planning process that depends entirely on professionals, agencies, or political leadership outside of the community. For a community to achieve and maintain self-reliance, it must itself develop the fundamental tools of planning. In REP these tools are communication, inventorying, goal development, evaluation, and decision-making.

EXURBIA: THE CHANGE AND THE CHALLENGE

An increasingly important issue that many rural jurisdictions and small towns will have to deal with in the 1990s and into the twenty-first century is a new kind of low-density growth that is not suburban in character and not even directly connected to an urban area. This phenomenon, called "countrified cities" by Joseph Doherty[20] and "the new heartland" by John Herbers, is a new form of exurbia. Herbers observes that

the new-growth areas are different from any kind of settlements we have known in the past . . . [and] of such low density that they make the old "suburban sprawl" seem dense. Subdivisions, single-family housing on five- to 10-acre lots, shopping centers, retail strips, schools, and churches, all separated by farms, forests, or other open spaces, are characteristic.[21]

They are seldom found on flat, rich farmland, which continues to lose population in all regions. Nor are they part of the back-to-the-land movement of the 1970s that drew those disenchanted with American civilization to rural communes. Rather, the new communities are made up of a prosperous, adventurous middle class superimposed over small towns and countryside in a way the suburbs never were.[22]

According to Herbers, the U.S. Census Bureau data for the period from 1980 to 1985 shows the greatest growth to be in the farther reaches of the exurban areas—sixty to seventy miles in all directions from New York, two and three counties removed from such cities as Atlanta, Philadelphia, San Francisco, and Chicago—and in small metropolitan areas that are in themselves low density, anticity developments, such as Ocala, Florida, Edinberg-McAllen, Texas, and Chico, California. Herbers perceives that much of this growth

is a product of what some authorities call a post-industrial society. With the decline of heavy industry and the rise of a service economy, neither factories nor office buildings need to be clustered near sources of raw materials and water or rail transportation. For the first time in American history, both businesses and workers can settle pretty much where they please. And where they please is not the large city.[23]

This development is relevant to REP in the sense that rural and small-town beauty can be considered a potential economic resource. Development based on the appeal of a rustic, historic, or scenic place, if balanced with the community-defined concerns of health and well-being, can enhance economic diversity and hence sustainability in that place. Simply put, many small communities and remote rural areas are attractive to new residents and businesses precisely because they are small or remote. The risk, however, is that disconnected exurban development will overwhelm or destroy the rural quality that was the initial attraction.

Often the infusion of new settlers and enterprises in unspoiled rural environments is only indirectly connected to the traditional economic model of an urban-regional hinterland. Increasingly, economic activity can be geared toward a nationwide or even international market. Examples are the dulcimer crafts of Appalachia, the pottery of New Mexico, and the weaving of the Navajo Nation.

In a paper presented to the American Collegiate Schools of Planning Conference, Edward T. Ward, professor of planning at California Polytechnic

State University, expanded on the premise that a new nonmetropolitan reality is emerging.[24] Ward ascribed the reverse migration from urban to exurban places to the deeply rooted American tradition of small town and country living and Americans' ambivalent feelings about cities. Multiple surveys have consistently shown that "a majority of Americans would prefer to live in small cities, small towns and the countryside. The big change now is that more people are able and willing to *act* on their preferences, even to the extent of trading off higher incomes." The opportunity and challenge for the twenty-first century, according to Ward, is for "communities that foster diversity, not large concentrations of sameness; that have a continuity with the past as opposed to trashing it; that go beyond the suburbs in blending development with nature; and which provide choices, quality, and an aesthetic . . . that is meaningful to people."[25] Not achieving this diversity, continuity, and blending with nature risks the deterioration of the character and amenities that attracted people to the rural environment in the first place. Clearly, the quality of rural places is a finite resource.

Herber's and Ward's analyses suggest that in the preparation of a rural environmental plan it is important to identify valued aspects of rural areas and small towns and to make explicit how those aspects differ from traditional features of urban and suburban areas. Criteria for exurban development include maintaining differentiated population density, mixing income levels and age groups, providing services to both clustered and dispersed populations, protecting natural systems, enhancing agricultural and other biologic productivity, promoting a sustainable and self-regenerating economy, and managing an aesthetic environment where land, water, and vegetation, not buildings, are the dominant components.

CONCLUSION

Rural planning in America has a long and rich history that includes indigenous cultures as well as cultures introduced from Europe and elsewhere. For much of American history, though, rural planning was limited to new settlements, to the outskirts and suburbs of cities, and to large economic regions or natural-resource areas. Between the 1960s and the early 1980s, rural planning evolved from regional planning as a result of federal subsidies for small towns and rural jurisdictions. Rural planning as a discipline in North American universities and colleges is an even more recent development. A decade ago very few planning schools included rural planning in their curricula; the number is now increasing. It is becoming more generally recognized that rural communities are not just "unformed" or incipient cities but rather socially and culturally interdependent groups of people with lifestyles, public goals, political structures, and social values different from, sometimes sharply at variance with, those of urban dwellers. Diversity results in a need for rural planning strategies that will help people to pursue their public goals and to eschew the unwanted or unintended influence of urbanization.

3

Rural Environmental Planning: Organization and Process

LET US ASSUME that from your experience in your own community, from what you have read in this book, and from your knowledge of rural problems and opportunities, you would like to know how to get a rural environmental planning process started. What can you do? At first the task may appear to be so complex that you do not know where to begin. Although the issues to be addressed are complex, REP can be broken down into a series of steps that the citizens and leadership of any rural community can take, one after another, and achieve significant community goals. The entire planning process can be divided into three parts: start-up, create the plan, and implementation. The steps necessary for each of these parts are presented in this chapter.

START-UP

How does the process get started? In the experience of the authors, start-up activities fall into three common phases: initiation, discussion, and organization. While the hard work of data collection, goal development, and plan evolution comes later, start-up is so critical to future success that it requires special comment.

Initiation. In the beginning someone gets an idea that some aspect of the community could be improved through collective action. This initial spark may come from seeing or hearing what other communities have done. It may be a reaction to the chronic problem of high unemployment or exodus of young people. It may be touched off by rumors of a large development that is perceived as a threat to the rural way of life. Or it may result from the discovery of new opportunities for local development. This vision of a better community is all important, but it must be connected to an understanding of the political process, otherwise it will die. To translate the vision into a feasible plan of action that will appeal to a large portion of the community, a further step is needed—discussion.

Discussion.   All ideas for community improvement, even the best ones, need a lot of informal discussion before they can be successfully implemented. A substantial amount of give and take is necessary to test whether a new concept is worth the work required to bring it about. The more a concept is discussed, the more people there are who will feel a part of its development and who will be personally motivated to support it. A major advantage of informal community discussion is refining and improving a proposal. Objections can be met; details can be worked out; examples can be studied; possible opponents can be persuaded. Discussion in small groups and communitywide gatherings will show how the proposal fits into the overall scheme of things: how it relates to regional planning, how planners can take advantage of special opportunities for financial assistance, and how the special talents of local people can be drawn upon. A discussion period may also produce community participants and potential activists who will be indispensable in the next phase—organization.

Organization.   After discussion has informed the community of the possibilities of REP and interested individuals have stepped forward, it is time to proceed in a more structured way. Often by this time leaders have emerged who have the respect and support of the active citizen group. An ad hoc committee may elect a spokesperson to conduct meetings and a secretary to keep records, or an elected board may appoint members as a citizens committee.

At the first meeting a number of public goals may be discussed. Committee members may consider sources of professional assistance, discuss how to fit REP into the cogs of local government, and indicate their concerns and possible subcommittees on which they would like to serve. The makeup of the new organization will directly reflect the objectives of the members. If one goal is to plan for sustainable economic development, an effort should be made to include representatives of all groups with a direct interest in the economic structure of the community. If another goal is to develop a plan for environmental protection, the group should include those with a special interest in or knowledge about environmental issues. If interest is expressed in a trail system, members should include hikers, cross-country skiers, and bicyclists. If the priority is tackling poverty and unemployment, as reported in some recent REP cases, then members should include the appropriate representatives.

PROCESS AND ROLES

The creation of a rural environmental plan is a participatory process supported by expertise from public agencies, universities, nonprofit organizations, private individuals, and local citizens. A draft plan is reported and discussed in subcommittee sessions and in meetings involving as many of those affected by the plan as possible. The final plan, after adoption by town, village, county, tribal government, or other jurisdiction, then serves as a guide for long-term community development by public, private, and community-based organizations.

The process of creating a rural environmental plan requires a working relationship among three participants or groups: the client, the planner, and the technical team. The client initiates the plan. The client may be represented at various times by an elected board, an appointed or ad hoc advisory commission, a nonprofit organization, those who speak up at public meetings, or those who respond to a community survey. The ultimate clients of a rural environmental plan, though, are all those who are or will be affected by the plan.

At the end of the start-up phase the client group may organize in a number of different ways. It may become a conservation commission appointed by elected officials to assist with the development and implementation of the plan. This has been done in Massachusetts and other Northeastern states. Or the planning commission itself may undertake such planning. An ad hoc committee of citizens could provide the engine for developing an environmental plan. There are other possibilities, but whatever form this group takes, it will need to have committed leadership, good connections with local government and community organizations, and volunteers to help develop the plan.

After the REP committee is organized and there is general agreement on the direction of planning, subcommittees are set up. These should be few in number and organized according to inventories to be made and chapters to be written in the plan. To clarify the role of subcommittees, let us outline several of their typical assignments.

Public Goals Subcommittee.   Review chapter 4 of this book; draft goals questionnaire; obtain suggestions from full committee; get help from rural environmental planner to finalize questionnaire; distribute questionnaire to all households; collect questionnaire; tabulate it; write up results; report results to full committee and to public.

Natural Areas Subcommittee.   Review chapter 6 of this book; ask natural scientists and citizens for a list of natural areas; study identified public goals; write report describing natural areas and proposing protective measures.

Agricultural Subcommittee.   Review chapter 7 of this book; get information on agricultural activity, trends, and numbers from technical team; study public goals for agriculture; get technical recommendations for plan to achieve those goals; write report as a draft chapter for rural environmental plan.

Economic Subcommittee.   Review chapters 12, 13, and 14 of this book; make an economic profile of town; list alternative development strategies; find examples of other communities working on sustainable economic development; get suggestions from state development department; present and discuss findings in public meetings, then summarize as input to plan.

These examples show the general procedures of subcommittees. Members visit and observe their subject area; review literature; get help from the REP planner and technical team; study results of a public goals survey; discuss findings, options, and recommendations; and then summarize the results as a draft chapter for the plan.

The person who provides services should communicate all the steps and concepts of the planning process to citizens and town officials, facilitate the work of the subcommittee, oversee data collection and inventories, assist citizen subcommittees in drafting and editing chapters, and insure the input of citizens and local officials. This person should also provide drafting maps, collect all materials in the form of a plan, incorporate changes, obtain approvals, and publish the plan. These responsibilities can be performed by a person with formal training in planning or someone with skills in community development.

In states with a planning degree program at the state university, graduate students can participate in rural planning as part of their course work, professional projects, or theses. A graduate student or recent graduate can serve as the on-site planner. He or she, along with a professor of planning, may attend the first meeting of the elected board or planning commission; from then on, the student is the planner designated to attend local meetings. The student visits government agencies and other organizations to work on the inventory and receives advice and guidance each week from the university planning faculty in preparation for the next week's work.

A variation on the university model is for a class of students in an advanced-planning studio to assist in developing the plan. While a semester is a short period, experience shows that a team of ten to fifteen students, working under faculty supervision, can accomplish a lot. However, a semester or two of additional work by a graduate student and the citizen planning committee may be necessary to complete the plan.

Typically, the university planning faculty consists of a core planning group and a support group. The core group often includes an environmental or economic planner, a landscape architect, a geographer, a cartographer, or a civil engineer. The support group may consist of professors in various departments—geology, soils, hydrology, social planning, anthropology, recreation, health services, resource economics, business management, public administration, and law, among others—who help students to collect data and draft recommendations.

A university planner is limited by the number of plans that can be completed in university studios, by the number of graduate planners, and by the funds available to rural jurisdictions. Even if there are dozens of villages, counties, small towns, or Indian pueblos that would like rural plans, a university may be able to serve only a few clients each year. In states without planning programs at the state university, rural communities can advocate the adoption of such, meanwhile contacting a nonprofit organization experienced in community development.

The technical team consists of professional and technical experts who help subcommittees to conduct inventories and draft recommendations. They may be employees of federal, state, or county agencies, or they may be retired persons, private-sector volunteers, or resident professionals. In some cases they may be paid by not-for-profit or philanthropic organizations. Paying for essential technical services is often necessary to assess problems correctly and formulate solutions. Whatever the arrangement, technical personnel should be selected on the basis of talent and experience so that sound decisions will be made.

In early REP projects the technical team consisted of a representative from the USDA's Soil Conservation Service (SCS), the county forester, a county agricultural extension agent, and a state university faculty member experienced in rural planning. With the Reagan administration's elimination of USDA section 111 planning grants, as well as grants to the Department of Housing and Urban Development and the Bureau of Recreation, access to many federal agencies was restricted. The administration also reduced personnel and cut technical-assistance programs in agencies such as the SCS and FmHA. Although the Reagan administration advocated the provision of comparable services at the local and state levels, in most states this did not happen.

By the mid- and late 1980s other more innovative strategies were utilized to obtain expertise and funding. These strategies attracted volunteer or resident professionals from the private sector; technical experts from state agencies and universities; private, philanthropic, church, and other not-for-profit funding sources; and community organizations. Examples of specialists who can supplement REP technical teams are state or county foresters, agricultural extension agents, fish and game biologists, housing specialists, and economic development specialists.

PARTICIPATION IN THE REP PROCESS

REP affords community residents many opportunities to participate and make a difference. In summary, citizens can do the following:

- Initiate the REP process
- Contribute ideas from the beginning and gradually refine them
- Suggest questions for the goals survey
- Volunteer for subcommittee work
- Organize and participate in field trips
- Conduct resource inventories with technical team assistance
- Review literature, especially case studies of successful projects elsewhere
- Draft chapters and sections for the plan
- Attend public hearings and other meetings
- Serve on decision-making and implementation bodies such as conservation or planning commissions

Public participation has become an accepted part of the community planning process. Usually, representatives from various parts of the community are invited to meetings, or meetings are advertised and all are invited to attend. In many rural communities meetings may work well. In multicultural communities the results are not always so good. Meetings, to be successful, should be viewed as forums for reporting and advancing work. Participants should leave a meeting with some idea of the steps that need to be taken before the next. The action can be just taking a set of questions back to a constituency group who may not be meeting-goers but who may have information, insights, or other contributions to make to the process.

Residents unable to attend can be encouraged to serve in many other capacities, for example, organizing and leading field trips for the subcommittees. Resource inventories, field trips, and goal surveys inform the community as well as the decision-makers. The gathering and presentation of information are crucial to participation and skills building. They are also the reason the REP process cannot be hurried. It is not enough to outline an issue and ask participants to decide on solutions. The vision of where the community can go and the information on how to get it there requires input from people within the community as well as from the technical team and project examples from other communities. The exchange of information among subcommittees, the technical team, and outside communities is necessary to stimulate involvement and accelerate learning.

Experience in REP cases has shown that one way to increase community involvement and confidence is to address and solve a specific problem early in the planning. An environmental problem such as toxic waste dumping or an overflowing landfill will draw out local leadership that can then be tapped to assist with long-term planning. Residents may want to meet basic needs before moving on to the creation of new businesses or complex kinds of environmental preservation. Some services, such as meal delivery to senior citizens, can be developed into a business that both serves basic needs and provides jobs for some residents. This gradual movement from preliminary planning to more comprehensive planning is not just for less experienced groups. As John Dewey and John Friedmann point out, "Through experience we come not only to understand the world but also to transform it. As in a spiral movement, from practice to plan and again back to practice, it is the way we learn."[1] The process of discovery will engage people in authentic learning where, collectively, they create a vision, determine community goals, and then gain the skills needed to take steps toward realizing their vision.

GETTING UNDER WAY

A successful plan requires a core of active citizens who understand their community and desire to improve it through the instrument of self-government. In communities where elected officials do not recognize the value of planning, concerned citizens may have to initiate projects themselves with the hope that official attitudes will change over time.

Rural towns, districts, or counties become ready to plan at differing rates.

Communities, like families, go through cycles of growth, stability, decline, and resurgence. Community leadership also varies in strength and quality over time. A prosperous community may feel no need to plan until a crisis arises. A declining community that has lost its leaders may need help in getting started. Or thc existing leadership may lack the vision and imagination to try new ways. It is important for the rural planner and the people in an area to recognize their own unique situation in order to estimate the potential return of time invested in a plan. There is no precise measure of the factors involved, but there are some general REP guidelines that have evolved over the years.

If there is a small group of recognized community leaders who want to consider the REP process, then a start can be made. *If* the community has an annual fiesta, holiday celebration, library fund-raiser, or other similar event, it probably has enough leadership and cohesion to consider REP. *If* the community has recently undertaken, primarily through its own effort, some major collective enterprise—such as building a baseball field, a fire station staffed with volunteers, or a community center—it has the necessary leadership for planning. *If,* at a public meeting called to discuss REP, there is a good turnout and a majority of those speaking are ready to take positive action, then REP will probably bring results.

THE UNIT OF ORGANIZATION

Local government serves as the framework for planning. Without such a political unit—many unincorporated communities in the South and West lack one—a community can have a local organization provide the framework for planning. The town or village government serves for rural town planning, and county or tribal government for rural area planning. However, if the planning area is synonymous with a natural-resource area or region, such as a river basin, a multiple-town lake basin, or a mountain region, then a special organization separate from local political units must be established. This multijurisdictional board can represent, communicate with, and provide feedback to the political units that must implement the plan. For example, to plan the Camels Hump mountain region and the Winooski River valley in Vermont, special state legislation setting up multiple-town administrative units was sought and enacted.

In some natural-resource areas, alternative agencies, nonprofit organizations such as nationwide environmental organizations, community-development organizations, or subunits of the state such as soil and water conservation districts or irrigation associations provide a framework for natural resource planning. In special cases, a coalition of interest groups can serve as the public's representative in the development of a plan. Such a coalition might include representatives of a farmers' or ranchers' co-op, the local wild-life preservation society, or representatives of natural resource and planning disciplines at the state university. The plan is submitted to the elected representatives of constituent communities. In some unincorporated areas, constituents served by the plan may be represented by a nongovernmental organization such as a grange, an irrigation association, or a nonprofit development corporation.

SCHEDULE AND PROCEDURE

How long does it take to develop a rural environmental plan? What is the procedure? The longest and most difficult period is often getting ready to plan. It may take the people in a rural area or small town a long time to move from the perception of concern to identify needs, goals, possible futures, and then to get organized, to identify agencies and resources to assist in the planning process. The time needed for getting started can vary widely, from a few months to a few years. The amount of time actually needed to develop the plan is determined more by the ability of participants to learn and to set goals than by the actual number of hours that go into inventorying and planning. A six- to twelve-month period is usually sufficient in a small community or rural area to conduct the technical tasks of inventorying resources and drafting a plan. Experience shows that interest tends to decline after a year of effort. Following public review and adoption, implementation of the plan may take several years.

The procedure for developing the plan also varies widely from case to case. There is no single prescription to fit all cases. The options and steps outlined below are general suggestions that have emerged from two decades of diverse experience in rural environmental planning.

CREATING THE PLAN

The first step in creating a plan is to hold a special information meeting with the town or village council or with the county or other jurisdictional board. This meeting provides an opportunity for the citizens and community leaders to express their concerns, objectives, and priorities. It also informs community officials about the concepts, purpose, and process of rural environmental planning. Typically, the prospective planner explains the method of developing a plan and the need for participation of all interested parties. The dual goals of economic development and environmental protection are explained, and the need for local approval of recommendations is clearly stated. Citizen input and planning costs are discussed. Also, local officials are invited to visit other communities where rural environmental plans have been completed to learn about REP and observe its results.

A project budget should be discussed at this meeting. Even if planning is done by salaried public servants, it is still necessary to estimate a price tag for additional planning costs. If a rural community gets planning service free, it will tend to attach less worth to the resultant plan. However, if the jurisdiction is charged something for mapping and publishing the plan, then the elected board and citizens have a stake in the outcome. If planning occurs under the auspices of a community-based organization, the budget process should include the preparation of funding proposals.

After a decision is made to proceed, the elected officials or sponsoring organization may send a letter to the rural planner stating the scope of work to be done and requesting assistance for the development of a rural environmental plan. The letter should include a budget and identify the liaison person. The planner then responds to the letter, confirming the agreements and describing how planning will draw on the skills of the technical team.

APPOINTING COMMITTEES

When a rural jurisdiction is involved from the outset, it is a good idea to appoint a REP committee or, in some larger areas, a natural-resource district or other multiple-jurisdiction board to work on the plan. An existing planning commission may serve as the REP committee, or the new committee may be a subcommittee of the planning commission. This arrangement achieves two objectives: it prevents an existing planning commission from feeling that it is being bypassed, and it insures that all subcommittee work will be fed to that commission and therefore into the established planning procedure. An alternative is for the elected board to establish a separate conservation commission or to designate a community-development organization to work on the plan. If this procedure is followed, then the proposed plan is submitted as a recommendation to the planning commission, which in turn considers and processes it just as they would any plan presented to them by other planning consultants.

The composition of the REP committee is determined by several factors, among them the scope of the planning task and which individuals have volunteered their services. Special effort should be made to inform and involve all interested groups. This will reduce unforeseen friction and help to balance conservation and development goals.

Much of the fieldwork, creative thinking, and concrete proposals that produces a community plan takes place in subcommittees. As we have seen, they are organized by matching inventory subjects with the interests of volunteers. Subcommittees vary according to local situations and interests; typical subcommittees include those on agriculture, recreation, water resources, economy, natural areas and wildlife, and history and rural character. Individuals may join more than one subcommittee, or a subcommittee might complete its work and the members join another subcommittee that needs more hands. In general, half a dozen subcommittees should be enough for a full environmental plan. Related subjects may be combined in subcommittee to keep the number at a manageable level. With the assistance of the planner and the technical team, each subcommittee gathers data, collects recommendations, considers goals, and then drafts a chapter for the plan.

DISCOVERING PUBLIC GOALS

One of the first tasks in creating a plan is to conduct a goals survey of as many members of the rural community as possible. The purposes of this survey are to get opinions on issues and on the potential goals identified in the start-up period or at the first information meeting; to discover additional issues, unrealized opportunities, or goals; to establish priorities; and to attract interested people for work on subcommittees.

Experience in the REP process has demonstrated the importance of a 100 percent attitude survey as one of the foundations of a democratic planning process. In small rural communities a one-page survey can be mailed or hand-delivered to every household. Even in larger rural areas the cost of mailing a single-page questionnaire to all households can be more than offset by the benefit of quick, inexpensive input into the planning process. A majority response indicates prevailing views; a minority response identifies goals for further study. There are additional benefits to questionnaires: information can be transmitted through them, and citizens often feel that their views are valued as a result of being asked for an opinion. Public goals are not permanently determined by a goals survey, but may continue to evolve as the planning process proceeds.

INVENTORYING RESOURCES

Inventorying the assets of a community—natural, cultural, and human—is a major task in planning and can take a significant amount of time. Inventorying is done by citizens on subcommittees working with the rural environmental planner and with the technical team. The objective is not to produce a detailed research report on each subject but rather to collect information, both from published sources and from direct observation, to get the whole picture of a community, including its history, character, and potential. Inventories are not just background information; with help from the best experts on each subject, they provide an opportunity to collect proposals. Combining inventories with the advice and guidance of experts results in a list of general and specific recommendations to take to the public for consideration in the next step, public review. The importance of the inventory step is marked by the fact that eight chapters in Part II of this book address this aspect of rural environmental planning.

DRAFTING AND DISSEMINATING THE PLAN

After inventorying, collecting recommendations, and holding public hearings, it is time to assemble, publish, and distribute a draft of the plan, that is, a *proposed* plan. The compiling and publishing may be carried out by the planner or by a small subgroup of the citizens committee. Citizens usually distribute the plan, making an effort to provide a copy to every household in the community.

To increase the potential for implementation, the plan must develop over time in the minds of people—not just be presented in a final publication. To help accomplish this, the vocabulary of the plan should be that of the client—not that of the academician or scientist. This advice does not imply that either vocabulary is better, but only suggests that if the plan is to be implemented by the people of the area, then the language of the client should be respected and used. The layout and design of the report is equally important. It should be designed for ready reference to and clear illustration of specific recommendations. Each chapter should be complete and self-explanatory, covering one subject from inventory to recommendation to implementation. A summary reviews the contents of each chapter for the reader's understanding.

IMPLEMENTING THE PLAN

The best plan is of little value if it is not followed by effective implementation. When governmental bodies are involved, four groups are responsible for implementing an adopted plan: elected officials (board of commissioners or select persons), the planning commission, the conservation commission or other citizens committee, and special-project committees, which may include an implementation committee or a joint partnership between a community-based organization and the appropriate political jurisdiction.

Elected officials shoulder most of the responsibility for implementing an adopted plan. State legislation establishes their duties. Among other responsibilities, the elected officials enact subdivision regulations and zoning ordinances and adopt a capital program and budget.

The planning commission may be advisory or may have its responsibilities delegated by elected officials. The planning commission deals with the myriad details of land use, including drafting subdivision regulations and zoning ordinances, setting conditions for development, and making recommendations to elected officials on all aspects of plan implementation. They should be acquainted with the methods of guiding land use listed in chapter 15 and should select the type needed for each step of implementation.

A separate special commission (or subcommittee) may be appointed by the elected body for the specific purpose of assisting it and the planning commission in developing and implementing an environmental plan. In New England this role is frequently filled by a conservation commission. Conservation commissions were introduced in Massachusetts and later sprang up in other northeastern states.

Special project committees are ad hoc subcommittees appointed by the elected body or the planning commission to assist in implementing a single project or goal. The Indian Brook Reservoir project discussed in chapter 1 is one example. Another is a citizens implementation committee or an advocacy group like the one described later in Chapter 5.

Implementation usually consists of three distinct actions. The first and most important is identifying and adopting specific implementation procedures. The second is for the appropriate jurisdictions to enact bylaws or ordinances to achieve the plan's goals. In small towns or villages implementation strategies often include zoning or a permit system with districting, subdivision regulations, an official map of the planning area, and a budget and program. In more sparsely populated areas, or in natural resource areas, only some of these elements are usually required. The third action is delegating the responsibility of evaluating implementation to the planning commission, a citizens advisory committee, or a community organization.

ADOPTING IMPLEMENTATION PROCEDURES

A plan is only as good as its implementation. The methods for implementation should be contained in the plan itself. One approach is to lay out a grid with goals, time frames, responsible entities, and resources so that progress can be tracked. Another is to include in each chapter of the plan what resources are available and what entity will be responsible for implementation objectives. For example, a proposal for a cross-country ski trail network may include a statement concerning the type of agreements to be worked out with landowners and the persons to negotiate the agreements. Another proposal, for establishing group credit for property owners served by an irrigation association, may indicate the source of funds, the procedure for obtaining funds, and the person(s) responsible for obtaining them. Information on procedures provides the tools crucial to plan implementation.

ENACTING ORDINANCES OR BYLAWS

When ordinances or bylaws must be enacted for plan implementation, it is helpful to draw up a map showing the various districts or zones within the plan area and defining the uses to which each will be put. Community ordinances or bylaws should include subdivision regulations for new housing or for commercial or industrial development. The local government should also adopt a long-term capital program and a more detailed short-term capital budget. Performance-based zones or alternatives such as permit systems— as opposed to the traditional land-use zones of urban areas—can make zoning more acceptable and enforceable in rural areas. When unduly detailed zoning is enacted in rural areas, it can lead to frequent zone changes or to a pattern of granting exceptions on request. This can destroy confidence in the planning process and in the notion of equitable administration.

Where land-use controls or guidelines are necessary, all methods should be considered and the most acceptable selected. Alternatives to zoning include building codes, plumbing codes, health regulations, setback ordinances, easements, and a building permit system.[2] In a rural area whose citizens are opposed to zoning, the rural plan should not rely on that method of implementation.

The adoption of simple, clear, functional zoning and subdivision regulations is one method of implementing a plan. Zones or districts should be designed to fit the rural territory and its requirements. There are three important zones for rural environmental planning. The first is the central activity or development zone. This is an area around the village or community center where commerce and small-lot residences are encouraged. Second is the ring around that center, a limited development zone where lot sizes may be larger and efforts are made to avoid commercial development. Third is the rural zone, the surrounding area where lots are sized to protect agricultural land, forests, or wetlands. The rural zone may contain or be surrounded by conservation zones in which building is not permitted if it would damage the environment. Conservation zones may consist of higher elevations, stream banks, lake shores, arroyos, ditch-irrigation systems, wetlands, steep slopes, or ridges. These zones often cross or weave through the other zones.

In urban areas the official projected land-use map is an indispensable tool for implementing a master plan. In rural areas a land-use map is less useful, as it assumes definitive knowledge of the rates and type of future development. Prediction in rural planning is very speculative. A general map, though, showing development and conservation zones and major access roads, does provide a clear framework for a rural area and can help participants make more detailed decisions about future growth.

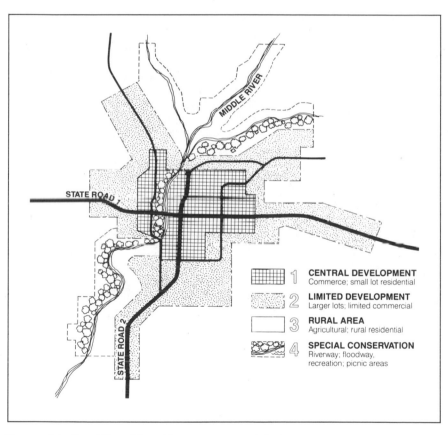

FIGURE 3.1. Rural Zone Map. *The components of this zone map are typical for a small rural community. General areas defining residential density, commercial or industrial use, rural or agricultural districts, and special open or conservation areas, as well as major access roads, serve as a guide for more detailed decisions in the future.*

PART I: START-UP

1. *Initiation:*   recognition of problem, need, or opportunity.
2. *Discussion:*   informal exchange of ideas, options.
3. *Organization:*   ad hoc citizens committee formed; REP process studied.

PART II: CREATING THE PLAN

1. *Hold an information meeting* with elected board, planning commission, rural environmental planner, citizens.
   a.   Discuss objectives, procedures, assistance available, costs, schedule.
   b.   Exchange letters of agreement.
2. *Appoint Rural Environmental Planning Committee.*
   a.   Form subcommittees around inventory subjects.
   b.   Include representatives of all groups with an interest in the Plan.
3. *Discover public goals.*
   a.   Draft and deliver goals questionnaires; collect questionnaires.
   b.   Tabulate results of goals survey and distribute.
4. *Inventory natural, cultural, human resources.*
   a.   Describe resources.
   b.   Obtain data, guidance, recommendations from technical team.
   c.   Conduct field trips for direct assessment.
   d.   Present and discuss inventory reports at public meetings. Incorporate recommendations.
5. *Draft plan. Review, publish, and distribute.*
   a.   Assemble draft of findings, goals, recommendations, priorities, implementation methods.
   b.   Organize in chapters, based on inventory subjects (or goals, or geographic areas).
   c.   Distribute to all households.

PART III: ADOPTION AND IMPLEMENTATION

Hold public hearings, adjust, then adopt Final Plan with implementation strategies.
Action 1: Pursue implementing strategies, identify funding sources, parties responsible for actions.
Action 2: Enact ordinances, bylaws, adopt official map, capital budget.
Action 3: Establish responsibility to monitor progress and implement the plan.

FIGURE 3.2. The REP Process

A capital program sets forth the long-term capital expenditures anticipated by a municipality or a rural planning district. A capital budget establishes specific expenditures for a projected period, usually five years. Proposed expenditures are based on findings for needed physical improvements in such areas as transportation, public facilities, utilities, and land acquisition. The capital program and budget establish commitments for public investment in accordance with the specific goals and needs identified in the plan. As such, they prevent haphazard public spending and block the potential for selectively ignoring established goals. Although detailed programming for a five-year budget may require special assistance, every rural community or individual unit in a planning district should prepare a capital program and budget as a guideline for public investment.

DELEGATING RESPONSIBILITY FOR EVALUATING IMPLEMENTATION

When people are directly involved in defining goals and strategies, implementation is much easier. Participation creates a sense of owning the plan; it creates a constituency. Still, after the plan is adopted and the ordinances or bylaws are enacted, participants must make sure that action takes place. Often the planning commission or REP committee develops a sense of responsibility for, or feels it has a special stake in the implementation of, the plan. Involvement of such citizens in a conservation commission or on the planning commission can provide continuity and help to implement the plan. Plan implementation is aided by clear declarative statements in the adopted recommendations, by effective ordinances or bylaws, and by minimizing the number of variances granted.

CONCLUSION

REP differs significantly from conventional urban planning in both organization and process. The organization recommended in REP includes a working relationship among three parties: the client (a town or county government, a tribe or Indian pueblo, a community-based organization, a multijurisdiction, or a regional board); the planner (a faculty member or a student in rural planning at the state university, a rural-planning graduate, a state agency, or a paid or volunteer professional); and the technical team (personnel from state or federal agencies, private-sector volunteers, or other professionals).

PART II

The Components of Rural Environmental Planning

4

Discovering Public Goals

GOALS ARE IMPLICIT in any planning process. For example, urban planning generally assumes and projects the goal of continuous growth. The urban planning process consists of separating land uses by zoning, supplying municipal services to new or revitalized areas, and allocating space for anticipated residential, industrial, and commercial growth. In rural planning, goals may be quite different. They may include minimizing land-use controls, protecting natural resources, fostering cultural resources, preserving rural amenities, or simply maintaining a rural way of life. Such goals are not determined by the planner but rather discovered through surveys and discussions with people in the community.

Special attention must be paid to identifying community goals in rural planning as the public goals of past decades may be progressively less relevant to present conditions. For example, a former goal of unqualified economic growth may have given way to the goal of controlled development. Past goals, moreover, may give little or no consideration to quality of life, for example, preserving scenic views, rural byways, access to public lands and waters, natural areas, cultural resources, and historic sites.

Wishes expressed by people in rural communities must be translated into specific objectives and methods for implementation; priorities must be established. If the goal is clean water, for example, actions such as building a sewage treatment plant or providing comparable waste water treatment in dispersed or cluster systems must be agreed on. Economic goals must be compatible with environmental protection, cultural values, or other local priorities. Many questions of tradeoff and equity arise. Should cleaner water, say, be accessible to all, or just to a few cottage owners on the lakeshore? Should land be bought now for wilderness reserves or should the money be spent for parks? Do we transfer water rights from traditional agriculture to recreation or second-home developments? These questions of appropriate goals and the priority they take can be answered by systematic survey and analysis.

TYPES OF PUBLIC GOALS

There are three types of public goals to be identified: established goals, goals under development, and proposed goals.[1] An *established* public goal is a policy decision that a village or county legislative body has incorporated into an ordinance, regulation, or administrative directive. An example of an established community goal would be a decision to enforce public-health controls by hiring a health officer. A *developing* goal would be one for which a few steps have been taken by the body politic but which has not been definitely established in law or practice. For example, if a community sets a goal to provide parks to serve all town residents, the building of one park would only partially fulfill that goal; more parks may be needed before the goal is achieved. *Proposed* goals are those that some people say should be public goals but that have not yet been accepted and acted on. The protection of a natural area would be a proposed goal until it was included in an adopted plan.

METHODS OF DETERMINING GOALS

There are three methods that can be used in identifying and establishing public goals: following tradition or the example of other communities, employing consultants, or using attitude surveys and open planning. Following tradition has often proved a useful tool for determining public goals, and it continues to be useful in areas where growth and an urban infrastructure are still relevant. However, previous goals may be an inappropriate guide to the management of a rural community as new community goals evolve. Many good ideas may be gleaned by a study of the past; however, new concepts for land use cannot be discovered by only studying past procedures. Following the example of other communities has the advantage of letting them stand the expense of testing new methods. Hawaii's experiment in scenic zoning may be copied by other states. The Massachusetts conservation commissions are worthy of study and possible use elsewhere to serve as citizen boards advocating natural resource conservation. Similarly, conservation authorities and small watershed programs in the province of Ontario, Canada, can be studied to learn about interagency cooperation in river valley planning. This method of reviewing how things are done elsewhere should be used constantly and assiduously. Rural communities may better achieve sustainable economic development by developing new goals or new methods fitting to their region. They either devise new ways or apply concepts used elsewhere and adjust them to the local area. However, the most direct and effective method for discovering goals is simply to ask those people who will be affected by the plan.

GOAL SURVEYS

In REP projects, 100% attitude surveys have been developed as a major device for determining public goals. An effective attitude survey must satisfy three requirements: it should provide accurate information from a significant percentage of people concerning public goals; it should be conducted, analyzed, and reported inexpensively and quickly; and it should have an educational objective, that is, it should explore new concepts by asking questions about them. Methods to determine community goals inexpensively and quickly and to stimulate learning through participation in the planning process are described in the following paragraphs.

To increase accuracy and inclusiveness in rural environment planning, the survey questionnaire is developed by the rural planner in close collaboration with the goal subcommittee. The survey is sent to all households, not to some small or random sample of them.

The cost should be included in the REP budget, funded by the local jurisdiction. To conserve money the questionnaire may be printed by the local newspaper, placed in local stores, or taken home by children from school. The form is short—one sheet, both sides—and leaves enough space for new suggestions to be written in. The restriction in length to one sheet is not too severe. Ten to twenty questions can be put on a single sheet; this will provide sufficient information to a planning commission in the initial stages of discovering public goals.

A brief survey reduces the cost and time involved in analysis, thus permitting the survey to be an input into the first phase of the planning process rather than a subsequent review or critique of it. Brevity can be compensated for later, in public discussion of the issues. When the wide range of options are reduced to a few specific choices, a second survey may be conducted to determine preferences. The rural environmental planner should assure citizens and community officials that within one month after the attitude survey is conducted, the results will be made public.

The goal survey is designed to give information as well as to elicit it. Questions may be included for several purposes. A question can establish a general goal, for example: "Should Shelburne have more public access on the lakeshore?" A question can be directed toward a specific objective: "Should the village of Pajarito establish a public market for farm produce and handicrafts?" Questions can be drafted to ascertain lack of information and to set the stage for education: "Are you familiar with the plan for a Connecticut River valley recreation area?/Would you like to know more about it?" Through a question, a new concept can be introduced to the public for purposes of further discussion: "Do you think the communities in the Jemez Valley should work together to coordinate regional services?" See figure 4.1 for further questions.

One of the most important purposes of the questionnaire is to determine whether local citizens are willing to support a specific program through the allocation of tax money: "Would you agree to have your taxes increased by $3 next year in order to raise $10,000 for the acquisition of land for recreational purposes?" In many instances, positive replies to questions like this have transformed local elected board members from guardians of the status quo into active leaders. One survey, conducted in South Burlington, Vermont, resulted in a complete reversal of the town officials' concept of public goals. Initially, officials assured the planning team that taxes were too high and that the voters would not support an appropriation of money for acquisition of park and recreation land. When the survey was completed, however, 60 percent of the respondents indicated they would be willing to spend money for parkland. Other pro-environment issues gained the support of 60 to 90 percent of the respondents. In light of results, elected board members reversed their position and proceeded to implement the wishes of the community.

The purpose of goal survey in the REP process is to formulate public goals as people see them at a certain time within a continuing planning process. The survey is for planning purposes, not for academic or statistical analysis of people's attitudes correlated with multiple demographic and economic factors.

The REP survey may utilize professional assistance from specialists in attitude surveys. However, the specialists assisting with a rural survey must understand how the rural planning process differs from traditional statistical techniques used for large population sampling. In a small community or rural area, a survey that reaches all households is psychologically superior to as well as more accurate than the random sampling recommended by statisticians in surveying large populations. Responding to a survey generates a positive feeling of participation. Random samples in a small community where most people know each other run the risk of kindling resentment in those not surveyed.

The results of attitude surveys are biased to some degree. In any democratically governed society, decisions are made or influenced by those who choose to participate in the process. From previous attitude studies we know that respondents usually represent a disproportionately larger number of a community's higher-income and better-educated people. Those who do not participate are left out of this stage of the planning process.

Fortunately there are other opportunities in an open-planning process for all citizens to express their attitudes on public goals. The survey process includes a public meeting for presentation and discussion of questionnaire results. This meeting should be held as soon as the responses are tabulated. An announcement for this gathering might read: "If you returned a questionnaire, come and discuss your recommendations and hear what others have to say. If you did not return a questionnaire, you will have an opportunity to fill one out at this meeting."

A survey to formulate public goals, no matter how well conducted, should not be confused with a vote in town meetings or on a referendum. The survey is more like an opinion poll in an electoral campaign when attitudes are changing. It may be an accurate representation of opinion, but only that of the actual respondents, and only based on the knowledge they have at one point in time, that is, the initial phase of planning. A survey is not the final word; rather it is an invaluable first step that far surpasses a few elected officials making a decision in isolation.

Many situations and unforeseen opportunities may arise that make it logical and justifiable for town officials to take action not given a high priority in the survey. For example, a survey might indicate little interest in developing access to fishing areas. However, the sudden availability of state funds for fishing access might lead to action to acquire them. A proposal to beautify a town plaza or to mark historical buildings might receive low priority, but it could be implemented if a small group of interested volunteers does the work.

PUBLIC PARTICIPATION

Basic to the determination of public goals is a concerted effort to involve as many people as possible in the planning and decision-making process. There

The Henniker Conservation Commission and the Planning Board are developing a comprehensive master plan for the town. Please fill out the following questions and return the questionnaire at the town meeting or to the selectmen's office. Please read each statement carefully and check one response for each.

	Agree	Uncertain	Disagree
1. There is a need to preserve and protect wetlands, unique natural areas, and significant wildlife habitats in town.	186 / 90%	9 / 4%	6 / 3%
2. To prevent unsound development and the destruction of the floodplains, we must enact floodplain zoning.	145 / 70%	16 / 8%	36 / 17%
3. We should strengthen present land use legislation to cover those areas not presently protected, while improving the tax base and protecting the town's valuable natural resources.	141 / 68%	13 / 6%	39 / 19%
4. We should encourage the keeping of agricultural land in production.	186 / 90%	7 / 3%	8 / 4%
5. Efforts should be made to keep forest lands in production.	175 / 85%	7 / 3%	18 / 9%
6. To preserve the rural character of the town, selected roads should be designated as "scenic" and should retain their present characteristics.	152 / 73%	15 / 7%	33 / 16%
Please specify any roads which you feel should be designated as "scenic."	(tabulated separately)		
7. We should encourage the preservation of structures of unique and distinctive architectural character or historical importance.	166 / 80%	12 / 6%	22 / 10%
8. There is a need for more open space in the central area of town.	68 / 33%	76 / 37%	54 / 26%
9. Adequate housing is available in Henniker to meet the current needs of residents.	68 / 33%	47 / 23%	84 / 41%

10. If you disagree, please check the types of housing you would like to see in town to meet these needs:

Single family	22	Condominiums	4
Mobile home	1	Apartments	22
Cluster housing	8	Low-cost housing	22
Other	4		

	Agree	Uncertain	Disagree
11. There is a need for expanded recreational facilities within the town.	149 / 72%	36 / 17%	14 / 7%

FIGURE 4.1. Henniker, New Hampshire: Attitude Survey[2]

12. If you agree, which of the following recreational activities should be added or improved? Please rank in order of preference the top three choices (1 is top preference, 3 is lowest).

Recreational Activity	Priority 1	2	3	Recreational Activity	Priority 1	2	3
Swimming	34	17	13	Scenic lookouts	0	2	5
Camping	3	2	8	Nature trails	13	13	9
Fishing	2	4	5	Bicycle paths	15	19	21
Public hunting	1	0	2	Hiking and			
Picnicking	4	5	4	walking trails	16	12	10
Power-boating	0	0	0	X-country ski trails	1	13	4
Nonpower-boating	1	9	6	Snowmobile trails	3	2	3
Motorbike trails	9	3	4	Skating	7	13	16
Playgrounds	12	10	15	Other	5	2	0

	Agree	Uncertain	Disagree
13. An effort should be made to increase the use of the flood-control area for recreational purposes (other than the land already leased for agriculture).	118 57%	28 14%	46 22%

14. Would you support purchase of land and development of facilities for outdoor recreation if it meant an increase in your 1976 tax bill of:

$0	28	$5	22
$10	22	$15	3
$20 or more	16	Uncertain	22

	Agree	Uncertain	Disagree
15. A revitalization program for downtown should be undertaken to make it more aesthetically pleasing.	110 53%	55 27%	27 13%

16. Would you support the idea of a conservation easement for Cascade Falls?   Yes: 103   No: 33

17. How long have you lived in Hennikier?

College students	83	0–5 years	31
5–10 years	28	10–15 years	12
15–20 years	12	Over 20 years	17
All your life	19		

18. Sex:
      male   116 (56%)   female   82 (40%)

19. Would you be willing to assist in the drawing up of the comprehensive plan for the town?   Yes: 97   No: 69

Thank you for your time.

          Signature (optional) _____

are several techniques that may be employed in addition to attitude surveys. Field trips, news releases, and public meetings and hearings are all useful. The planning process should include field trips—for the technical team, the citizens committee or planning commission, or the public—can be made to study soils, natural areas, and sites for irrigation ditches, recreation grounds, or trails. The success of field trips should not be judged by the number of people attending but rather by how much information they gather and disseminate. Results of the trip can be published in the local newspaper or broadcast as a public-service announcement on local radio or TV.

Public hearings and meetings are a common and effective method of determining citizen reactions to proposals and of refining community goals. They are also a good method for determining public goals when conducted for that purpose. A checklist (see fig. 4.2) can be used to track the progress and accomplishments of open planning. An intensive effort during the process to inform and involve people who will be affected by a plan is the key to community approval and implementation of the plan.

CASE: SAN YSIDRO, NEW MEXICO

In December 1984, the mayor of the village of San Ysidro de los Dolores, a two-hundred-year-old community in north-central New Mexico, asked for assistance from the community and regional planning program at the University of New Mexico in preparing a plan for the future of their village. San Ysidro, with a population estimated at two hundred in 1985, is located at the confluence of the Jemez and Salado rivers in north central New Mexico. The Rio Jemez drains portions of a pine-forested, 11,000-foot-high volcanic caldera providing spring and summer irrigation to the villages and Indian pueblos along the river, while the Rio Salado drains the more arid, alkaline plateau lands toward the Continental Divide to the west.

According to a special census conducted by the New Mexico State government in the spring of 1984, San Ysidro had a population of 198 people, slightly less than in 1978 when the village had 204 people. The 1984 census showed decreases since 1978 in the age groups 1–4 and 5–17, with a substantial increase in the age group 18–64 and a slight increase in the age group 65 and over. The residents of San Ysidro have subsisted for a long time on the small farms and gardens in the irrigated valley, their small herds of cattle grazing the mountain slopes, and part- or full-time mining on nearby mesas. Gypsum, gravel, rock, and pumice are extracted intermittently to serve fluc-

Activity	Number of Participants	Summary of Accomplishments
Planning meetings		
1. Meeting of planning committee	_____	_____
2. Meeting with elected officials	_____	_____
3. Subcommittee meetings	_____	_____
Public information meetings		
4. Required by law	_____	_____
5. Additional meetings	_____	_____
Informal contacts		
6. Elected officials	_____	_____
7. Planning commission	_____	_____
8. Special interest groups	_____	_____
Media information		
9. Newspaper story reporting planning progress	_____	_____
10. Newspaper story announcing public meeting	_____	_____
11. Radio or television reports	_____	_____
12. Handouts distributed at meeting	_____	_____
13. Newsletter	_____	_____
Field trips		
14. Soils/irrigation ditches	_____	_____
15. Trails	_____	_____
16. Natural areas	_____	_____
17. Community parks	_____	_____
Reports to special interest groups		
18. Coffees (total attendance)	_____	_____
19. Exhibits (total attendance)	_____	_____
Plan dissemination		
20. Systematic collection of comments leading to revision of draft plans	_____	_____
21. Proposed plan distributed to public	_____	_____

FIGURE 4.2. Planning and Participation Checklist

tuating construction markets in Albuquerque, Santa Fe, and other cities of the region.

San Ysidro had been experiencing a substantial increase in traffic on the two highways that converge in the village and provide access to high-altitude recreation areas—cross-country skiing, archeological sites, mineral hot springs, and local festivals. A recent widening of these highways, the purchase and marketing of some of the village lands by outsiders, and other pressures for change led the mayor and chair of the village council to request university assistance in preparing a plan for the future. Preliminary meetings with University of New Mexico planning faculty led to a recommendation for a public meeting to define planning objectives.

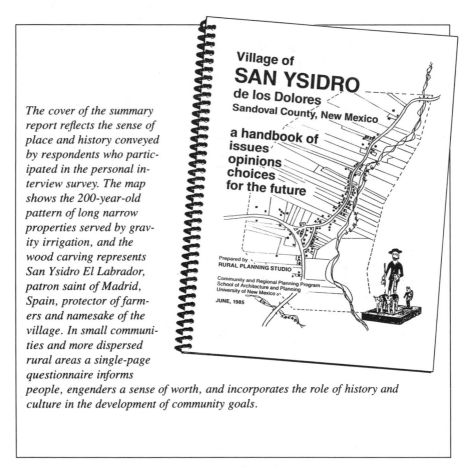

The cover of the summary report reflects the sense of place and history conveyed by respondents who participated in the personal interview survey. The map shows the 200-year-old pattern of long narrow properties served by gravity irrigation, and the wood carving represents San Ysidro El Labrador, patron saint of Madrid, Spain, protector of farmers and namesake of the village. In small communities and more dispersed rural areas a single-page questionnaire informs people, engenders a sense of worth, and incorporates the role of history and culture in the development of community goals.

FIGURE 4.3. Goal Survey.

In January 1985 a meeting was called by the village council so that people in the community could voice their opinions about local issues, problems, and needs. Graduate students from the rural planning studio at the university attended this meeting and heard a wide range of concerns and strong opinions about how to address these concerns. Problem areas included water availability and quality, jobs and economic survival, tourism and traffic, areawide recreation, and the village park. Also discussed were health services, childcare, programs for the elderly, zoning, and the management of growth.

In light of the diversity of issues and opinions, the village council requested that members of the planning studio conduct a survey of the entire community to better define issues, goals, and priorities. After a period of research the students designed, tested, and in the spring of 1985 conducted an attitude survey of all village households. About 85 percent of the families chose to respond. A summary of the planning studio's findings follows.

The house-to-house survey revealed that the people of San Ysidro commanded a wealth of job skills—managerial, mechanical, secretarial, construction, retailing, ranching, farming, logging, hair-dressing, dental hygiene, and handicrafts. These represented a significant resource that could form the basis of new economic activity in San Ysidro.

Of the families surveyed, 92 percent indicated a desire for more jobs in the village and 73 percent a desire for more local businesses. Half of the families had children who had moved away because of employment, marriage, or school. A general goal emerged from this information: to reduce outmigration by increasing jobs and business opportunities.

Ninety-two percent of the respondents said they had to travel outside of the Jemez Valley for such things as shopping, medical appointments, and entertainment. Thus another general goal emerged: to reduce the need for external travel. Within a year of the survey, a new health clinic had been established in conjunction with an adjacent community.

The primary concern of San Ysidro was water. The quality and quantity of the supply was perceived as a serious limitation to all future village plans. Almost half the people surveyed were concerned about the water's safety, taste, and appearance. More than a third had concerns about irrigation, for example the condition of community ditches and the quantity of water they made available. Almost 30 percent had problems with septic tanks that needed frequent cleaning and maintenance. The implied goal—good-quality water—was already being addressed by a separately funded program to install point-of-use water purifiers in each home and business. In addition, options for financing water pumping and storage were being discussed with state agencies.

The survey showed that San Ysidro residents prized the rural qualities of their village. Newcomers and new businesses would be welcome in small numbers as long as rural quality was not affected. Most residents, though, were not willing to sacrifice the "specialness" of the village just to bring in more jobs and income. Many felt that village development brought with it a price, and they had chosen to live in San Ysidro precisely not to have to pay such a price. The implied goal was balanced growth, that is, accommodating new growth but in such a way as not to sacrifice the qualities that made San Ysidro a special place.

The results of the survey and of the students' research were incorporated in a report to the village council and summarized on large display boards exhibited at the village fiesta in May 1985.[3] The report suggested various goal categories and recommendations for action. It also identified people in agencies that could be of help in addressing problems and achieving community goals.

CONCLUSION

One of the major differences between conventional urban planning and rural planning lies in the determination of public goals. Urban planning goals are strongly driven by the requirements for growth. Often they are determined by elected or representative boards and tested through opinion sampling or voting.

In rural planning, public goals vary widely depending on community values, life-styles, and available resources. They may include a desire to restrain or manage growth. Because of the potential for a more direct relationship among people in small communities, the process of formulating public goals is important. In REP, goal determination is not a delegated responsibility but rather a process that requires conducting a 100% goal survey designed to gather ideas and suggestions, the drafting of recommendations based on survey findings, and public meetings to discuss the community's natural, cultural, and human resources and their relationship to public goals. The survey also provides information about priorities and alternatives and helps to identify citizens interested in working on inventory and planning subcommittees.

5

Inventorying the Resource Base

INVENTORYING THE RESOURCE base is a major activity in any planning program. In large-scale urban planning the emphasis is on physical resources—land-use zoning, utilities, transportation, and other parts of the urban infrastructure. In rural planning the emphasis is on natural, human, and cultural resources, the building blocks of the local economy. There are a great many ways to inventory resources.

Inventorying starts immediately after the formation of subcommittees, as described in chapter 3. It takes a few weeks to several months, until the components of a plan can be put together. Information about community resources provides the data base for recommendations and the rationale for policy decisions. The data base teaches subcommittee members, and through them the community, more about the technical aspects of their situation. Resources identified should be seen as raw material, basic stuff for the discussion of goals discovered by survey or by the technical team. The inventory and classification of resources supply the descriptive part of each chapter in the plan.

There are a number of standard planning inventories included in comprehensive plans that may or may not be useful in a rural environmental plan. They are mentioned here briefly, in case any should be necessary.

A population projection is basic in all planning. The projection can be estimated from regional population projections prepared by state planning or budgeting agencies or the U.S. Bureau of Census surveys available at public libraries or county offices. Alternatively, planning or demography students at the state university can make the projection. Road and highway inventories and plans are obtained from the state highway department. Inventories of educational facilities are made with assistance from school district administrators and teachers. An inventory of parks and recreation land, or of criteria to define such lands, can be supplied by the town recreation committee or by a county or state agency responsible for parks and recreation lands. Inventories of police, fire protection, and utility services are made by contacting the providers of these services.

COMPREHENSIVE AND FOCUSED INVENTORIES

There are two approaches to inventorying: the comprehensive and the focused. The comprehensive inventory presented in planning textbooks is frequently used in urban and regional planning. It consists of collecting all the information available on all subjects relevant to the planning area. This data is tabulated and published in the planning study. The advantage of this approach is that it provides information to answer any questions that may arise.

The focused inventory is especially designed for rural planning requirements. To conduct a focused inventory, first draw up a tentative list of hypotheses or recommendations from the technical team for developing a plan in accord with public goals. Then gather only data needed to support these proposals. For example, in a focused inventory of Glover, Vermont, recommendations from a plan for a neighboring town were studied along with the technical team's suggestions. These recommendations were then discussed with reference to Glover. Some were dropped, others were added, and a list of anticipated recommendations was agreed on. This list was used to guide data collection. Only currently available data that supported these recommendations was collected.

The focused inventory takes between a third to a tenth of the time required for a comprehensive inventory and can bring considerable savings in time and money with no apparent loss in the quality of the plan. A focused inventory follows the scientific method, which states that a tentative theory or hypothesis should guide data-gathering. As planning proceeds, some hypotheses may be dropped and others requiring different information may be proposed. As this happens, data gathering is adjusted accordingly.

The relationship between inventorying and goal determination is very important. The two processes should be kept distinct in order to achieve the real goals of the people (uninhibited by considerations of resource limitation) and to compile the best information and recommendations from the technical team (uninhibited by concern for local attitudes). After the goals are determined and the inventories made, the two processes can be combined. Thus some new goals may appear from the results of resource inventorying, and some additional inventorying may be required to provide data for new goals.

SOURCES OF DATA

There are four general sources of information that may be tapped to supply inventory data: this book and others on rural planning; government offices and data bases at the federal, county, and state levels; state university libraries, faculties, and technology-application centers; and subcommittee field surveys.

The local extension service office, the USDA's SCS, the U.S. Fish and Wildlife Service, the Forestry Service, the U.S. Census Bureau, and the Department of the Interior's U.S. Geological Survey are especially good sources of help. Many of these agencies have recently developed geographic information systems (GIS) utilizing computer-assisted cartography and database files to collect, analyze, display, and print statistical, spatial, and cartographic information from a digitized base.

The state university is another good source of information. Fortunately, most focused inventory information is readily available in local libraries, extension service offices, or the nearest regional repository libraries designated by the federal government. Information should be selected, organized, and interpreted by someone familiar with the subject and then checked with the appropriate specialists on the technical team.

The most direct way for subcommittees to collect inventory information is through field observation. This method is good for studying waterfront access, scenic roads and overlooks, school facilities for outdoor recreation, pedestrian or cross-country ski trails, and natural areas, among other subjects.

NATURAL, CULTURAL, AND HUMAN RESOURCES

We need clear definitions to organize and present the results of inventories. The following distinctions and definitions reflect general usage. For the purposes of discussion, we divide the field of resources into three categories: natural, cultural, and human resources. Natural resources are further divided into the following categories: physical setting; land ownership pattern; soils; agricultural land; water resources; groundwater aquifer, water supplies, and recharge areas; wetlands; forested lands; wildlife habitats; elevations and slopes; and historic sites, landscapes, and buildings.

PHYSICAL OR GEOGRAPHIC SETTING

An inventory of a physical setting is a general geological, meteorological, and geographic description of an area. It covers the relation of the area to the region and includes major physical features, population densities, and special positive or negative factors.

Natural resources such as wetlands, forests, unique geological formations, and wildlife habitats, and some modified resources such as agricultural lands, dams and irrigation systems, buildings, and rural landscapes, require special inventories because of their importance to the community or their special requirements for management. Special inventories are discussed in greater detail in this and in later chapters of this book.

THE LAND OWNERSHIP PATTERN

One of the most important parts of an inventory is a description of the land-ownership pattern. In states where ownership maps are maintained in county clerk's offices, it is not difficult to study ownership patterns. In states where ownership maps are not used and acreage descriptions in warranty deeds are estimates, only research will reveal ownership patterns. To analyze ownership for rural planning, it is not necessary to identify and measure every lot but to develop a general idea of the pattern of ownership. This can be obtained by identifying and locating larger ownerships and the predominant uses of smaller ones. A study of land ownership enhances understanding of the political economy of land use and increases the relevance of the planning process.

Knowledge of ownership, for example, assists in the protection of natural areas. Such areas can often be protected by designation. This method works well if natural areas are owned by people receptive to suggestions for protection and preservation. If a rural community wishes to acquire access to public waters, it must understand ownership patterns along these waters. The potential effects of future development at high elevations may be discovered by determining who owns land at those elevations and what the long-term vision of the owners is.

In rural areas, larger land holdings are sometimes underassessed relative to smaller holdings. An ownership survey and a comparison of assessments of record may reveal the need for a professional reassessment of large holdings. As a result, some owners of large holdings end up with higher taxes—an inducement for them to trade tax concessions with the rural jurisdiction for water access, park or recreation land, or trail easements.

SOILS

An inventory of soils is basic to rural planning. In most every county in the United States since the early 1930s, the SCS has been analyzing, mapping, and interpreting soils as well as recommending their proper use to prevent erosion and maximize agricultural productivity. Until the 1950s, such efforts focused on advising farmers how to reduce erosion, improve drainage, and maintain wildlife habitats. Since the 1950s and increasingly since the 1970s, the SCS has also considered soils with reference to suitability or limitations for roads, leach fields, wetlands, natural areas, community development, and industrial sites.

SCS soil surveys are either general or detailed. General surveys combine associated soil units, complexes, or undifferentiated groups of soils into larger units appropriate to more extensive use. General soil maps show from ten to twenty or more main patterns of soils called soil associations. Each of these associations may, in fact, contain several major soils and several minor soils in a pattern that varies through the association. The soils within a given association often differ in significant ways, for example, in slope, depth to bedrock, stoniness, natural drainage, or wetness. Thus, the general soil map shows not the kind of soil in any particular place but rather several different patterns of soil made up of the many separate soils in each association.

Detailed soil reports are also prepared by the SCS. Maps and descriptions in detailed reports are based predominantly on field surveys and on the analysis of soil borings or layers in road cuts or pits. While a general soil map may show ten to twenty different soil associations, as many as fifty or sixty different types of soils may be shown in the area covered by a detailed map. Detailed soil maps and reports are available in SCS offices, located in nearly all counties and all soil and water conservation districts in the United States.

A map of soil potential and limitation for on-site sewage disposal by septic tank and leach field can be useful in REP. It should be noted, however, that even detailed soil maps are not site-specific. Within each soil classification there may be a number of areas that have better or worse potential for its indicated purpose. A more definitive soil investigation or engineering analysis is needed, for example when evaluating specific sites for on-site sewage disposal or for the design of other sewage disposal systems.

Similarly, a detailed soil map indicating potential or limitation in certain areas for sanitary landfill is useful. This type of map shows the general potential for sanitary landfill of the predominant soils in each area. To learn the specific locations that might be most suitable in each proposed site, the planning commission or the landowner should have special soil samples taken of proposed sites. SCS personnel as well as the state department of water resources or environmental protection should be consulted about locating sanitary landfills.

AGRICULTURAL LAND

Although economic returns on agricultural land have varied greatly over the last twenty years, the most basic resource for many rural areas is soil with agricultural potential. Whenever there is extensive agricultural land in a region, it must be inventoried and classified in order to consider its potential future use in relation to competing uses. Several methods of classification have been developed since land-use planning evolved in the early 1930s.[1]

The system outlined here is based on a combination of soil and economic data. The starting point of classification is SCS information concerning soil's characteristics and soil's suitability for farming. Added to this are data on land-use trends, the minimum size for viable farm units, and the economics of location in relation to markets. This information is available from state university departments of agricultural economics or from the local agricultural extension agent.

Classification is done in three steps: mapping land into four suitability classes based on agricultural productivity and the economic potential of soils; mapping present land use; and mapping ownership, with overlays indicating private or public and identifying the managing agency. After these steps are completed, recommendations for future land use can be made.

This classification system provides a relative, not an absolute, means of comparison. The most suitable land is the land most suitable within the county or that particular soils analysis area—not necessarily in the state or region. Land is classified in four categories: class 1, best suited to row- or field-crop agriculture; class 2, moderately suited to such agriculture; class 3, poorly suited to such agriculture; and class 4, unsuitable to such agriculture. Land devoted to nonagricultural uses and not likely to be returned to agriculture is included in class 4. Land rated in categories 1, 2, or 3 should be distinguished as active or inactive farmland.

The land most suitable to row- or field-crop agriculture, class 1, is usually in flood-deposit plains, in river valleys, and on level or gently rolling landscape. Flood-deposit plains, because of their soil and topography, are excellent for farming. Class 2 land is less suitable to agriculture than class 1 land. Class 2 land is generally level or gently sloping and mostly sandy or silty, often with a clay subsoil. Class 3 is the least suitable of all for row-crop agriculture. Soils vary considerably in this class. Some are sandy, some stony, but all lack the natural fertility and ease of cultivation found in more productive soils.

The remaining land is placed in the classification 4, "Unsuitable for Traditional Agriculture." Class 4 land is mostly hilly or mountainous. The classification, however, evaluates land only for traditional flatland cropping and harvesting. Hilly or mountainous land can be used for grazing, intensive terraced agriculture, silvaculture (growing trees as a crop), and other productive uses.

Highly developed or urbanized areas also are placed in class 4. Urban developments may be located on soil with good agricultural potential. Such areas are usually considered lost to traditional agricultural use. However, special note should be made of suburban or cluster developments located on rich soil. These, suitable for intensive agriculture, aquaculture, and bio-mass recycling, can help to meet urban food and energy needs in the future and should be identified as potentially valuable community resources.[2]

Who inventories and classifies soil? The ideal team is made up of the local SCS representative, the county agent, or a successful agriculturalist who knows the soil in the area, and an agricultural economist from the state land-grant college. As an alternative, a planning student can interview these specialists and subsequently assemble and map the information. After classifying and mapping soil areas, the classification team should make a preliminary assessment of their "best use" with reference to the owners' interests and the public's. A map outlining present and projected future use provides a basis for a dialogue among citizens that will help them to plan land uses for the future.

WATER RESOURCES

Water is as important as soil in REP. In fact, soil may be considered a filter or conduit for the ground phase of the hydrologic cycle. Most state governments have water resource departments or, as in the Western states, a state engineer with highly competent technical staffs. However, obtaining information on water may be difficult because in many state universities its study is not considered a discipline. Water experts are often scattered among the departments of civil engineering, limnology, soils, geology, resource economics, law, and public administration.

An intensive effort must be made to describe existing conditions and actions necessary to achieve community goals for domestic water, irrigation, and recreational water use. A rural environmental plan should include a section on water resources that describes these resources clearly and comprehensively but also in terms that people affected by the plan can understand. Additionally, this section should make recommendations based on public goals and within the framework of quality control required in federal and state legislation and health department criteria.

The task of the rural environmental planner is to interview water experts in state agencies and university departments in order to collect data on the present situation, such as quantity, quality, process of allocation, ownership, historic use, or legal aspects. The biologists, hydrologists, limnologists, and geologists of the state universities or water resource agencies tend to use technical vocabulary that is basic to their scientific method. This vocabulary may not be suitable for community planning process. For example, many water scientists do not use the term *pollution*. They speak instead of "levels or eutrophication" and "levels of nutrients." And health departments have very precise definitions of pollution with reference to swimming and drinking water. This data, then, should be organized, translated into layman's language, and included in the plan's water resources chapter along with the recommendations that have been collected.

GROUNDWATER AQUIFERS, WATER SUPPLY, AND RECHARGE AREAS

Knowledge of the location of groundwater aquifers and recharge areas is desirable for wise land use planning. This information is obtained by surficial geologists who study soil, bedrock, slopes, and other data and infer the location of aquifers accurately enough to make their protection possible. Protection of these aquifer recharge areas is important for maintenance of potable water. They must be located and protected from intensive development. The source of this information is the state geologist or the university department of geology.

An inventory of the domestic water supply will require assistance from the state or county health department, water resources department, county or adjacent municipal water district, and local water-supply administrators. The report should include the number of samples taken, the number that have passed, and the number that have failed.

It should also describe water quality without fear or hope of favor. Sometimes water quality is treated as "sensitive" information. Research at the University of Vermont demonstrates, however, that if the public is given clear, concise, and frequent information about the public water supply, and if the quality is inadequate, people will take immediate steps to correct it. The University of Vermont experiment used a computer program to summarize and map data on water quality around the state; information was supplied to newspapers, which published a map indicating the number of samples taken for each public water supply system, the systems that passed, and the systems that failed. Citizens responded by informing the agency responsible of their concern. Local health officers unanimously concluded that the news reports were effective in promoting public awareness of and concern for water quality.[3] Information on water sources, water quality and quantity, and recharge areas should be mapped and made available to inform citizens and their elected officials.

WETLANDS

Wetlands—marshes, bogs, and ponds, as well as river and arroyo (dry-wash) floodways—require special attention, as they play a vital role in life cycles, flood prevention, and the hydrologic cycle. They are often also scenic natural areas. They should be identified, described, and appraised from the viewpoint of hydrology, botany, and wildlife biology. Then appropriate recommendations should be made to protect the functions that they serve. Wetlands are invariably unsuitable for building sites, and because they frequently act as flood retarding reservoirs or water-table recharge areas, there is strong justification for proposing in the plan that they be maintained as natural greenbelts.

FORESTED LAND

Forested land is a common feature of rural communities. An inventory of its type, acreage, ownership, and market value is an important component of the natural resource base and the economic base. Data for this inventory may be drawn from the state forestry department, professional foresters, federal regional foresters, and owners of extensive woodlands. Special care must be exercised in reporting acreage, as definitions of forested land vary from one agency to the next and some categories of agricultural land fit into the forested land category.

Forested land introduces special problems because it often represents residual land use. When the size of a holding is small, say, a hundred acres or less, and the quality poor, it is usually unprofitable to manage the land for timber production. Much forested land is held for non-timber production purposes such as water recharge, game management, even for aesthetics and recreation. To inventory forested land, assistance should be sought from county or state foresters on the production potential of forests, from botanists and hydrologists on the role of forests in the hydrologic cycle, from resource economists on the economics of multiple uses of forested land, and from environmental planners on the future role of the forestland in a quality environment.

WILDLIFE HABITATS

Three sources of information about wildlife habitats are available: SCS soil maps, biological surveys and interviews with state and university wildlife experts, and interviews with local game wardens, hunters, and farmers who know the wildlife of the area. Habitats may be studied by referring to soil and topographical maps, but while maps are useful in general planning, they lack precision. Biologists can make field surveys of wildlife. This method is precise but too expensive for most rural area planning.

Game wardens, hunters, and fishermen, as well as farmers and ranchers with a knowledge of wildlife habitats, may be interviewed to determine the location and size of habitats. Supplemental information is available from state fish and game department experts and range specialists at land grant colleges. An inventory of bird habitats, nesting and feeding areas, and migration routes, provided by local Audubon Society members, can add environmental perspective to a plan. Data from several sources permits comparison and the compilation of a consensus. Wildlife habitats can be mapped by species, location criticality, endangerment, etc., depending on the specific proposal for a natural area or conservation zone.

ELEVATIONS AND SLOPES

In rural areas, an inventory of slopes and higher elevations is essential to prevent expensive mistakes in the location of residences or other more intensive uses. Steep slopes are generally poor locations for roads and buildings, or other active uses, because of increased impact on local ecosystems. On steep slopes plant species are fewer, soils are shallower, erosion is more likely, precipitation damage is heavier, damage from roads or logging is greater, risk of fire is greater, and after-damage recovery is much slower. Early settlers in the eastern United States were aware of these disadvantages, and in northern New England farmland was not usually cleared above 2,000 to 2,500 feet elevation. In the West, most permanent agricultural communities were located at the edge of a valley, not on the steepest slopes and not on land that could be irrigated.

While steep slopes require protection primarily for conservation, higher elevations should be protected from intensive development primarily to minimize long-term costs to the local jurisdiction. Although local conditions vary, in general the higher the elevation, the more costly the road upkeep, snow removal, and other municipal and county services. Concentrating development in villages or residential clusters at lower elevations or along the edges of valleys is cheaper and more efficient from the point of view of development and services.

Elevations may be mapped directly from topographical maps of the U.S. Geological Survey. Slopes are calculated by counting the number of contours per inch, or of some other unit on the map scale, and then plotted according to steepness.

HISTORIC SITES, LANDSCAPES, AND BUILDINGS

Historic sites remind people of their cultural heritage; identifying them adds an attractive dimension to a rural area, village, or town. Inventorying historic sites is usually one of the easiest inventories to accomplish. In most communities there are interested individuals who will volunteer to review records in the state archives and the local library, interview community elders, and write a brief history of the important sites and buildings.

The National Historic Preservation Act of 1966 authorized financial support for the preservation of historic buildings and unique landscapes or sites for practical, economic, historical and aesthetic reasons. Title 1 of this law authorized the secretary of the interior to expand and maintain the National Register of Historic Places and to provide grant funds to states for historic resource planning, acquisition, and development. Funding under this act was reduced when the Economic Recovery Tax Act of 1981 was amended in 1986. This act allows tax incentives for accelerated depreciation and for rapid amortization for rehabilitation expenses of commercial and income-producing properties on the National Register of Historic Places. The 1986 amendment reduced tax credits from 25 to 20 percent and required credits to be applied to properties themselves.

University history departments, state and local historical societies, and the state office of cultural affairs provide technical assistance to local officials and assist rural inhabitants in recognizing and preserving historic places. Citizens may want to form a history subcommittee as part of an overall planning effort. Members can interview community elders to derive oral history information about events; cultural traditions and their origins; significance of valued sites, buildings, landscapes, rituals, and observances.

Fortunately REP subcommittees do not have to conduct all eleven inventories. The number of inventories and the amount of work they require are reduced in several ways. In most REP projects three to six subcommittees are sufficient to address all the inventory subjects with critical importance to planning at one time. Small municipalities with a population of a few hundred to a few thousand are essentially rural, their principal interests probably being agricultural or open space. In municipalities of a few thousand to ten thousand REP may supplement a conventional master plan; the focus would be on types and uses of open land not covered in a master plan. Also, the technical team provides much of the inventory information either directly or by guiding additional subcommittee research. Focused inventories also help to make inventorying a process that can be conducted in a few months.

CULTURAL RESOURCES

Surveying the resource base means looking into the social and cultural heritage of a community. Every place has a cultural as well as a physical history, even those places that have no remaining historic buildings or artifacts. This history may not be as well known as the rich histories of places such as Roanoke Island, Taos, or Mark Twain's Calaveras County, but in each location the events of history, whether recent or ancient, create a community bond that is as valuable as other more tangible resources.

To understand the social groups of a planning area, community leaders such as teachers, clergy, or officers in a local cooperative can be interviewed. Churches, fraternal organizations, and sports clubs attract various social subgroups.

In most rural communities there are individuals with knowledge and genuine interest in cultural resources. Just as with physical historic resources, when these issues gain recognition and respect through the public meeting and survey process, people with such knowledge may volunteer to contribute information, research, conduct interviews, or draft a cultural history.

A Rural Environmental Plan may identify and honor the historical sites and events of their own place as the roots of people's memory in a community. Even the name of the community can have a story behind it that interests local citizens.

CASE: ALBUQUERQUE, NEW MEXICO

An example of planning that recognizes traditional and cultural values is the Tonantzin Land Institute, headquartered in Albuquerque, New Mexico. Tonantzin is a private, nonprofit organization of Mexican- and Native American land-based communities from throughout the Southwest. In a 1987 contract with the Southwest Regional Office of the U.S. Forest Service, the institute assessed the natural resource needs of traditional communities adjacent to the Cibola National Forest in central New Mexico. In all, nine communities participated in the survey: the Acoma, Laguna, Sandia, and Zuni Indian Pueblos, the Canoncito and Ramah Bands of Navajos, and the towns of Cubero, San Mateo, and San Fidel. The survey stated values and goals and proposed procedures for the development of a forest management plan.

The Cibola National Forest encompasses expansive grassland, timber woodland, mountain recreation areas, and fragile desert. No other forest management plan affects so divergent an environment and so diverse a population. Native American tribes such as the Navajo and Apache, aboriginal Pueblos, and Mexican-American land-grant settlers have used the resources of this land for centuries. That portion of the Tonantzin Land Institute report covering Cibola Forest, completed in August 1988, assesses needs and suggests ways in which the U.S. Forest Service and traditional communities can work cooperatively, rather than competitively, in natural resource planning. The proposals accommodate the day-to-day needs of communities by allowing and supporting their customary use of natural resources for food, timber, and livestock. The report explains alternative viewpoints regarding historically pressing concerns such as water rights and land tenure, and it states the indigenous people's preference for collective use of natural resources, their commitment to stewardship, and their aspirations for the right to self-determination.[4]

In addition to needs assessment, the contract issued to Tonantzin called for the design of a program to train Forest Service personnel in the dynamics of traditional communities and how such dynamics affect their relationship with the Forest Service. When completed, the program will help Forest Service personnel to increase community participation at all levels of decision-making about the management and joint use of forest resources. Together, the report on resources management and the training program signal a new beginning in U.S. government relations with indigenous and traditional communities. In spring 1989 the Southwest Regional Office of the Forest Service extended the contract with the Tonantzin Land Institute to encompass all five national forests in New Mexico.

HUMAN RESOURCES

The collective knowledge, skills, and memory as well as the network of associations among rural residents *are* the human resources of a place; they provide the framework of its existence. When economic conditions or other circumstances change, the ability of a people to take group action can mean the difference between economic decline or renewed prosperity.

One way to find out about the skills of a people is to ask them. A human resources survey can ask people to list their skills, even such things as crafts for which they may not be paid. The reservoir of job skills in a community where people are unemployed or undervalued is the foundation for new economic activity. An ability to repair complex machines, traditional sewing, quilting, weaving, or food preparation, a knowledge of soil and plant properties—all these represent valuable skills that can be transferred to similar tasks that bring greater economic return. Applying old skills to new activities to fit a changing local or world market might be one way of revitalizing a community.

CASE: CHAMA, NEW MEXICO

In 1980, the primary employer in the New Mexico village of Chama, a lumber mill that at its peak employed more than 250 people, shut down. With an FmHA planning grant and technical help from the Design and Planning Assistance Center at the University of New Mexico, the mayor, village council, and citizens and neighbors of Chama prepared a development plan for the village and surrounding area.[5] In preliminary information meetings they decided they needed a newsletter or newspaper to keep people informed of happenings in their area.

Subsequently, volunteers on the citizens committee, composed of residents and landowners, developed a questionnaire in the form of a newspaper and mailed one to each household in the village and the surrounding valley. In the "newspaper," *The Chama Valley Voice*, area residents were told about the planning process and were asked to fill out the questionnaire, which covered such subjects as the local economy, public improvements, recreation and tourism, and health and human services. The response rate was just under 30 percent. Over 90 percent of those who responded to questions on the economy agreed that local resources should be used to expand local employment, and that employment opportunities should be broadened to include more women and young people. Respondents also said it was important to develop locally owned and controlled industries. Further, a large proportion stated that they would be willing to put time or money into a local business or co-op.

One question dealt with the establishment of a skills bank. The survey asked what skills a respondent or family member had that might be used if there were a market for them, and what skills he or she, in turn, would like to learn. Answers to this question were long and varied, revealing that in addition to lumbering and mill work, many residents were skilled in areas such as wood carving, carpentry, plumbing, sewing, quilting, and animal care and husbandry. Many others expressed interest in learning these skills.

Many of the recommendations of this community development plan were implemented by local quasipublic or private agencies. For example, two non-profit organizations, a community-based clinic, and a community-based economic development corporation (Ganados del Valle) each took sectors of the plan and implemented them with a mix of philanthropic and public funds and with the help of professional, paraprofessional, and volunteer staff.

CONCLUSION

Inventorying for a rural environmental plan tends to be more extensive and detailed on some subjects than it is for many urban plans. In an inventory, the productivity of the land and of the people and the connection between natural resources, human activity, and location are surveyed, tabulated, and summarized. The process, which takes a substantial amount of time, becomes manageable when it focuses on aspects germane to community goals. If new concerns or different opportunities arise, an inventory can be supplemented. The task also becomes more manageable when shared with volunteers, supported by planning students, and assisted by a technical team of experts from public agencies and private organizations. A task can be divided and the parts delegated to subcommittees; with the help of technical experts and, in some cases, university students, each subcommittee focuses on one subject and produces data for classification, analysis, and specific recommendations.

Additional methods to inventory natural areas are explained in chapter 6; water quality is addressed in chapter 9; scenery inventories are covered in chapter 10 and information on social impact assessments is presented in chapter 11. Economic base inventories are described in chapter 12 with additional information needed for economic development in chapter 13. Inventorying covers many subjects, including technical recommendations and steps for future action. It is the foundation and the heart of the Rural Environmental Planning process.

6

Protecting Natural Areas

ALL RURAL AREAS have unique natural features—a bog, a stand of old trees, a waterfall, a fossil site, a desert canyon, a blue heron rookery, a mountain summit. These are often highly valued by the citizens, who may wish to protect them for present and future generations. A rural environmental plan can help protect natural areas if they are properly identified, rated, designated, and incorporated as elements in the plan.

A natural area classification and evaluation system should satisfy three objectives:[1] it should be readily understandable to citizens, community planners, and officials; it should be based on the judgment of natural scientists as well as local citizens; and it should be able to withstand legal challenge. To satisfy the first two requirements, the evaluation system should have two parts: a rating by natural scientists and a rating by the planning commission or citizen committee. To satisfy the third requirement, the system must be based on legal precedent or, where judgment is involved, must be systematic, reasonable, and objective. The classification and evaluation system described in this chapter is designed to meet these requirements.[2] There are a number of special areas that should not be rated by this system: white waters for rafting, canoeing, archeological sites, land reserved for environmental management, and wilderness areas. These areas should be classified and rated by experts in each respective field.

THE NATURAL SCIENCE RATING

The first step in developing a natural science rating is to classify suggested areas in accordance with a system adapted from the New England Natural Areas Project.[3] The system divides natural areas into five categories as follows:

1. Land Forms
   Mountain peaks, notches, saddles, and ridges
   Waterfalls and cascades
   Gorges, ravines, and crevasses
   Deltas
   Peninsulas
   Islands
2. Geologic Phenomena
   Cliffs, palisades, bluffs, and rims
   Natural rock outcrops
   Manmade rock outcrops
   Volcanic (geologic evidence)
   Glacial features (moraines, kames, eskers, drumlins, and cirques)
   Natural sand beach and sand dunes
   Fossil evidence
   Caves
   Unusual rock formations
3. Hydrologic Phenomena
   Significant and unusual water-land interfaces (scenic stretches of shore, rivers, or streams)
   Natural springs
   Marshes, bogs, swamps, and wetlands
   Aquifer recharge areas
   Water areas supporting unusual or significant aquatic life
   Lakes or ponds of unusually low productivity (oligotrophic)
   Lakes or ponds of unusually high productivity (eutrophic)
   Unusual natural river, lake, or pond physical shape
4. Biologic-Flora
   Rare, remnant, or unique species of plant
   Unique plant communities
   Plant communities unusual to a geographic area
   Individual specimen of unusual significance

Plant communities of unusual diversity or productivity

Plant communities representative of standard forest plant associations identified by the American Foresters and American Geographical Society

5. Biologic-fauna (classification is the same for fish, birds, and terrestrial animals)

Habitat area of rare, endangered, and unique species

Habitat area of unusual significance to a fauna community (feeding, breeding, wintering, resting)

Fauna communities unusual to a geographic area

Habitat areas supporting communities of unusual diversity or productivity

The list of natural areas in each rural community, of course, would be different. Archaeological sites are omitted from the classification system to reduce the possibility that they might be plundered.

The second step in rating is to evaluate natural areas and determine their potential for preservation in the public interest, a task accomplished by a natural scientist, or the planning committee with scientists' advice. Each natural area is rated for an array of selected characteristics: size; elevation; frequency of occurrence; diversity or variety within the natural area; national, regional, or local significance; and fragility, that is, the degree to which it is subject to deterioration by human activity or encroachment (fig. 6.1, Natural Science Rating). Each natural area is rated from 1 (low) to 5 (high) for each attribute; the ratings are compared with ratings for other natural areas in the region or state.

SIZE

The larger the area, the more important it is for preservation in the public interest, other things being equal. A five-acre bog with unusual plants would be more desirable to maintain than a one-acre bog. A mountain peak with a thousand acres, all other considerations being equal, should receive a higher priority for protection than a similar mountain peak with only a hundred acres of open space.

ELEVATION

Natural areas occurring at higher elevations are generally more critical from the point of view of environmental quality. For example, an elevation of

Area name: _____ Date of combined rating: _____

Town: _____ County: _____

Map reference number: _____ Natural science category: _____

Ownership: Private _____ Public _____ Mixed _____

I. NATURAL SCIENCE RATING		II. PLANNING RATING	
1. Area (in acres)		**1. Recreation Uses**	
1,000 and over	5 ___	5 or more	5 ___
500 to 999	4 ___	4	4 ___
100 to 499	3 ___	3	3 ___
10 to 99	2 ___	2	2 ___
Under 10	1 ___	1	1 ___
2. Elevation Above Adjacent Land Area		**2. Education/Research Uses**	
		5 or more uses	5 ___
2,500 feet and over	5 ___	4 uses	4 ___
1,500 to 2,499	3 ___	3 uses	3 ___
Under 1,499 feet	1 ___	2 uses	2 ___
		1 use	1 ___
3. Frequency of Occurrence		**3. Integrity**	
Rare	5 ___	Safe, 5 years or less	5 ___
Infrequent	3 ___	Safe, 5 to 10 years	3 ___
Common	1 ___	Safe, indefinitely	1 ___
4. Diversity		**4. Management Status**	
High	5 ___	Mismanaged	5 ___
Average	3 ___	Poorly or not managed	3 ___
Common	1 ___	Well managed	1 ___
5. Established Significance		**5. Planning Status**	
National	5 ___	Federal plan	5 ___
Regional	4 ___	Regional plan	4 ___
State	3 ___	State plan	3 ___
Substate/regional	2 ___	Substate regional	2 ___
Local	1 ___	Local	1 ___
		No plan or designation	0 ___
6. Fragility		**6. Natural Cycle Protection**	
High	5 ___	High	5 ___
Medium	3 ___	Medium	3 ___
Low	1 ___	Low	1 ___
TOTAL	___	TOTAL	___
Combined total (natural science rating plus planning rating)			___

FIGURE 6.1. Natural Area Evaluation Rating Sheet

2,500 feet is recognized in Vermont's Act 250 as being one above which development can take place only under special conditions and with suitable restrictions. Vermont law sets 1,500 feet as the elevation above which "pristine streams" are to be identified and designated by the Water Resources Board. In high desert or mountain states in the West, the cutoff point is higher, but the principle is the same. Research has shown that natural phenomena at higher elevations are more fragile, take longer to recover if disturbed, and are more likely to be rare.

FREQUENCY OF OCCURRENCE

As a criterion for evaluating natural areas, rarity may be explained by reference to a market-driven economic system that attributes higher value to attractive objects of greater scarcity. The concept of scarcity applies to natural areas. Any such areas that are unique are popularly regarded as more valuable than areas of which there may be many. Niagara Falls is highly valued because it is the only major falls in a large geographical area. The Troy colony of great laurels in Vermont is highly valued as a natural area because it is unique in the state. A similar stand of laurels in the Carolinas, where there are many, would be valued much less.

DIVERSITY OR VARIETY

A mountaintop with rare plants would be rated more highly than another mountaintop with no rare plants. A wetland area that is also a migratory wildlife feeding ground would be rated more highly than a similar wetland area not used as a feeding ground.

SIGNIFICANCE

Recognition of a natural area also is important. A mountain peak designated as a national natural landmark, or one identified by a local REP committee, is of greater significance to protect than a peak of similar elevation and configuration that has not been so designated or identified.

FRAGILITY

Fragility of a natural area is a criterion that duplicates or reinforces other factors used in evaluating the area. In general, fragility is correlated with higher elevations. However, there are also fragile low-elevation natural areas, for instance, rare-bird nesting sites in a bog or a rookery on a cliff. If disturbed, these sites may be abandoned.

THE PLANNING RATING

After the natural science rating is completed, other factors, based on the comparative characteristics of each natural area, must be considered. The planning rating (see fig. 6.1, Planning Rating) is based on six categories that represent public use of, or public interest in, natural areas: the number of recreational uses, the number of education and research uses, the potential for or likelihood of development, the quality of management, the planning status of the area, and the function of the area in a natural cycle.

The number of recreational uses reflects the importance of an area to the public in terms of how many would benefit directly from its maintenance. For example, if an area is of interest only to hikers, it has one use and gets one point in the planning rating. If it is of interest to hikers and photographers, it has two uses and thus earns two points. If it is of interest to hikers, photographers, and cross-country skiers, it has three uses and receives three points.

The number of educational and research uses is also counted. If school-children visit the area, that is one educational use. If it is additionally used for geologic research, it would be rated two, and so forth.

The probability of loss of a natural area to development is determined by the citizens committee or the planning commission on the basis of their evaluation of the land market pressures. For planning purposes, the greater the danger of loss or misuse of a natural area, the more urgent the need for action to protect it, therefore the higher rating.

The quality of management of a natural area is another basis for judging how urgent it is to acquire the land. A natural area with private owners who arrange for it to become a public conservation zone (or to receive greenbelt tax status) may have a lower priority for additional public protection than a natural area on land held for speculation. An area under good management is less urgent to acquire than an area being mismanaged.

The planning status of an area can be a useful basis for setting priorities. If an area has been designated in local, regional, or state plans as a natural area, it would be rated more highly than an area not so designated. This category attaches weight to areawide plans; an area designated in a regional or state plan is given a higher rating than those not so designated.

Finally, the degree to which the area functions in natural cycles and/or food chains as well as its aesthetic appeal must be considered in a planning rating. If a marsh filters water before it reaches a lake, this function needs to be considered and added to the rating. An area that functions in the hydrologic cycle as a groundwater recharge area should get a relatively high rating. Similarly, an area that functions as a buffer zone between incompatible land uses might be rated highly.

THE COMBINED RATING

The natural science rating and the planning rating are combined in a composite rating (see fig. 6.1). The two classifications, each with six criteria and a maximum of five points for each, gives a possible total combined score of 60 for a given area. The lowest score would be 12. The higher the composite rating, the higher the priority for protection or acquisition and for ultimate inclusion in a rural environmental plan. This system encompasses both scientific and popular definitions of natural areas. Residents may propose a beaver pond as a natural area, and it will be so designated even though the natural scientists say it is a transitory phenomenon. A geologist may propose a roadcut, which seems pedestrian to the citizenry, as a natural area to demonstrate to students the geologic history of the area.

THE NATURAL AREA CLASSIFICATION SYSTEM

The purposes and limitations of the classification and evaluation system should be understood. It is a rating system for *planning* purposes, based on scientists' judgment augmented by planners' judgment to accommodate the requirements of community planning. The system is designed to utilize the best of scientific knowledge and the best of planning judgment in the interests of developing an acceptable rural plan.

If one area is rated lower than another, that does not mean the first will not be protected. The procedure is designed to help a community decide where to act *first*. All natural areas listed in an adopted plan may eventually be protected. In some instances, a lower-priority natural area might be acquired before a higher-priority natural area because it becomes available sooner.

In any classification system based on combined factors, questions are raised concerning the weighing of factors. The system as shown here is not excessively sensitive to any single factor of the twelve. Even if the rating of a single factor is doubled or halved, the total index does not change by much. and hence the relative priority of the area will not change significantly.

The major purpose of the natural area classification and evaluation system is to inform people of significant or unique natural phenomena during REP development and implementation. The system is designed so that any interested citizen or community group can follow the instructions, obtain a list of natural areas from state agencies, supplement these with a local survey of additional natural areas, and then conclude their work by developing a description and rating for the community plan.

This system has been tested in a number of regional and community planning projects. Natural scientists from state or federal agencies or students from the state university provided the natural science rating data; and citizens committees or town planning commissions provided planning ratings. In these cases, the process has proven comprehensible, inexpensive, and effective. The chapter on natural areas is usually one of the most interesting and acceptable in a rural environmental plan.

METHODS OF PROTECTING NATURAL AREAS

There are three conventional methods for protecting natural areas: purchasing, zoning, and designation. Outright public purchase is recommended when a natural area is part of a larger purchase area such as a park. Zoning is recommended to protect a natural area in a conservation zone such as a higher elevation, a lakeshore, or a wetland.

Designation consists of identification, objective evaluation, and incorporation of the description, evaluation, and statement of public interest in a master plan or declaration. Designation is recommended as a land-use control when the objectives of the public and of private owners coincide. Through designation, decisions about acquisition or easement purchase to achieve public objectives can be deferred until public and private objectives differ. Designation, by itself, is not a taking of value or a limit on existing rights of ownership. Rather, it serves notice that if a change in use is proposed by the owners, that change must be adjusted to accommodate the public interest.

Designation has often proven successful in protecting natural areas. An owner who discovers that his or her land is prized as a natural area may become interested in, knowledgeable about, and protective of that land. In fact, the owner may initiate steps to protect it. Designation of natural areas, and incorporating designations in a master plan, enables the planning commission to set requirements respecting the integrity of those areas in the event of proposed changes in their use. For example, such areas can be included in the 10 to 15 percent reserve usually required for public purposes.

Unlike purchase in fee simple, designation does not cost the taxpayer money. Unlike zoning, it is not likely to be challenged in the courts, as it does not deprive owners of their rights. On the contrary, the effect of designating a natural area on private land may be to increase the value of the property as well as the value of adjacent properties.

Figure 6.2 is the natural area section from the Ferrisburg, Vermont, rural environmental plan. It illustrates citizen action taken to designate and protect natural areas in the community and surrounding area. The eight locations were inventoried by two graduate students in the course of developing an environmental plan with the town.[4]

CASE: CAMELS HUMP PARK, VERMONT

Camels Hump is one of the highest, most distinctive, and visible peaks in the Green Mountain range, which runs the length of Vermont and gives the state its license-plate nickname. The summit of Camels Hump is in a state forest. Its slopes were once owned by lumber companies, and it is surrounded at the base by small towns. Unlike other high peaks in Vermont it is untouched by ski slopes, and it has long been a favorite destination for bear hunters, hikers, hawk migration watchers, rugged cross-country skiers, and snowshoers. In late 1966 a rumor circulated that a lumber company planned to sell the east slope to a developer who was going to cover it with Swiss-style chalets accessible by cable car. Concerned citizens were quick to respond. The conservation committee of the Audubon Society called a meeting to save Camels Hump. The meeting was well attended by representatives of hunters, hikers, bird-watchers, and conservationists. They decided that a specific plan for extensive public use of the mountain would bring more support to save the mountain than a negative campaign against the developer alone. They asked an environmental planner from the University of Vermont to work with them, and together they collected data, discussed appropriate land uses and controls, and produced a proposed plan.

The planning report, "Camels Hump Park," was published by the Extension Service of the University of Vermont in October 1967.[5] The plan proposed that different zones of the mountain be distinguished by elevation. The highest zone, a fragile environment, was to be used by hikers and hunters only. The middle zone would allow cross-country skiing. The lower zone

Following are eight natural areas that the Ferrisburg Citizens Committee regard as top priority areas to be protected for our enjoyment and the enjoyment of our children's children.

Button Bay. Button Bay is a unique geological formation of lime deposits that form small buttons visible on the ground. Located on the shore of Lake Champlain covering an area of approximately 10 acres, the area is regarded as significant on the state, regional, and local levels. The Button Bay natural area is well protected, as it is owned and recognized as a natural area by the State of Vermont.

Porter's Lake. Porter's Lake is adjacent to Otter Creek, about 2 miles from the mouth of the Creek at Ft. Cassin. It is an aesthetically pleasing, shallow, marsh-like lake consisting of approximately 200 acres, at 100-foot elevation. The lake is rich in aquatic flora, such as pond lilies, coontails, duckweed, and other submerged aquatics. During times of high water, the lake is accessible by boat. Forests bordering the lake are dominated by silver maple, red elm, and hemlock.

The lake is a prime spawning area for fish as well as a natural habitat for many animal species, including certain varieties of water-fowl. It is an excellent area for canoeists, photographers, and bird watchers. The lake is privately owned.

Presently, there is no development bordering this area. Developments of any kind, however, will certainly destroy the value of this lake. The town should recognize the value of this natural area and provide protection of the area by strict water surface and lakeshore zoning.

Danyow Marsh. Danyow Marsh is a rich, aquatic area, bordering the Otter Creek. The area displays various species of pond weed, such as coontails, cattails, and pond lilies. The Marsh serves as an important waterfowl resting area in the north-south flyway. Bordering the river side of the Marsh is a very distinct towpath used by horses to tow barges up the river to Vergennes during the pre–Civil War era. The Marsh is approximately 250 acres in size and 101 feet in elevation. The Marsh is privately owned.

At present, there is no development encroaching on the border areas of the Marsh. The danger of home construction on upland areas of the Marsh is prevalent and if allowed to develop, the value of this Marsh as a natural area would be lost. This Marsh should be zoned as a natural area.

Little Otter Creek Marsh (South and East Slang). This is perhaps one of the finest natural wildlife areas in the entire state because of its great diversity and size. This 1,000-acre expanse of shallow-water marshland contains one of the largest wild rice stands east of the Mississippi River. Located 1 mile from U.S. 7 at Ferrisburg Center, the area presently is surrounded by open agricultural land.

Because of the Marsh's environment, it is well recognized as a migration stopover for many types of waterfowl. Likewise, it serves as one of the finest duck hunting marshes in the state.

The dominant vegetation of the Marsh is broad-fruited bur reed and wild rice. There are also small stands of cattails, and submerged aquatics such as pond lilies

FIGURE 6.2. Natural Areas Inventory, Ferrisburg, Vermont

and duckweeds. The Marsh is shallow with a soft bottom of organic debris; a rich assemblage of plants found along the Marsh include hummocks of ferns and sedges.

The Little Otter Marsh has been recognized by several natural scientists as a natural area of national significance. The Marsh is relatively safe from destruction for a good deal of it is owned by the State of Vermont. Although well protected as a natural area, Ferrisburg planning officials should prevent high intensity development in ring-like fashion around the Marsh. This fine and rare natural area should be protected by zoning.

Gorge and Waterfall on Little Otter Creek. The waterfall at Ferrisburg Center offers a fine example of a spectacular natural area that is readily accessible. A 10-foot waterfall is spread over a 100-foot wide sheet of redstone. Privately owned, this natural waterfall once served as a power site for an old grist mill. Below the falls is a gorge 75 feet deep carved by the natural motions of rushing water.

The value of this area is greatly enhanced by the number of people to whom it would be readily accessible. In addition to serving as a rare geological formation, the area could be combined into an extensive community recreation area. The town should acquire this area and maintain it in its natural condition.

Ft. Cassin Site. Located at the mouth of the Otter Creek, this historic natural area served as an Indian site and village as well as a location of the famous Ft. Cassin, used as a naval defense point against the British Navy during the War of 1812. A small area over-looking Lake Champlain, marked by a monument, designates this spot. Of state, regional, and historical significance, the site is inaccessible, privately owned, and serves as a setting for several summer cottages. The immediate threat to this area is high. The town's plan should recognize this threat, attempt to provide public access, and offer protection to the site by a historic zone.

The Birches Area. An outstanding wildlife area of several hundred acres adjacent to the East Slang, this area is valuable to the Town of Ferrisburg as a nature park. Serving as a rare example of an unaltered wilderness, the Birches is a living museum of varied types of plants and animals. Well recognized as a fine hunting ground for deer and birds, this wildlife area is owned by the State of Vermont. With the proper protective regulations, this area should be open and accessible to the residents of Ferrisburg as an outdoor classroom for nature study on a daily basis.

Kingsland Bay. Kingsland Bay (Eagles Breast Vicinity), a part of Lake Champlain, borders a unique scenic area composed of a rocky shoreline of deep projecting inlets. Consisting of both open and forested areas, this bay area has long been recognized as a predominate winter deer yard and fossil-collecting area.

Privately owned, the site is viewed as a unique and irreplaceable spot because of its natural beauty. Land use controls, official recognition, and/or public acquisition of the site should be enacted to preserve and maintain this site in its natural state—undeveloped.

would be for multiple use under regulations to protect the environment. The three zoning levels would include state-owned forestland at higher elevations and privately held land at the two lower elevations. This citizen proposal appeared necessary as the State Department of Forests and Parks, which owned the summit, did not recognize the need to change policies that were geared toward timber production and harvesting and ski-slope development.

The Save Camels Hump (SCH) committee took their plan public with news stories and a series of open meetings. Considerable support was quickly forthcoming from the Vermont Federation of Sportsmen's Club, the Green Mountain Audubon Society, the Vermont Natural Resources Council, and the Vermont chapter of the Society of American Foresters. There was no organized opposition; however, the State Forest and Parks Department continued to withhold support.

In May 1968 new stimulus to the SCH movement came when U.S. Senator George Aiken persuaded the U.S. Department of the Interior to include Camels Hump in the National Registry of Natural Landmarks. People living in small towns around the base of the mountain formed the Camels Hump Area Preservation Association (CHAPA) and launched a publicity campaign. They held public meetings and distributed a newsletter. The effort was successful—there was wide support and no opposition.

The State Department of Forest and Parks was now ready to support the SCH plan. Because they could control land use on their own acreage but had no authority to zone the lower slopes, special legislation was necessary. The SCH and CHAPA committees approached state Representative Arthur Gibb, chair of the House Committee on Natural Resources, who persuaded the commissioner of forests and parks to appoint a nine-member committee to draft a statute. This committee was broadly representative, including foresters, conservationists, and hunters. A bill to establish a special park was drafted and Representative Gibb introduced it to the state legislature. When the House and Senate held a joint hearing on the proposed bill, all testimony was favorable.

On April 18, 1969—two and a half years after the initial citizens' meeting—the Vermont legislature passed act 71, chapter 57, establishing the Camels Hump State Park and Forest Reserve. The statute incorporated the objectives of the SCH and CHAPA ad hoc committees. The State Department of Forests and Parks, now a strong advocate of the new park and reserve, changed its priorities and proceeded to purchase additional land on the flanks of the mountain to assure its protection from intensive development.

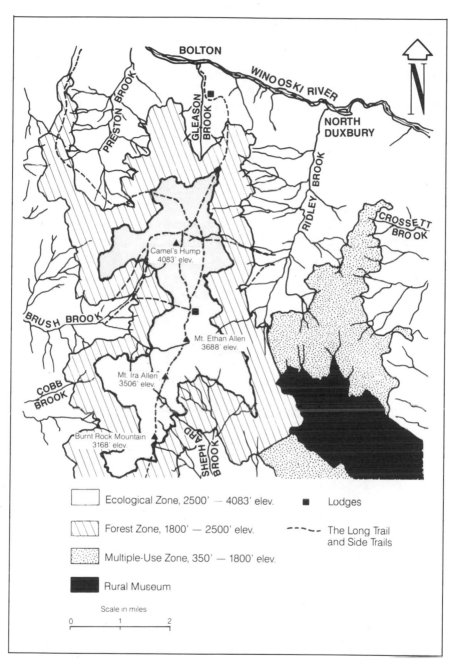

FIGURE 6.3. Proposed Camel's Hump Park Showing Elevation-Determined Use Zones

CONCLUSION

Identifying and planning the protection of natural areas can be one of the most enjoyable parts of developing a rural environmental plan. Schoolchildren may discuss natural areas and suggest the ones they would like to have protected. Nearly everyone supports natural area protection, and everyone can participate. Further, nearly every political jurisdiction has several such areas to classify, designate, and protect. The manner in which this is done should be objective, fair, inexpensive, and of immediate benefit to the community. While defining and evaluating natural areas were difficult tasks in the past, they are now relatively easy. A two-part classification system can be used to define natural phenomena in both scientific and popular terms. The system provides a list of priorities for incorporation in a community plan.

7

Keeping Land in Agriculture

THERE ARE MANY commonly recognized motives for keeping land in agriculture: economic, cultural, and environmental. Even the aesthetic quality of open farmland is an incentive to retain land for agricultural use. The varied topography and textures of rural landscapes across North American farms provide interesting patterns, colors, and tones—pastures, fields, orchards, woods, fence rows, gardens, picturesque farm buildings and homestead lots. Techniques to preserve farmland are outlined and compared in this chapter.

NATIONAL PERSPECTIVE

In America public action to support family farms goes back to Thomas Jefferson and continues in the expression of goals in many state and community plans. Social scientists have long confirmed that communities that are made up of a variety of small to large farms have richer social interaction than communities dominated by only large corporate farms. On a national level, the conversion of prime farmland to nonagricultural uses takes away land needed for the food supply of future generations. Once farmland is converted to more intensive development, the process is considered irreversible.

Many interest groups support public policies intended to preserve farmland. Farmers located near cities would like to continue farming where it is most profitable—close to urban areas. Farms close to cities, though, are located in markets where competing demands for land are the most intense. Many urban residents desire locally available fresh fruits and vegetables; however, to increase community self-sufficiency in food production requires

93

maintaining truckcrop farming near population concentrations. Conservationists also see advantages in maintaining agricultural land: it is a way of providing wildlife habitats and protecting ecological cycles. Knowledgeable taxpayers realize that it costs more to provide services to and maintain most residential developments than they yield in taxes. When agricultural land is turned into housing developments, tax bills rise.

There are other concerns as well. Landowners want to maintain their right to cash in on the increased value of agricultural land caused by urban growth around them. Recreation interests believe that the public should benefit from special tax policies that favor agricultural land. Such benefits include the right to recreational activities such as hunting, hiking, and fishing.

But tax and other incentives do not always produce the desired results or benefits. Since the 1930s, in spite of continuous political pronouncements in favor of preserving the family farm, federal laws in the United States have had an opposite effect. Federal farm policy has favored farmers with larger holdings, allowing them to purchase adjacent small farms. During the late 1970s and early 1980s, tax laws encouraged non-farmers to buy farms as tax losses. Thus further reducing the ranks of small and moderate family farms. The net result of the last fifty years of federal agricultural policy has been a continuous decline in the total number of small to moderate-sized family farms in America. By contrast, many Canadian provinces implemented laws and programs to maintain family farms, and at least one U.S. state, South Dakota, prohibits corporate farming.[1]

A significant obstacle to keeping land and small farmers in agriculture has been the ineffectiveness of traditional zoning methods. Often considered the only method of solving the problem, zoning is subject to change when economic forces are sufficiently strong. Those who would profit by a change in zoning from agriculture to development usually succeed in obtaining the change. Planners must look for zoning methods that satisfy voters, taxpayers, and landowners. Landowners should not be deprived of the potential for increases in land value, and the taxpayer should not be burdened by inefficient development or an inequitable allocation of taxes. Ideally, preservation methods must allow agricultural land to remain economically productive as long as possible under existing land-control institutions.

TECHNIQUES FOR RETAINING FARMLAND

For many years tax incentives have been used to keep land in agriculture. Most of these are income tax credits and preferential tax assessments of real property, where greenbelt land is taxed at agricultural value instead of market value. In addition to tax relief, a number of other techniques have been proposed and implemented. If in the development of a rural environmental plan alternative techniques are analyzed and compared on the basis of public and private cost, and of political and social acceptability and permanence, a technique, or more likely a combination of techniques, may be found to retain a significant amount of prime land in agriculture. Techniques from which to choose are described below.[2]

RESTRICTING SUBDIVISION DEVELOPMENT TO SEWERED LOTS

Municipal and county subdivision regulations may require that all duplex, apartment, or mobile home park construction take place on municipal sewer and water lines. Although not effective in restricting single-family dwellings using septic systems or composting, or cluster-home package-treatment systems, this technique allows the planning commission to control more intensive suburban expansion. This limits leapfrog development in open country and allocates the concentration of development in urbanizing areas. While this method can be effective, it has not been widely used by rural towns. Sprawl occurs slowly and is often not recognized by the community until it is too late to remedy.

CONSERVATION ZONING

A conservation zone may be included in a zoning ordinance to restrict building in areas subject to flooding, on steep slopes (greater usually defined as gradients greater than 15 percent), along stream banks, on wetlands, or at higher elevations. Agricultural or recreational uses are permitted in designated conservation areas. The extent to which this technique keeps land in agriculture depends on the percentage of agricultural land that falls into one of the protected categories. In rural areas where a considerable portion of the farmland lies within a defined floodplain, conservation zoning protects much of the prime agricultural land from unwarranted development; in other places, only a small percentage of land is covered. One benefit of this technique is that it can protect public health by protecting water supplies for all users during floods. Protecting public health is an acceptable criterion for land-use zoning. Conservation zoning for flood hazard areas can be justified on this basis alone.

CLUSTER DEVELOPMENT

Clustering keeps land in agriculture by requiring that all buildings be concentrated on a specified, proportional area of a total acreage. To be effective, this requirement should rate building sites according to some functional criterion such as soil suitability for on-site sewage disposal, degree of slope, or the erodibility of soil. The clustering provision in a zoning ordinance should indicate the maximum number of building units per acre. Bylaws can be adopted by the local jurisdiction that set aside one-half or more of a parcel for agricultural use or open space while still allowing the same number of lots that conventional subdivision permits.[3]

For example, cluster zoning could require a minimum of ten acres for a development. The prospective developer may be restricted to building on only 25 percent of the acreage and only on a portion of the land with permeable soil or some other specific criterion. Approval may depend on development rights on the remaining land being dedicated to the town or county jurisdiction. The land not built upon could thereby remain in agriculture or be kept open without being a burden to other taxpayers. The seller, meanwhile, would still receive full value for the land.

TRANSFERABLE DEVELOPMENT RIGHTS

This technique prorates development rights equally to all landowners, for instance, one development right for each dwelling allowed by the existing zone. The planning commission publishes a schedule showing how many development rights are required for each type of development throughout the municipality. For example, if 1 development right is required for each housing unit, then a person wanting to build a 200-unit condominium would be required to have 200 development rights. If the particular area proposed for development had only 100 development units on the land, the developer would have to purchase 100 TDRs from other landowners within the TDR area. Hence, the total amount of development is controlled and all landowners have development rights to sell or use. This procedure calls for accountability, management skills, and flexibility in planning.

Great interest has been shown in this technique, as it controls growth while allowing landowners to profit from the sale of development rights. Experience with TDRs demonstrates that they are applicable in urban and surrounding areas where land is synonymous with "developable space" and the principal land value determinant is location. The TDR process is less

FIGURE 7.1. Clustering Development to Preserve Farmland. *The site drawing, left, depicts a conventional approach to development where infrastructure encroaches on and breaks up agricultural land. The other drawing shows how clustering can guide development so that density is achieved with minimal intrusion into surrounding farmland and greenbelt spaces.* (Courtesy of and copyrighted by the Center for Rural Massachusetts, University of Massachusetts; design by Dodson Associates, Kevin Wilson, illustrator.)

applicable in rural areas where land is not in short supply or where much land is unsuitable for development because of location or topography.[4]

SCENIC EASEMENTS

A scenic easement is the acquisition by purchase, dedication, or other means of the right to an unhindered view at a particular location or over a certain area of land. This may include purchasing development rights and restricting advertising signs or other obstacles at strategic locations to protect views. Scenic easements have been used effectively in Wisconsin to protect the scenery along the Great River Road, which runs parallel to the Mississippi River. Maine passed enabling legislation for conservation easement in 1970.

Even though the most common use of scenic easements is to preserve vistas, on some sites this method may require the purchase of development rights on wide strips of agricultural land so as to protect it. Scenic easements should be considered for floodplains along major rivers where their combination with flood protection reinforces their benefit to the public.

AGRICULTURAL ZONING

Agricultural zoning has been used by many states to keep land in agriculture. This technique works well until economic pressure builds to the point, for example, that a prospective buyer and the landowner demand a zone change. Experience shows that zoning is effective only if it is associated with accountable tax appraisal, that is, land is appraised at a value consistent with its legally zoned uses, not at a value based on more intensive, speculative use. Agricultural zoning can be effective for the period of time required to develop a more permanent procedure.

COMPENSABLE REGULATIONS

Compensable regulation is a technique that lies between conservation zoning, which may be too confiscatory, and public acquisition, which may be too costly. Compensable regulation limits the use of land, say, to open space but also compensates the owner for any drop in value attributed to the regulation. Under compensable regulation, a greenbelt may be designated as part of an overall plan to enhance the productivity of agriculture as well as to maintain its aesthetic quality. Land use in the greenbelt is restricted to farming, recreation, or other low-density uses. Landowners are guaranteed that if they wish to sell their land, they will receive an amount equal at least to the value of the land before the imposition of regulations, or equal to the new market price of similar land not under restriction. The government obligates itself to pay the difference if the actual sale price falls below this evaluation. Land subject to compensable regulation remains in private ownership, continues to yield tax revenue, and requires no public expenditure for maintenance. The political jurisdiction is required to pay only when a parcel is sold, and then only for the amount of the difference between the sale price and the guaranteed price. Compensable regulation is not a suitable method of protecting a whole rural area, but it is suitable for specially valued and designated scenic areas.

TAX STABILIZATION CONTRACTS

Some states, for example, California, New Hampshire, and Vermont, have developed tax relief programs authorizing restrictive agreements where a landowner receives a preferential tax assessment in exchange for a written contract to retain farmland in agricultural use on a long-term basis. The particulars vary from state to state and sometimes county to county. The Vermont program was enacted in 1967 when the state legislature passed a bill allowing towns to contract with farmers to stabilize their taxes. In Vermont, towns may stabilize the tax rate, the tax appraisal value, or the dollar amount of the tax. The tax stabilization program can be initiated by a favorable two-thirds vote at a town meeting. Elected officials then negotiate contracts with farmers who wish to participate. A number of Vermont towns have implemented this program. Some towns have opted for each of the three stabilizing procedures.[5]

Several conclusions can be drawn from experiences such as Vermont's. First, the program is useful in a town with a small number of farms and a large number of citizens who appreciate keeping land in agriculture. In a town with much farmland the program is not likely to be adopted for tax stabilization implies that the tax burden will be transferred. In a rural area made up largely of farmers it would not be equitable to transfer farmers' taxes to a small group that did not farm. Second, tax stabilization is a holding action. It may not keep land permanently in agriculture. It may, however, keep it in agriculture until other methods of so doing are developed or become acceptable. Third, the towns in Vermont with tax stabilization have not experienced a significant tax transfer. This is because farms in that state are generally assessed according to agricultural productivity, even though Vermont statutes require that land be taxed at fair market value.[6]

PUBLIC PURCHASE: RESTRICTING AND RESALE

Agricultural land may be protected from conversion by public purchase in fee simple. After purchase, the government agency sells or leases the land on the open market, in this case, for farming purposes only. This can be an effective way to supplement other methods of maintaining land in agriculture.

An experiment of this type was carried out in Saskatchewan, Canada, in the 1960s. In an effort to promote family farming, a land bank commission was established. The commission was authorized to purchase agricultural land of any quality and resell it in viable units to small or new farmers. During the course of the experiment the commission purchased 517,000 acres and subsequently leased 1,400 acres to farmers. It charged tenants an annual rental fee of 5.75 percent of the property's value. This program permitted a new generation of farmers to get started in agriculture without mortgaging their future. To enhance the economic effectiveness of the program applicants were restricted to families whose annual income had averaged $10,000 or less over the previous three years and whose net worth was not greater than $60,000. Thus the program served people who would not otherwise be in farming. In contrast to many U.S. farm programs, this one, the "state land development corporation" program, was designed to assist the lower-income farmer rather than the large-scale or corporate farmer.

FLOODPLAIN ZONING

Agricultural land can be protected by the local jurisdiction through floodplain zoning. Protecting floodplains means protecting public health, a justifiable aim. There are three possible steps to zoning a floodplain. First, obtain a soil map that delineates flood-prone areas from the local SCS office. Transfer this information onto a planning map. Two, inspect the floodplain in person to see if it corresponds to the locally accepted notion of what floods cover. Three, draft a zoning regulation stating the permitted uses of the floodplain—agricultural, no buildings, and so forth.

PRIVATE LAND TRUSTS

A private land trust is a nonprofit corporation whose objective is to hold land for the particular purposes of the trust. Some land trusts are established to hold land in an open and natural state. The land trust concept can be adapted to protect agricultural land by purchase of development rights from farmers. The Maine Coast Heritage Trust is an example. It was founded in 1971 for the protection of Maine's coastal islands. Land trusts of this type work well when public interest in maintaining agriculture for aesthetic or environmental protection reasons is high and the number of operating farms is low. Such land trusts have been effective in the hilly tourist areas of northern New England and New York.

LAND EVALUATION AND SITE ASSESSMENT

The LESA is a program developed by the SCS to help to implement the federal Farmland Protection Policy Act of 1981. The program basically assists local governments in protecting farmland. The importance of LESA is that it is not a system of regulations but rather a tool for rating the *relative value of land* in terms of agricultural potential. Land evaluation helps local government planning commissions and elected officials to identify lands with present and future agricultural value.

Site assessment consists of helping local officials to evaluate the impact of proposed development on an agricultural tract. Assessment criteria, developed by local decision-makers, include such considerations as the size of a site, its existing or potential agricultural use, the agricultural infrastructure, land-use regulations, the availability of alternative nonfarmland, transportation networks, water and sewer lines, and environmental factors.

LESA is not a method of regulating development but rather an information system that establishes comparative values. Each local government decides which land and soil classifications to apply to an area based on relevant technical information obtained from the SCS. In addition to scientific data, local representatives are free to include other criteria they consider important as individual development plans come up for review: proximity to a city, environmental effects, and traditional values, among others. Each factor is awarded points that are then converted according to a weighting scheme; the result is a factor score. Site assessment points serve as one more piece of information for planning and zoning commissioners to use in deciding whether a specific site should be approved for nonfarmland development. Information regarding the uses of LESA may be obtained from any SCS office.

Apart from specific techniques to preserve farmland adjacent to urban areas, where pressure to convert land to nonfarm use is greatest, mention should be made of a strategy to maintain farmland in less threatened locations: keep current land in active production and convert potential farmland to productive use by trying new agricultural products that generate jobs and increase local incomes. Regulation of land use to protect agricultural holdings is not a substitute for working directly with farmers and ranchers to increase the productivity of their land.

As reported recently in *Growing Our Own Jobs,* projects involving vineyard development in rural Tennessee, specialty vegetables in Mississippi, a hydroponic greenhouse in Georgia, and shiitake mushrooms in Iowa have demonstrated how alternative crops can diversify production, open new markets, increase crop yields per acre, create jobs, and stabilize local economies. Other projects—beef jerky processing in North Dakota, a wool mill in Pennsylvania, cucumber and pickle processing in Texas, and a corn wet-milling plant in Minnesota—serve as examples of how agricultural products can be processed on-farm, adding value to the products, capturing a larger percentage of consumer dollars, and growing new jobs at home.[7]

COMPARISON OF METHODS

Keeping land in agriculture requires judgment; options must be compared and related to planning principles. The state's political and legal framework, public attitudes, and regional agricultural, economic, and land-use trends must also be considered. The suitability of methods for keeping land in agriculture varies according to many factors: the intensity of the trend toward nonagricultural land use; land productivity; income levels of people in the area; level of understanding, experience and sophistication in planning; skill and leadership of people in government; and public attitudes toward land-use control. A technique such as restricting development to sewered lots would be most applicable in an urban setting or in an adjacent area subject to the pressure of urban expansion. Public purchase may be more feasible in a large metropolitan state than in a small rural state. Conservation zoning applies more to areas with many part-time farmers. Tax stabilization contracts are useful where the total number of farmers in a village area or township represents a small percentage of the citizenry. Easements are applicable in special situations, such as a river basin parkway or flood damage reduction.

Above all, no single technique is sufficient to protect farmland in any given community or state. Effective programs should incorporate various measures to maintain and support the economic viability of agriculture. Land-use controls and incentives by themselves are not sufficient. The loss of farmland is the result of many factors, and any attempt to further curb it should be multifaceted, comprehensive, legally defensible, and tailored to local conditions.[8]

In several REP projects the comparison of methods for keeping land in agriculture has been useful and effective. It has led to broadened discussion of alternatives for enhancing agricultural viability and, in several cases, to specific action to stabilize agricultural land use. For example, in Colchester, Vermont, this type of analysis resulted in the zoning of prime farmland for agriculture. In Charlotte, Vermont, a university planning class provided information that prompted the town to adopt a tax stabilization program for farmers. In South Burlington, Vermont, an agricultural land analysis strengthened the concept of containing development in already developed areas and reducing strip development in agricultural land and related open spaces.

CASE: RIO ARRIBA COUNTY, NEW MEXICO

Rio Arriba County, in the north-central part of New Mexico, is characterized by magnificent mountains and narrow, stream-fed valleys.[9] This sparsely settled county covers 5,856 square miles. Its estimated population in 1988 was 32,600. Española is the only incorporated city in the entire county. In the rest of the county there are only two incorporated villages, Chama, near the Colorado border, and Dulce, headquarters of the Jicarilla Apache Reservation. The county does not have jurisdiction over the reservation. With mountain elevations ranging from 5,600 to more than 13,000 feet, and with both natural and manmade lakes, Rio Arriba County, especially the Chama area, attracts visitors, fishermen, and hunters. Some efforts were made to establish resort and second-home subdivisions in Rio Arriba County in the 1960s and 1970s; however, much of this activity was suspended by federal and state authorities because of fraudulent sales of lots.

From the late 1970s and throughout the 1980s, state revenues from extractive industries and federal spending decreased throughout New Mexico. State policy during this period was to promote tourism and other potential sources of revenue. A number of proposals were made, including the development of a major ski resort in the Chama valley. Some ranchers considered subdividing all or part of their property to capitalize on the ski resort.

Under New Mexico law, water resources belong to either the state or prior users. Prospective developers must acquire water rights as part of the property purchased or from other properties in order to obtain approval for the development. Water rights can also be sold separately from land. To sell water rights, though, means permanently severing them from the land, diverting the water from its present use, and retiring any irrigated agricultural land from cultivation forever. For many long-time residents traditional agriculture provides subsistence and preserves cultural roots. Diversion of water to other uses is seen as a threat to economic and cultural survival.

In Rio Arriba County many subdivisions were developed before stringent environmental controls were enacted under the New Mexico Subdivision Act in 1973. Some illegal subdivisions were also developed after the 1973 law. Subsequent to the installment of these poorly controlled subdivisions, evidence showed up of increasing groundwater contamination.

In 1986 the Rio Arriba County Commission amended their existing subdivision regulations in order to strengthen control of land subdivision and to prevent the loss of agriculture. The subdivision amendments declared one of the public interests of the county to be preserving agriculture through traditional community ditch irrigation.

The new regulations require a water system for each proposed subdivision, putting the burden on the developer to obtain rights to sufficient water for all the planned lots. Water rights are allocated by the state engineer's office, however, and the state engineer must consider the public interest of all affected properties in deciding on the transfer of water rights from one area to another.

Rio Arriba County also developed strict regulations for liquid-waste disposal, requiring larger lots for septic tanks in areas with poor soil or a high watertable. These regulations require the preparation of sufficient information to allow the county commission to determine whether a proposed development will disrupt traditional rural communities and the county's limited supply of irrigated agricultural land.

CASE: DOÑA ANA COUNTY, NEW MEXICO

Doña Ana County in southwest New Mexico is the state's second most rapidly growing county, with a population estimated in 1987 at 128,800.[10] Las Cruces, the county's burgeoning city, population 54,100, is home to New Mexico State University and is relatively close to the White Sands Missile Range. Las Cruces's mild winters have also made it an attractive place for retirees. To accommodate new growth Las Cruces recently engaged in some intricate land exchanges with the city of Albuquerque and the Bureau of Land Management (BLM). The trades enabled Las Cruces to nearly double in size through planned annexations. The rush for urban expansion made the sale of prime agricultural land attractive to some area farmers.

Immediately to the west of Las Cruces, along the lower Rio Grande Valley, is the town of Mesilla, an historic village with low residential density and extensive farmland. Some in Las Cruces see Mesilla as an attractive bedroom community, and Mesilla is feeling the pressure of that city's expansion. Many people in Mesilla dislike the prospect of becoming a suburb and would like to keep their agricultural land under cultivation. The town developed an innovative plan to accomplish this.[11] The plan draws on precedents in the area involving land trades with the federal government.

The BLM controls land on the urbanizing fringes of Las Cruces, dry, agriculturally insignificant alluvial mesas above the irrigated valley. The BLM plans to release this land for urbanization. To retain its farmland Mesilla has proposed a scheme to utilize the BLM land as a "receiving area" for development rights that Mesilla farmers own in their own lands presently under cultivation. The scheme, for example, would have a farmer in the Mesilla area with a 40-acre pecan orchard, located on prime agricultural soil (as identified by the SCS) and with attendant water rights, voluntarily exchange urban-use development rights on his/her farm for a tract of land on the mesa. The mesa land, now owned by the BLM, has no agricultural value; identified by the BLM and by the State of New Mexico as being suitable for urban expansion, it is scheduled for public sale. The value of the land received by the farmer would equal the difference in value between the farmer's value per acre for farmland and its potential development value per acre, as determined by independent appraisal.[12]

Once the exchange is completed, the farmer would continue to own the farm and use it for agricultural purposes. The farmer can also sell it at any time as a farm, for as much as the market will bear, but the deed excludes urban use. The land area of the farm would remain under private ownership; however, development rights would be included as part of a prime agricultural trust for the benefit of current and future New Mexicans. The farmer also owns a parcel of mesa land that can be put to urban use. Such use would have to be approved by federal, state, and local officials. The farmer retains the option of developing this land, selling it for urban use, or holding it for later development.

The federal government does not give away its land; it must be compensated for the market value of any property released. To compensate the BLM for releasing its land, Mesilla proposes to set a transfer tax at a percentage of sales price. The tax would be applied to each sale of mesa land that had already been exchanged for agricultural development rights. The government would then have a steady, long-term source of income to compensate it for the public lands used in the exchange. In addition, a local tax can be applied to each sale for the express purpose of supporting the development of an areawide infrastructure.[13]

Mesilla does not have the authority, under current state enabling legislation, to levy an additional gross receipts tax for the purpose of paying the federal government. Thus the town needs to find an alternative source for payments. Town planners and officials are publicizing their proposal to state and congressional officials to get support for an additional tax. They also want to present the proposal as a model to be followed in other areas of the country where farmland lies near federal lands scheduled for release.

The town of Mesilla believes that those government entities that would participate in the original exchange of development rights would also benefit from increased land values resulting from future sales. Farmers would be compensated for maintaining agricultural lands in a voluntary system combining free-market principles with land-use planning that respects long-term public goals. The local governments of Mesilla and Las Cruces would thereby gain a new means of "mining" the land and have a perpetual land bank as their source of income. Developers would have a clear idea of where and how urban growth is supported by the government. Agriculture in Doña Ana County would continue to benefit the people. Planning by local government would recognize defined agricultural areas and protect important natural resources, and officials would have a clean slate on which to plan urban growth on the mesa.[14]

CONCLUSION

These techniques for keeping land in agriculture, with all their variations, have one characteristic in common—to implement them, they require strong public support and a high level of planning expertise. Public support grows as understanding develops of the reasons for conserving agricultural land. Experts who can help to nurture public understanding can be found at the agricultural extension service, the department of agricultural economics or planning, the department of public administration at the state university, or the state department of agriculture. If all of these techniques for keeping land in agriculture are studied and appraised, a method or a combination of methods will emerge to meet that goal. It may be, as the two case examples here show, that some new variation of existing methods develops to satisfy local conditions of financial feasibility and political acceptability.

8

Planning Lake Basins

ONCE CONSIDERED A limitless resource in the United States, water has in recent decades become an important policy concern in most regions of the country. The era of extensive water development based on federal subsidies for the construction of large dams, aqueducts, and intrabasin water transfers has ended. Disputes over the allocation and use of water, however, have just begun. In the eastern states, for instance, Florida has problems of aquifer depletion and saltwater intrusion. Many large cities suffer from groundwater pollution and would like to get future water supplies from nearby rural areas. In those areas, though, citizens may want to reserve the water for their own future growth. In the western states, particularly those governed by the water-rights doctrine of prior appropriation, there is a growing need to resolve water-use conflicts among energy producers, expanding municipalities, recreational tourists, commercial farmers, and Native American and Hispanic communities.[1]

Because of the expanding demand for water, small towns and other rural jurisdictions are finding it necessary to protect their long-standing claims to regional water supplies. Competing interest groups such as municipalities and industries can typically afford lawyers, engineers, hydrologists, and planners to lobby on their behalf. Small-scale water users, on the other hand, do not always have the means to present their unique interests on an equal footing. The transfer of water resources from agricultural and other rural uses to so-called higher uses is becoming more common. Many rural communities unable to compete in the water marketplace have lost their water rights to urban areas and developers.

As noted in chapter 5, the REP technique is for rural communities to inventory and classify their resource base. Nowhere is such a need better demonstrated than in the case for documenting and planning water supplies. To protect existing rights, and to preserve water supplies for the future, rural communities must take the offensive in water policy planning. The final plan for a small town, a county, or a region, therefore, should set out community goals with respect to present and future water use.

Lakes are among the most valuable public assets in communities fortunate enough to have them. Multiple use of a lake entails an understanding of its impact on the area that drains into the lake and on water quality and quantity, and protection of water quality through appropriate land-use controls. Both objectives can be incorporated into a rural environmental plan. Fortunately, techniques for lake basin management are well developed and readily available.

Most lake management and water-quality classification programs developed to date have been produced by state agencies. These programs are designed according to the standards of state water resource departments. The planning method presented here emphasizes local initiative and aims at lake management with local goals in mind. From this perspective a lake basin management program must meet two basic criteria: it must be scientifically sound, and the cost must be modest. In addition, some results should be obtained within a season to maintain public support, and the management system should be implemented by rural officials with minimal assistance from sources such as the state department of water resources and water resource specialists from the state university.

In the development of a lake watershed plan, the REP process suggests four specific indices or ways to measure the potential for maintaining lake quality in balance with existing or proposed uses: an index of the lake's vulnerability to accelerated eutrophication (aging), an index of the degree of lakeshore land use intensity, an index of land use in the upland watershed (the land that drains into the lake), and an index of present water quality. These four indices are combined to develop a lake water-quality monitoring component and a watershed land-use component for the rural environmental plan. Although the tasks sound complicated, much of this information is available from state university departments, state or regional agencies responsible for water quality, environmental health, and game and fish, or state engineers and planning agencies. The task of the rural planner is to contact these sources, obtain the information identified in the sections that follow, fit them into the indices as shown in the examples, and incorporate them into goal formulation and planning.

INDEX 1: LAKE VULNERABILITY[2]

Some lakes are very susceptible to what natural scientists call accelerated eutrophication, that is, speeded-up aging. Accelerated eutrophication, which makes the lake environment less conductive to many species of fish, is often caused by human use of the lake and its shore. Some lakes, however, withstand considerable increase in nutrients and pollutants without adverse affect on their aging. To understand the urgency of various land-use controls, we need a measure to determine the relative vulnerability of a lake to loss of dissolved oxygen, rapid increase in algae, and silting and sedimentation.

A lake vulnerability index is developed by first collecting morphological data (that is, lake size, shape, depth, and flow) for all lakes in a specified region. These data should be available from the university sources or state agencies identified previously. A list is then made of the range of variation in each category. This list can be divided into three gradations (low, medium, and high), with a rating number assigned to each (1 for lowest vulnerability, 2 for medium, and 3 for most vulnerable). The list is arranged according to rating numbers for a lake vulnerability index (see fig. 8.1).

Five items that contribute to lake eutrophication are included in the vulnerability index: the ratio of lake volume to drainage-basin area, shoreline configuration, mean depth, shoalness ratio, and mean hydrologic residence time. Each of these has an effect on the growth of algae and loss of fish habitat in the lake. A discussion of each follows.

Drainage-Basin Area to Lake Volume Ratio. The drainage-basin area divided by lake volume provides a ratio that tells a lot about the potential rate of change in the quality of lake water. The larger this ratio, the more vulnerable the lake to a change in quality. The supply of nutrients and nutrient-bearing sediments from the area that drains into the lake tends to increase in direct proportion to the size of the watershed, if other things such as rainfall, slopes, and land use remain the same. That is, the smaller the lake volume in relation to the land area that drains into the lake, the less able the lake is to assimilate nutrients in inflowing water.

Shoreline Configuration. The total shoreline length of a lake divided by the circumference of a circle with equal area will produce another indicator of vulnerability. The higher this ratio, the more likely the lake is to have embayments with shallow water and, thus, the more likely to have more aquatic vegetation and to produce algae (as opposed to a lake with a more circular shoreline). Nutrients are more likely to be retained in embayments because the average depth of bays is usually less than that of the main part of the lake. Consequently, embayments are more likely to experience photic-production (vegetative matter produced in water that is penetrated by light) and eutrophication (vegetative and algae production).

Mean Depth.   The mean depth is another indicator of vulnerability. The deeper a lake, the less vulnerable it is because of its greater capacity to absorb nutrients and hold them in sediments below the zone of light penetration. In the hypolimnion (cold) zone of stratified lakes nutrients cannot be

Lake _____ Location _____ Surface area (acres) _____ Average depth (feet) _____ Volume (acres-feet) _____ Shoreline length (feet) _____ Drainage area (acres) _____			
Morphological Characteristics	*Vulnerability Rating*		
	Low 1	Medium 2	High 3
Drainage Basin- to lake-volume ratio __ acres/ __ acres-feet = __	_____	_____	_____
Shoreline configuration or compactness ratio Shoreline length/circumference of circle equal to lake area __ feet/__ feet = __	_____	_____	_____
Mean depth ratio Volume (cubic feet)/lake area (square feet) __	_____	_____	_____
Shoalness ratio Lake area with depth less than 20 feet to total lake area __ acres/__ acres = __	_____	_____	_____
Residence time	_____	_____	_____
Total lake vulnerability index _____			

FIGURE 8.1. Index 1: Lake Vulnerability Compared to Other Lakes in Region *Note: Indicators of lake vulnerability to accelerated aging are based on morphological characteristics.*

utilized during the critical summer months. The shallower the lake, the more likely it is to have excessive vegetative and algae production.

Shoalness Ratio.   The percentage of lake bottom areas that lies 20 feet or less below the water surface may be used as a vulnerability indicator. Light penetration to bottom sediment depends on various factors such as water color, turbidity, mineral content, and algal biomass. Twenty feet may be taken as the lower limit of the photic zone. Nutrients in sediments at this depth are readily available for the growth of water plants and algae under normal circumstances. This area of the lake is therefore most likely to exhibit the symptoms of excessive fertility, given the introduction of sufficient levels of nutrients. Thus, the greater the percentage of lake bottom that is less than 20 feet below the surface, the more vulnerable the lake is to accelerated eutrophication.

Mean Hydrologic Residence Time.   The amount of time that inflowing water stays in a lake is called residence time. The shorter the residence time of a lake, the less high-nutrient inflows will affect it because they will be flushed through the basin more quickly (again, assuming all other factors to be invariable).

The above indicators of lake vulnerability were chosen for two reasons. First, although not exactly predictable, such relationships do exist and they are direct. Second, information pertaining to these indicators is readily available from state agencies or else can be collected inexpensively.

INTERPRETATION OF INDEX 1

Once the data are summarized, they can be taken to an expert in the water resources department or at the state university for interpretation. All five indicators are considered separately and then rated as follows: low (1), medium (2), or high (3) vulnerability. The three rating numbers are based on an approximate division into thirds of the values obtained for each factor in a survey of a number of lakes in the region. A comparative basis for evaluation is necessary, for there is no accepted criterion that pinpoints the value or range of values for low, medium, or high vulnerability.

In the absence of comparative data on other lakes, index 1B may be used (see fig. 8.2). This interpretation is based on an average of data from similar technical reports. It will give a preliminary indication of vulnerability for a single lake. This can also be interpreted by experts in the water resources department or at the state university.

INDEX 2: LAKESHORE LAND-USE INTENSITY[3]

The intensity of land use in the entire watershed is a measure of the lake's vulnerability to pollution or eutrophication. It is also an indication of cultural, that is, manmade and therefore controllable, contributions to the aging process. The lakeshore land-use intensity index is based on a rating of the major types of human-influenced land uses that are recognized as having an effect on lake water quality. The intensity of each type of land use is rated on a scale from low to high, indicating its potential impact on the lake. The watershed assessment is then divided into two components: lakeshore land use within 1,000 feet of the shoreline, and watershed land use in the rest of the area that drains into the lake.

Index 2 (fig. 8.3) displays four factors to determine the impact on water quality of lakeshore land use. Each factor deals with shoreline use that di-

	Morphological Characteristics	Vulnerability Rating		
		Low 1	Medium 2	High 3
Drainage	Ratio: Drainage basin area (acres) to lake volume (acres-feet)	Less than 0.3	0.3–1.0	Greater than 1
Shoreline	Ratio: Shoreline length to circumference with area equal to this lake area	Less than 1.5	1.5–2.0	Greater than 2.0
Mean depth	Ratio: Lake volume (cubic feet) to lake area (square feet) in feet	Greater than 30	10–30	Less than 10
Shoalness	Ratio: Lake area with depth less than 20 feet to total lake area	0–40%	40–80%	80–100%
Residence time	Varies widely	Determined by hydrologist		
Vulnerability index (add ratings)		_____	_____	_____

FIGURE 8.2. Index 1B: Lake Vulnerability for a Single Lake

rectly affects water quality: traditional on-site sewage-disposal systems, developed lot size, road proximity, and intensive public use areas.

On-Site Sewage Disposal Systems.   Inadequately constructed or maintained on-site septic tank and drainfield sewage systems are potentially significant polluters. When septic systems are installed within 200 feet of a lakeshore, there is a risk that some of the nutrients, bacteria, and other pollutants can enter the lake. Traditional septic systems, however, are not inherently inappropriate. Adequately sized, properly maintained, and regularly inspected septic systems provide on-site wastewater treatment that is biologically equivalent to that provided by many centralized town or village sewage treatment plants. For such systems to function properly, though, they must be located a suitable distance from all water sources, and, most importantly, drainfields must be placed in living, loamy soil to allow aerobic bacteria to perform their biological and mechanical cleansing actions, which is equivalent to tertiary treatment at a centralized waste treatment plant.[4]

Developed Lot Size.   Crowding structures along the lakeshore affects water quality directly because it increases the potential for pollutants from improperly designed or inadequately maintained septic systems or from boating and swimming. Crowding also means more runoff from near-shore areas. Development of houses, roads, and related support systems usually brings with it an increase in paved surfaces and a reduction of those plants and grasses that absorb rainfall. Lots averaging less than 100 feet in width may

Lakeshore Characteristics	Intensity			Rating
	Low 1	Medium 2	High 3	
Serviced by traditional septic tank sewage systems	0–33%	33–67%	67–100%	_____
Developed lots averaging 100 front feet or less	0–10%	10–50%	50–100%	_____
Main road within 200 feet of lake	0–5%	5–25%	25–100%	_____
Devoted to intensive public use	0–3%	3–10%	10–100%	_____
		Total		_____

FIGURE 8.3. Index 2: Lakeshore Land-Use Intensity

have inadequate surface area to absorb increased runoff or to mitigate the effect of contaminants.

Road Proximity.   The proximity of a road to the lakeshore is important to water quality. Roads 200 feet or less from the shore often define the boundary lines of lakeshore property. This can limit the space available for well-designed septic systems. Also, roads mean less vegetative cover, which increases the amount and reduces the quality of runoff.

Intensive Public-Use Areas.   These areas include marinas, boat-launching sites, public and private beaches, youth camps, picnic areas, campgrounds, and other intensively developed public and private lands. Land use contributes to lake water deterioration in several ways. Motorboats introduce oil and other chemicals into the water and cause shore erosion through wave action. Effects can be especially harmful when public areas concentrate several intensive water uses in relatively small areas.

INDEX 3: UPLAND WATERSHED LAND-USE INTENSITY

The remaining land-use categories that directly affect water quality are intensive development, agriculture and open space, and forest cover (see fig. 8.4). These relate to upland land use, that is, the rest of the watershed area.

Upland Characteristics	Intensity			*Rating*
	Low 1	*Medium* 2	*High* 3	
Watershed area intensively developed	0–5%	5–25%	25–100%	_____
Agriculture or open, cleared space	0–25%	25–50%	50–100%	_____
Covered by forest	75–100%	25–75%	25–0%	_____
Intensity of Upland Development Total				_____

FIGURE 8.4. Index 3: Upland Watershed Land-Use Intensity

Intensive Upland Development. The higher the percentage of total watershed area covered by development, the greater the potential for accelerated eutrophication from sediments and nutrients. Intensive development in the upper areas of a watershed, like intensive development on a lakeshore, may have adverse effects on lake water quality as it implies a concentration of human-related activities which directly increase runoff flowing into the lake. Intensive development is defined here as any commercial or industrial development, any urbanized area (including villages and hamlets), and any cluster of five or more dwellings on five or less acres in the watershed.

Upland Agriculture and Open Space. Research demonstrates that runoff from cleared land (including both active and inactive farmland), some of which may be partially grown over, is a relatively heavy contributor of nutrients and pollutants to lakes and streams. Because cleared land is often used for human activity, it increases the probability of eutrophication.[5]

Upland Forest Cover. Forested land (except commercial tree farms or logging areas) is beneficial to the larger watershed area. Mature, established forests do not contribute to eutrophication because their sediments and nutrients are largely absorbed by the vegetative cover and soils of the forest floor. Note that the percentage of forest cover in table 4 is inversely proportionate to land-use intensity, that is, the more mature forest there is, the less the negative impact on a lake.

INTERPRETATION OF INDEX 3

As in the interpretation of the lakeshore area, here each development area is measured as a percentage of the total watershed area and then located in one of the percentage distributions. Rating values (1, 2, or 3) are then added to get a numerical total.

Seven ratings may now be generated from the examination of land use at the lakeshore and in the watershed. The first four ratings are added to arrive at an index number indicating the relative intensity of lakeshore development. The final three ratings are added to produce the lake basin land-use intensity index. Note that for the forest-cover component, the larger percentage of forest has a lower negative impact. Figure 8.6 gives an example of how an index is constructed from land-use ratings. The range of index numbers for upland land use is from 3, for a relatively undeveloped watershed, to 9, for a highly developed watershed.

INDEX 4: LAKE WATER QUALITY

Obtaining complete, objective, and scientific information on lake water quality can be time consuming and difficult. The best way for a rural planner or citizen to obtain this information is by interviewing experts in state agencies and at the state university. Experts include employees at the state department of water resources, health, and fish and game, and professors of limnology, aquatic biology, hydrology, geology, and planning. Interviews are easier when questions are organized in the form of a questionnaire (see fig. 8.5). On the basis of interviews, lake water quality can be given a rating of low

---

Date _____

Lake _____   Respondent _____
                             Department _____

1. What data has been collected on this lake by your department? (List reports available.)

   _____
   _____

2. Based on the information available, how would you rate this lake in comparison with other lakes in the region with reference to:
   (a) Eutrophic level:
        (1) lowest ⅓___; (2) middle ⅓ ___; (3) highest ⅓ ___
   (b) Human-caused pollution:
        (1) lowest ⅓ ___; (2) middle ⅓ ___; (3) highest ⅓ ___
3. In your judgment, what are the principal characteristics of the uses of the lake and watershed land areas that contribute to this rating?

   _____

4. What are the principal sources of point and nonpoint pollution?

   _____

5. In your judgment, what types of lake or lakeshore controls, or changes in land use, are necessary to improve lakewater quality?

   _____
   _____
   _____
   _____

FIGURE 8.5. Index 4: Lake Water Quality Questionnaire

(1), medium (2), or high (3) eutrophic level, and low (1), medium (2), or high (3) pollution level with reference to other lakes.

INDEX 5: COMBINED LAKE QUALITY INDICES

Now, combine all four indices to produce a four-digit number. The first digit indicates the level of lake vulnerability, the second and third digits indicate the intensity of lakeshore and upland land use, and the fourth digit indicates the level of water quality. The highest (negative) level in each category is 3, and the lowest (positive) level in each category is 1. A combined index may be constructed for each lake (see figure 8.6).

With the combined indexes, lakes may be classified to provide a basis for prescribing monitoring and management programs and for developing a comprehensive watershed plan. These indexes, which combine direct observation

		Index		
Lake	*Lake Vulnerability*	*Lakeshore Land-Use Intensity*	*Upland Watershed Land-Use Intensity*	*Present Quality*
A	3	3	3	3
B	3	1	2	2
C	2	2	1	1
D	1	2	2	1

The index numbers have the following possible interpretations:

Lake A (3-3-3-3)   High vulnerability, high development of lakeshore, high development of upland watershed, advanced deterioration

Lake B (3-1-2-2)   High vulnerability, low development of lakeshore, medium development of upland watershed, medium deterioration

Lake C (2-2-1-1)   Medium vulnerability, medium development of lakeshore, low development of upland watershed, low level of deterioration

Lake D (1-2-2-1)   Low vulnerability, medium development of lakeshore, medium development of upland watershed, low level of deterioration

FIGURE 8.6. Index 5: Combined Lake Quality Indices

with the advice of state agency and university experts, permit local officials and local water committees to work with the environmental planner in forming a comprehensive plan for the lake basin as part of a rural environmental plan.

Examples of the practical application of this concept are the Granite Lake watershed in New Hampshire[6] and the Seymour Lake watershed in Morgan, Vermont[7]. These two projects demonstrate the value of a special watershed plan to protect a community's lake water. A lake basin plan includes land-use recommendations that have been agreed upon and that can be implemented by the local jurisdiction, the lakeshore owners' association, and individual lot owners.

ALTERNATIVE WASTEWATER TREATMENT SYSTEMS

Because of their impact on water quality, the plan should give special attention to the location, number, and arrangement of building lots with access to a lakeshore. Strings of narrow lots with inadequately designed filter-field sewage disposals can lead to a polluted lake with low land values and reduced tax revenues. By requiring a 200-foot setback for buildings from the high-water mark and reserving a strip of public land along the shore, the local jurisdiction maximizes the number of people who use the lake and contribute to the local tax base. Minneapolis, Minnesota, has successfully planned some lakes in this way. Increased tax returns can be used for a sewer with watertight joints, cluster wastewater treatment, or other biologically sound systems. The costs and benefits should be studied carefully by a community planning a lakeshore.

Alternative on-site systems may be appropriate in low-density or cluster lakeshore developments where distances between lots, soil quality, or shallow bedrock conditions make traditional septic systems or sewer excavations inappropriate. For example, where space allows development but soils are inadequate, evapo-transpiration (ET) drainfield beds use replacement soil over contained, impermeable liners, which allow evaporation of drainage and biological processing of nutrients in the vegetated soilbed. A properly designed and constructed system can process 100 percent of the effluent with no discharge to surface or groundwater. Evapo-transpiration/absorption (ETA) beds are a variation that discharge to both the atmosphere and the groundwater when site size, configuration, and subsurface conditions are appropriate.

Other biologically sound on-site or cluster systems can be utilized in ecologically sensitive areas when environmental or economic conditions and community health requirements warrant. For small clusters, subdivisions with up to a few hundred units, aerobic, multichambered septic systems can produce effluent meeting federal standards for discharge to potable waters.[8] For subdivision or large-scale developments, advanced centralized treatment systems such as enclosed solar aquaculture or constructed wetlands may be appropriate, particularly where water or discharge limitations make reuse and recycle options attractive.[9]

Where there are shallow soils, rock ledges, or severe limits on access to water, individual compost toilets are an option. A rural environmental plan for a town, lakeshore, or remote mountain area can specify performance requirements that allow individual waste-treatment choice and still reflect concern for public health and community utility and service costs. For example, in Sweden, which has extensive shallow soil and exposed bedrock, it is common to use in-house compost toilets in combination with water-conserving appliances. Small-scale, gray-water drainage systems are also extensively used. In Sweden and in other Scandinavian countries with long, subzero degree winters and shallow rocky soils, manufactured fiberglass interior toilets with a sloping composting chamber and a contributing chute from the kitchen for vegetable cuttings and other biodegradable wastes are fully sanctioned by environmental health agencies. These units have low-level air inlets and above-roof air outlets. They function as a low-temperature furnace volitolizing 90 percent of solids into harmless carbon dioxide gas and water vapor leaving a small, nearly odorless residue to be removed on an average of once every two to three years for a typical household of four persons.[10]

CASE: VERMONT ASSOCIATION OF CONSERVATION DISTRICTS

In Vermont, responsibility for management of on-site sewage disposal rests with local government. Although all towns have a health officer, many lack regulations governing on-site disposal. To induce them to adopt regulations and provide a service to homeowners, the Vermont Association of Conservation Districts (the coordinating organization for fourteen natural resource conservation districts) developed a multitown septic system design and inspection program in 1973. By 1988 the system had been adopted by over 107 towns.

To implement the inspection programs, a few changes were required in state health regulations and state law. One was to authorize on-site sanitary specialists and engineers, trained by the SCS, the Vermont Agency of Environmental Conservation, the extension service, and the state health department, to make inspections. Another measure was to replace percolation testing with soil analysis for determining a soil's suitability for on-site disposal. SCS soil scientists assigned Vermont soils to ten categories according to their suitability for on-site disposal and established design standards for each soil type. The SCS provided maps and a classification and interpretation of soils for each of the ten classes.

Vermont's Agency of Environmental Conservation and Department of Health also provide on-site sewage-system design criteria for each of the ten soil classes. Designs include recommended site modifications such as surface and subsurface drainage, benching, and filling to overcome site limitations.

The key to the program is the on-site sanitary specialist, employed by the natural resource conservation district, who performs an inspection at reasonable cost. The area covered by each specialist is determined by a workload of approximately two hundred sites per person per year. It amounts to five to fifteen towns per specialist. The specialists maintain an "open working schedule" and make many calls on weekends. Although sanitary specialists are assigned to specific towns, they may assist neighboring towns when the workload requires it.

The on-site sanitary specialist arranges for site inspection with the homeowner, installer, or contractor. The resulting report includes soil type, classification, and suitability for on-site disposal; recommendations for soil-related problems such as surface drainage, slope, and vegetative cover; basic criteria or a complete design for a disposal system; and provisions for compliance checks of the installation and an inspection report to the town board of health. The latter report is based on an inspection of the system before it is covered with earth. The SCS soil scientists and engineers assist when unusual site problems are encountered.

To participate in this program, a town first must adopt health regulations maintaining minimum standards for septic tank and leach-field installations. The town also must adopt a building-permit system and set a fee for inspection services. The on-site specialist assists the town in adopting these bylaws.

The Vermont program has grown at an encouraging rate. By 1988 all of the state's fourteen natural resource conservation districts were sponsoring the on-site inspection program, employing a total of ten sanitary specialists. In 1987 specialists evaluated 1,120 sites alone. Since the program began in 1973 they have evaluated over 10,000 sites.

CONCLUSION

Goals for water resource planning are either obvious or relatively easy to determine. Goals in lake basin planning can be for agricultural and domestic use, for aesthetics or for recreation including boating, fishing, rafting, sailing, and swimming. Inventorying water conditions and their causes, however, is a complex procedure. Complexity and cost have been a major obstacle to locally initiated community planning for water resources. To resolve this problem the University of Vermont conducted a research program to develop a less expensive but scientifically acceptable means of obtaining such information. The program, which uses the indexing techniques presented in this chapter, is designed to be conducted by rural planners, students, or citizens with assistance from the state university and state agencies. The advantage of this program is the low cost of gathering data for the development of local plans for the management and protection of lake basins.

9

Planning River Basins

UNTIL RECENTLY, RURAL towns and villages located in the drainage basins of major rivers did not play a significant role in water development politics. When federal agencies such as the Army Corps of Engineers, the U.S. Department of the Interior, and the Bureau of Reclamation planned a river basin, local officials and citizens were not often consulted and not often aware of the plans. If local people did recognize what was happening, it was difficult for them to break into the planning process.[1] Recently, however, a reduction of federal activity in river basin projects has changed the process and the politics of planning for water resources. Whether in humid or arid environments, rural communities can now get involved, even take the initiative, in planning their reach of a river basin.

Watersheds and rivers, not defined by political boundaries, frequently require planning at a regional scale. In the past, the division of authority among various levels of government rendered multipurpose floodplain planning nearly impossible. Since 1936 federal agencies have had responsibility for planning specific aspects of river basins, such as flood damage reduction, while county governments or towns have been responsible for local land-use planning, zoning, and zoning enforcement. In most instances the state has played no significant role in river basin planning. This system of divided responsibility without a mechanism for coordination among federal, state, and local agencies has obstructed multipurpose planning for the public interest. Single-purpose solutions have repeatedly been applied to multifaceted problems, for example, the construction of large-scale dams without the adoption of floodplain zoning.

122

Hydrologic principles concerning river basins and floods are well known. There is ample evidence, for instance, that dams without floodplain zoning fail to reduce flood damage and indeed increase flood damage in developments below dam sites. The most commonly cited case is that of the Colorado River in Texas. This river was almost completely controlled by dams in the 1930s. At one point, a storm front carrying heavy rains passed over the river valley at such a speed and angle that the waters overtopped some dams and resulted in severe damage. Had the dams not been built, and had the residents not built homes on the floodplain, damage would have been less. Fortunately, the single-purpose methods of the past are gradually being replaced by river basin planning undertaken by local-regional-state teams.

After the introduction of federal subsidies for state and local water planning in the Housing and Home Finance Agency Act of 1954, a new framework gradually evolved that fosters more coordinated, comprehensive river basin planning. It took several years for federal agencies to adjust to the new procedures. During this period, which lasted through the late 1970s, federal river basin planning continued with little coordination and little dissemination of information to local officials. Many towns developed master plans without knowledge of other plans then under consideration at regional and interstate levels.

MULTIPURPOSE FLOODPLAINS

Floodplains have a number of potential uses besides flood damage mitigation. With appropriate arrangements for on-site flood hazard protection, they can support a variety of outdoor recreational and economic activities as well as provide access to public waters (see table 9.1). Floodplains are invariably scenic, ribbons of green open space even in arid environments. Floodplains are indispensable to a quality environment, and together with streams, rivers, marshes, ponds, and wetlands, support prime fish and wildlife habitats. Floodplains also include some of the best soils for agriculture.

Rural Environmental Planning embraces consideration and analysis of all floodplain uses. River basins are useful for multiple purposes (see table 9.2). The river's role in the hydrologic and biologic cycles and the food chain must be considered and protected. A team of specialists can help local citizens to evaluate, appraise, and recommend how to manage a floodplain from environmental, economic, recreational, and public safety points of view. At least seven disciplines, in addition to engineering and planning, are directly concerned in this process—hydrology, geology, climatology, limnology, wildlife biology, forestry, and resource economics. All are represented at the state university.

PUBLIC GOALS IN RIVER BASIN PLANNING

Planning with reference to public goals became an established procedure in the 1960s after three federal agencies began supporting new planning programs. The U.S. Department of Housing and Urban Development increased subsidies for local efforts in town, county, and state planning. The EPA established environmental goals, introduced environmental planning, and encouraged states to set environmental standards. The Bureau of Outdoor Recreation inaugurated and subsidized state recreation planning and the development of local and state recreation facilities. As a result, local and state participation and leadership in river basin planning expanded, and local and state goals were recognized as significant parts of the planning process.

These changes in federal policies and the growth of state, regional and local planning have led to an emerging pattern of river basin planning. This new pattern has three components: First, today prime responsibility for coordinating the planning of river basin use is in the hands of the state, not the federal government. Second, plans are now developed through state-county-local coordination that recognizes and accommodates public goals at all levels. And third, when REP is utilized local government units determine local interests and incorporate them into the regional plan. These changing institutional arrangements have reduced federal emphasis on flood damage reduc-

TABLE 9.1

Floodplain Use and Compatibility with Flooding

Use of Floodplain	Compatible with Flooding
Flood damage reduction (spreading and slowing floodwaters)	Yes
Agriculture	Yes
Residences (intensive, urban)	No
Residences (seasonal)	No
Industry (intensive, urban)	No
Businesses (intensive, urban)	No
Recreation (access for fishing, boating, swimming, and hiking)	Yes
Greenbelts (open space)	Yes

tion via large, single-purpose dams. Recreation, agriculture, open space, and flood hazard mitigation in floodplain areas are given greater consideration and support at the local and state level.

WATER QUALITY CLASSIFICATION

Classification systems are useful tools for analyzing water quality in humid and arid environments. Each state or province may have its own system. If not, a five-class system may be used.

TABLE 9.2

Use of River Waters

Recreational
    Fishing (water and ice)
    Sailing (water and ice)
    Boating
    Water skiing
    Canoeing, rafting (flat and whitewater)
    Swimming
    Auto racing on ice
    Skating
    Scuba diving

Municipal and Industrial
    Municipal water supply
    Hydroelectric power production
    Treated sewage effluent dilution
    Industrial cooling, processing, and effluent dilution
    Navigation

Natural Area (Open Space)
    Aesthetic component of scenery
    Wildlife habitat
    Function in hydrologic cycle

Agricultural
    Irrigation
    Water supply

1. Class A waters, disinfected when necessary, are suitable for public water supply. The quality is uniformly excellent.
2. Class B waters are suitable for bathing and for recreation, irrigation, and agricultural uses. They are good fish habitats, may have aesthetic value, and may be acceptable for public water supply with filtration and disinfection.
3. Class C waters are suitable for recreational boating, irrigation of crops not used for consumption without cooking, habitat for wildlife and for common food and game fish indigenous to the region, and for such industrial uses that are consistent with other similar uses.
4. Class D waters are suitable for supporting aerobic aquatic life, for power, navigation and certain industrial process needs consistent with other Class D uses for restricted zones of water to assimilate appropriately treated wastes.
5. Class E waters carry untreated sewage in such concentrations that they constitute a public nuisance. They are unfit for body contact, fishing, and boating.

For planning purposes the complex chemical information collected by the state water resources or fish and game departments can be reduced to some simple statements about water quality. Where fishing is the primary planned use for a body of water, the most critical information may be the water's temperature and level of dissolved oxygen. When it is swimming, coliform count may be the most important criterion of quality. When it is boating or canoeing, a secchi disc (water turbidity indicator) quickly characterizes the suitability of a body of water.

The classification procedure consists of three steps: (1) preparing a map and a brief text describing present water quantity and quality in relation to proposed use; (2) preparing a text and a map projecting and explaining future water quality; and (3) in response to step 2, setting out dollar costs and discussing actions and agencies responsible for ensuring the adequacy of water quality based on anticipated use.

This report is the nucleus of the water chapter in a rural environmental plan. In drawing up the report, the rural planner or water resources subcommittee should obtain detailed assistance from state agencies responsible for water resources, health, fish and game, and from university departments of civil engineering, geology, public health, resource economics, and zoology. The water resources inventory should determine present water quality and sources of pollution and recommend methods to improve quality to permit the particular water uses identified in the community goals survey. The water chapter should also include recommendations concerning any other specific water supply and use problems identified by both citizens and water experts.

CASE: THE WINOOSKI RIVER VALLEY PARK DISTRICT, VERMONT

The Winooski, the largest river in Vermont, cuts through the Green Mountains, passes the capital city of Montpelier, flows through rich farmlands and greater Burlington, then empties into Lake Champlain. The gap the Winooski cuts through the Green Mountains is a route for a railroad, an interstate highway, and other state and town roads. The river provides hydroelectric power, transports sewage, and supports canoeing, fishing, swimming, birding, and boating. Near the mouth of the Winooski is the Intervale, an extensive wetland and floodplain that includes farmland, an historic site (Ethan Allen's homestead), an archeological site, a prehistoric Indian encampment, and a major feeding and resting ground for migratory waterfowl in the Champlain flyway.

As the city of Burlington grew, the Intervale migratory waterfowl resting area became threatened. The city was considering the Intervale as a site for a beltline highway, an industrial park, an oil storage tank farm, and a power plant. It was already used as a sanitary landfill.

In January 1967, at the request of the Chittenden County Regional Planning Commission, the University of Vermont's rural environmental planner conducted an attitude survey to determine the kind of resource development the people of Chittenden County wanted. The survey revealed that a large majority of the residents wanted cleaner water, open space, a Winooski park, public access to the river, a network of trails, and a natural area reserve. Seventy-five percent of the respondents mentioned stream pollution when asked what should receive prompt attention in Chittenden County. Seventy percent were in favor of creating a state park on the Winooski River, and over 60 percent wanted a trail system of some sort in their area.

In 1968 the city of Burlington decided to run a connecting highway through a corner of the delta floodplain. Led by the chairman of the Audubon Society's Conservation Committee, a group of citizens concerned about environmental impact decided it was time to act. Their objective was twofold: to develop a public goal for the protection of natural and recreational land use, and to develop a framework to implement the program on a multitown basis.

A public meeting was advertised and held in a Burlington school. The meeting provided a means of informing the public of the uses of the river and its wetlands; the threats to continuing its conservation, recreational, and aesthetic uses; and possible ways of better managing river valley land uses. A river valley district was proposed. At the next meeting, the Chittenden County Regional Planning Commission adopted the goal of protecting the Winooski and appointed a subcommittee to assist in creating a park district.

The university REP planner prepared a detailed plan for consideration by the planning commission. This plan described the river valley, outlined proposed developments (canoe trails, scenic overlooks, canoe access areas, wildfowl sanctuaries, and walking trails), and suggested sources of funds and organizations that could help in the implementation. This plan provided a definite statement of the park-district concept, and led to the next step, writing bylaws for a multimunicipality district (see fig. 9.1).

A committee of ten town representatives met regularly for a year with the director of the regional planning commission, an environmental lawyer, and

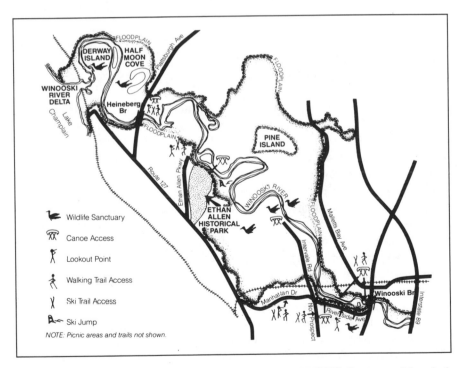

FIGURE 9.1. Winooski River Park: Proposed Locations of Wildlife Sanctuary, Historical Park, and Recreational Land Uses

a university environmental planner to draft bylaws. Park district bylaws were based on two enabling statutes: title 24, Vermont Statutes Annotated, chapter 95, enables the formation of intermunicipal unions, and title 10, Vermont Statutes Annotated, chapter 155, provides guidelines for property acquisition by intermunicipal unions. After the bylaws were drafted, public information meetings were held in all the lower-valley towns. At these meetings university environmental planning students presented a slide show depicting the beauty and uses of the Winooski, explaining the problems of pollution and erosion, and presenting the district park proposal.

By 1972 four towns had voted to join, and the Winooski Valley Park District (WVPD) started operation. By 1988 there were seven municipal members. After its organization the WVPD kept busy with high-priority conservation and recreation projects. A list of its land acquisitions tells the story (see table 9.3).

The board of trustees, which manages the WVPD, is composed of one representative from each member town. Trustees are appointed by the legislative body of each town and serve three-year terms. The budget, provided by member towns, increased from $8,950 in 1975 to $51,000 in 1988.

Early in its development the directors of the WVPD decided that they needed a master plan to state their objectives and guide their management decisions. In 1978 a graduate student in rural planning at the University of Vermont developed the plan for his master's project.[2] His plan focused on policy, in lieu of specific land use or economic and social impacts. As of 1990 the plan was still being used to guide park management and expansion.

This case illustrates four elements of the REP process: initiative by a citizens conservation committee; support from a regional planning commission and a state university rural environmental planner; student participation; and local municipal action to join and administer a proposal.

CASE: THE UPPER RIO GRANDE, NEW MEXICO

The growing importance of regional water planning is also seen in arid and semiarid environments. In 1987 the New Mexico State legislature authorized the development of substate or regional water plans to ensure an adequate supply of water for the future (New Mexico House Bill 337). Rather than establishing fixed or arbitrary boundaries for water planning, the legislature defined the regional level as "an area within the state that contains sufficient hydrological and political interests in common to make water planning feasible." Planning grants and loans provided for in the statute were designed as

TABLE 9.3
WVPD Parklands, 1988

Park River Frontage	Location Acreage	Acquisition Date	Uses
Ethan Allen Homestead 9,750 feet	Burlington 284	Purchased 1974, 1981, 1986	Historic site, picnicking, gardens, nature trail, canoe access, X-country ski trail, administration
Salmon Hole Island no. 1 Island no. 2 Mill Yard canoe launch 6,000 feet	Burlington Winooski Burlington Winooski 120	Leased 1974	Fishing, overlook, picnic conservation, natural area conservation, natural area canoe launch, picnicking
Island no. 3 3,900 feet	Essex 15	Leased 1976	Conservation
McCrea Farm 6,500 feet	Colchester 288	Purchased 1977, 1979	Nature study, canoe access, picnicking, trails
Muddy Brook 1,200 feet	South Burlington 8	Leased 1977	Canoe access, trail, fishing access

Delta Park	Colchester 55	Purchased 1984	Outdoor classroom, wildlife sanctuary, birding, geology
Essex Overlook	Essex 5	Leased 1985	Scenic overlook
Valley Ridge	South Burlington 18	Donation 1985	Wildlife reserve
Heineburg Wetlands	Burlington 11	Donation 1986	Wildlife reserve
Donahue Sea Caves	Burlington 15	Donation 1986	Natural area waterfowl observation

incentives to stimulate new approaches to planning, since an eligible region would have to be larger than a single jurisdiction but smaller than the state. The law also required "an appropriate planning process including opportunities for participation by those Indian tribes located within the various regions of the state."

Meanwhile, a team from the University of New Mexico (faculty members from economics, planning, and public administration) had been collaborating with a working group made up of Native Americans, Hispanics, and others concerned about water resources in the upper Rio Grande River basin.[3] Located in north-central New Mexico, the upper Rio Grande region supplies water to municipal, industrial, and agribusiness interests downstream. Water is supplied by the flow from melting snow and controlled by upstream storage facilities built at public expense.

Despite the fact that, historically, Indian pueblos and Hispanic villages were the first communities to appropriate New Mexico waters, their political ability to protect former water rights and to influence water policy had been declining as large-scale users expanded their control of Rio Grande waters. The purpose of the university project was to encourage a discussion among these land-based peoples on the community value of water and to articulate a strategy for water planning and policy development compatible with the culture of the region. In 1984 the university team invited community representatives to serve as members of the upper Rio Grande working group. The initial task of the group was to identify major local and regional problems and to develop a conference report declaring their own unique concerns. This was to be distributed to state legislators and water resources managers.

The working group's final report in December 1985 made twenty-seven recommendations for actions in five areas.[4] In the area of development, the report recognized the need for continued economic growth in the region but called for options consistent with the cultural values of Pueblo Indian and Hispanic rural settlements, including the retention of water rights for traditional uses. In the area of education, it was judged first that traditional water users themselves needed to learn more about water laws, procedures, and institutions, particularly with regard to the protection of existing water rights, and second that the general public and government officials should appreciate the crucial role water played in the continued survival of Native American and Hispanic cultures of the region.

In the area of water policy, the report noted that the state did not provide sufficient protection for the rights and needs of traditional users. State statutes considered water solely as a property right that could be severed from the land and then sold to the highest bidder. In the area of administration, problems were raised concerning lack of coordination among governmental agencies, overlapping jurisdictions, failure of state agencies to serve small-scale water users, and inadequate management in indigenous water organizations. Finally, in the area of infrastructure, the report described numerous problems associated with water delivery: inadequate maintenance of irrigation ditches; lack of control over erosion, flooding, seepage, and sedimentation; domestic supply systems with inadequate rate structures to finance needed repairs; and limited governmental financial assistance.

The university team and the upper Rio Grande working group continued their collaborative efforts through 1986 and 1987, this time developing strategic information to implement the report's recommendations. This second phase culminated in a conference on traditional water use held at St. John's College, Santa Fe, in October 1987. Community members, along with the university team and other resource professionals, presented strategy reports on various workshop topics: cultural philosophy, water rights protection, water education, the powers of acequia associations, alternatives to litigation, farmland preservation, agricultural marketing capacity, and water trusts.[5] At the conclusion of this conference, community members agreed to form a freestanding association of small-scale water users to protect and pursue their interests at the local, regional, and state level on an ongoing basis. This organization was established a year later and subsequently recognized in a legislative memorial bill during the 1989 session. University sponsorship of the upper Rio Grande working group ended there.

This case demonstrates the catalytic role of university projects in helping rural communities to participate in the changing politics of river basin planning. Without an effort such as this one, water policy for the upper Rio Grande basin would have continued to ignore the concerns of traditional small-scale users who appreciate water for its support of their way of life and not strictly as a commodity to be sold in the marketplace.

CONCLUSION

River basin planning has undergone dramatic changes during the past three decades. The picture has shifted from one of federal agencies focusing on a few water-related goals to local, regional, state, and federal cooperation aimed at multiple use of land and water.

Rural leaders and planners need to gear up to participate in this evolving process. They must play an expanding role as liaisons among rural water users, state water experts, water managers, institutions, legislators, and basinwide planning organizations. University advocacy planners in particular have an opportunity to help to resolve the inevitable conflicts between upstream and downstream water users, between urban centers and rural communities, and between small-scale and commercial/industrial users.

10

Planning for Rural Quality, Recreation, and Historic Preservation

RURAL COMMUNITIES HAVE unique opportunities to enhance rural quality, provide for outdoor recreation, and preserve cultural and historic resources. Each of these aspects of community affects the others. Recreational issues are economic as well as aesthetic concerns. They also affect access to resources, social equity, and cultural continuity. Ultimately, the plan for any rural community must strike a balance among these various concerns that accommodates the resources and values of that community. The components of a rural environmental plan that represent such concerns are rural character and sense of place, scenery classification, planning for rural recreation, and historic preservation.

RURAL CHARACTER AND SENSE OF PLACE

The most basic characteristics of a rural area or small town are the quality and natural beauty of its setting and its sense of place. With careful planning, rural communities can accommodate physical growth and new economic activity while maintaining rural character. Rural areas also have an economic incentive for aesthetic planning: enhancing the region's ability to attract visitors and thereby diversifying local sources of income.

At the beginning of REP projects, sections addressing ways to maintain rural character often include only a few paragraphs; by the time a plan is adopted they have grown to one or two chapters. For example, in the Shelburne, Vermont, plan, there is a whole chapter on aesthetics that discusses

135

seven land-use ideas for maintaining the countryside: rural byways, scenic turnouts, utility corridors, town commons/plazas, nursery and tree plans, beauty zones, and signs. The seven ideas are presented in this chapter for their potential application to other communities.[1]

RURAL BYWAYS

A great deal of the attractiveness of a rural area can be attributed to its roads. Narrow, winding, hilly, tree-shaded byways may not be preferred by a highway engineer, but they are a source of delight to both residents and visitors. Thus the people of the community may want to maintain and augment the aesthetic qualities provided by old country roads. An effective way to promote appreciation and protection of country road beauty is by designating selected roads as rural or scenic byways and representing them as such on official maps. Safety on these roads is promoted by setting lower speed limits, not by straightening, leveling, or widening the roadway, and not by extensive cutting of trees.

SCENIC TURNOUTS

Rural communities in the sierras of the Rocky Mountain states, in the coastal regions, and in the great river valleys and lakes of Middle America have access to spectacular scenery. However, even more prosaic rural locations need areas in which to watch a sunset, to view cumulus clouds over the distant hills, or to enjoy a pastoral scene. In decades past state highway departments, straightening bends in roads, would leave behind small crescents called turnouts for the benefit of travelers. These, however, often occurred without regard to the view. Today, automobile turnouts should be provided at scenic junctures. They should be designed with space for trash barrels and picnic tables for family outings.

UTILITY CORRIDORS

Transmission lines are often located and designed without regard to the damaging effect on a landscape. The effect on property values can be equally damaging. Each transmission line takes important acreage out of other more productive uses. Each line also casts a shadow of depreciated land value in a band on either side.

A number of techniques are available for reducing the aesthetic degradation wrought by power lines. For example, one corridor may be shared by several utility lines. Corridors should be as narrow as the safe transmission of electricity permits. Lines need not follow a straight line but should be fitted into the terrain to appear less imposing. The additional cost in design and construction for alignments may be more than offset by the reduced cost of property-taking or damages. The problem is that, most often, separate agencies account for costs and they do not consider the community context. Routes should be selected where the fewest people are affected. The cleared area under power lines should be "feathered," not clear-cut parallel to the utility lines, and landscaping should fit existing contours. In new subdivisions distribution lines should be buried underground.

TOWN COMMONS/PLAZAS

The town common or the village plaza is the heart of a community. Well designed, it is a place where people of all ages can go for recreation, cultural enrichment, socializing, or just relaxing. It should be within walking distance of population concentrations and include a field for free play as well as "tot lots" and benches.

Most rural communities lacking a common area at least have a site for one. A common area can be built without great cost, and it will increase the property value of abutting land. It is reasonable, therefore, to suggest to a landowner or group of adjacent property owners that if an acre or two is donated to the town for a common, it is possible for the abutting land to increase in value by more than the value of the acres donated.

NURSERY AND TREE PLAN

Trees and shrubs lining streets and bordering lots make a rural town beautiful. To maintain such beauty it is necessary to plant and replace trees as old ones die. Landscaping should be required when new streets are laid out. To accomplish these objectives it helps for a rural community to have a nursery and tree plan. A nursery can be established in a greenbelt and can be managed by volunteers working under the direction of a conservation or planning commission. A tree plan consists of an inventory of existing trees and a replacement and planting program. The inventory lists and locates all trees on community roads and other rights-of-way and classifies them according to size and vigor. The plan estimates how many trees must be replaced each year and the variety needed. Low-maintenance trees and native shrubs and plants reduce costs and increase survival, especially in arid environments.

BEAUTY ZONES

Commercial and industrial areas can be made as attractive as other sections of a rural town by landscaping the areas between roads and parking lots or other structures. These setback zones are planted with a mixture of trees, wildflowers, or other ground cover appropriate to the local climate and setting. Improvements can be low cost and can benefit both commercial properties and the community. It is a good idea to incorporate pulloff lanes in these zones to accommodate cars and reduce the potential of rearend collisions when vehicles enter the commercial area. A regulation providing for landscaped setback areas and pulloff lanes is justified on the basis of traffic safety and can often be funded under state or federal road safety programs.

SIGNS

In community efforts to plan and establish a quality environment, advertising signs represent a special challenge. Permissive planning, zoning, and variance procedures permit roadside businesses and advertisers to post signs in competition with their neighbors. This leads to such an intensive concentration of signs that they lose their effectiveness in communicating to the traveling public. A special committee should be appointed by the planning commission to review the issue of appropriate signing. Clear, legible, and attractive pictorial signs can provide needed information to people in any language. Reducing their number and controlling their size reduces costs for merchants and improves communication with potential customers.

SCENERY CLASSIFICATION SYSTEM

In order to designate scenic roads or to plan scenic turnouts more objectively, it is useful to first rate the scenic vistas. The scenery classification system presented here is a method by which several people can evaluate scenic qualities and arrive at an acceptable collective judgment. The REP scenery classification system consists of a simple numerical rating supplemented by notations on additional scenic attributes. The numerical rating measures distance and variety; the additional attributes are depth, width, continuity, special points of interest and scenic potential.[2]

Distance is a major factor in scenery classification. The distance one can see may be rated from a low of 1 to a high of 5 points. For example, a vegetated bank, a ledge, or a curtain of trees beside a road might score 1 point, while a view that includes a distant range of mountains might rate a score of 5. Intermediate views would be scored accordingly.

The variety of interesting items which can be viewed constitutes the second factor measured. Observations are rated on a 5-point scale. One refers to a single field or the side of a hill visible from the viewing point. Five, the highest rating, corresponds to a view including a pictorially significant number, five or more, of scenic components such as fields, canyons, ravines, hills, mesas, or forests.

By adding these two ratings, an index is produced which can vary from low − 2 to high − 10. To refine this index it is necessary to add notations on five additional scenic factors.

Depth of view is also important. Some views may contain all the elements of a high rating (a distant range of mountains, for example, plus a variety of four or five items) but within only a small area of the total field of view. Hence it is necessary to have some measure of the vertical depth of view. Depth, that is, the vertical angle covered by the view, can be approximated by holding your hand at a right angle at arm's length. If one finger blocks the view, that view is about 1 degree of arc or approximately 1 inch at arm's length; two fingers represents a view of 2 degrees, and so on. With views of distant mountains in particular, it is important to note the scene's apparent depth, not actual mountain height. Information about depth of view is recorded and mapped.

Width of view is also measured. A view seen over an arc of 180 degrees deserves a higher classification than one seen over an arc of 45 degrees. This measure is critical when comparing views from single points such as potential turnouts or scenic overlooks. Width of view is estimated with a protractor and then recorded.

Continuity refers to the degree of uninterrupted view. A view that has a high rating but is seen only intermittently is not as desirable as a continuous one. For example, intermittency occurs on lakeshores where a string of cottages and trees between the road and the water interrupts the view. Views with many scenic barriers receive a very low rating. Intermittency is noted and mapped with an appropriate symbol.

Special points of interest are noted in the comment section of the survey. These are defined as anything that many people may stop to see or photograph, such as a gorge, waterfall, historical monument, or a panoramic view.

The purpose of scenery classification is to generate action to improve scenic access. Therefore it is important to note "scenic potentials" that might be made accessible with small improvements such as clearing brush or constructing turnouts. Scenic potentials are places that will receive a rating of 8 or more by removing an obstruction or building a short spur and an overlook or picnic area. Potentials are noted in the comments part of the survey.

To prepare a chapter for a plan a large-scale reconnaissance survey may be conducted of all the roads in a town or county, of all the roads with potential to be scenic routes, or perhaps of the roads bordering a lake or

---

To classify scenery:

1. *Appraise the **distance** you can see:*

1 Close Foreground	3 Medium Foothills	5 Distant High Peaks

2. *Count the **variety** you see:*

1 None Just Trees	3 Pastoral Trees, Steeple, Farm	5 Maximum Peaks, Farm, Steeple, Brook, Bridge

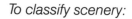  

3. *Add the two ratings.*

4. *Then add comments on depth, width, continuity, special interests, and scenic potential.*

FIGURE 10.1. Scenery Classification

running through selected river valleys. Scenery classification may also be done in greater detail at selected points on a road where overlooks or scenic spurs are considered. Odometer readings should be recorded at each viewing point and also at road crossings and town borders for map references. Each road must be driven in both directions for classification. Higher rated views observed while driving in one direction may be obscured or enhanced when driving in the opposite direction.

PLANNING FOR RURAL RECREATION

From the standpoint of public interest and plan adoption, a recreation plan is often the most important section of a rural environmental plan. A good recreation plan has something of interest for everyone in the community. A list of recreational activities is a useful starting point for the discussion of such needs. The list should be developed and revised as the local situation requires. Items that might be included in a survey of recreational development are community parks and plazas, tot lots, sports fields, community gardens, public access to natural areas, hiking trails, fishing access, lakeshore or river access, canoe or rafting access, cross-county ski trails, and bird sanctuaries.

The REP method for developing a recreation plan is to survey the development potential of the natural resource base, ask people what types of recreational facilities they want, at what cost and in what order of priority, and then match up resource potential with highest-priority, lowest-long-term-cost facilities. For each of these steps, assistance is available from public agencies and should be sought.[3]

To begin with, the recreation subcommittee should conduct field trips to investigate potential for the various types of development. Also, many states have a department of parks and recreation that can provide assistance to local communities regarding both appropriate locations for recreational activities and usage rates for comparable facilities.

The second step, the survey of citizens' attitudes about recreational goals, is conducted by the subcommittee on recreation. Chapter 4 described methods of and sources of assistance in determining public goals. REP experience shows that surveys of all households in a community not only gives residents an opportunity to state preferences and make suggestions but also serves to inform them about REP.

The third step, developing specific recommendations and priorities, will take considerable time as proposals are investigated with regard to cost, land availability, funding, and alternatives. Assistance in developing and evaluating specific proposals may be obtained from technical specialists in state parks and recreation departments, county or regional councils of government, or university departments with programs in recreation or planning.

COSTS

People often assume that outdoor recreation facilities are too expensive for rural communities. Experience in a number of REP projects demonstrates that a wide variety of such facilities can be provided at affordable cost. Trails for walking, hiking, and cross-country skiing can frequently be developed by volunteers through agreements with landowners. The cost of a community sports field becomes acceptable if an attitude survey shows that it is the number-one priority of a majority of the voters.

Once citizens have identified goals in a rural jurisdiction, all methods, even unconventional ones, should be investigated to achieve them. South Burlington, Vermont, a municipality previously landlocked, was able to obtain a 100-acre recreational park on Lake Champlain at no direct cost to the town. The cost was absorbed by a grant from the Bureau of Outdoor Recreation, state assistance, plus the sale of five acres to a power company for a substation that would provide the local portion of the cost. Another example is offered by the town of Ferrisburg, Vermont. Research of land ownership during development of an environmental plan there discovered state ownership of property adjacent to a body of water within the town's jurisdiction. This resulted in recreational access to the lake at no cost to the town. Similar opportunities may exist in other rural communities.

RECREATIONAL DEMAND

In planning outdoor recreation with rural people, it is useful to understand their motives for such in a cultural context. In traditional communities, including many farming communities, recreation includes hunting, fishing, and gathering. These provide opportunities for the generations to interact, for teaching the young, and for contributing to the family livelihood as well as escaping routine.

Recreation in more densely populated communities may focus on school and group sports. The textbook procedure for developing a recreation plan starts with projecting recreational demand. Three methods for estimating demand in large, regional, or urban areas are demand analysis, trend projection, and park planning standards. These methods are not relevant to rural areas for reasons explained below.

Demand analysis, based on a model of free-market resource allocation, is applicable wherever this system is functioning. Demand is defined in economic terms as the quantity of goods purchased during a period of time at various prices in a setting where relatively free choice reigns. It assumes large numbers on both sides of the equation, a mass-produced supply, and a growing population with increasing per capita income. These assumptions are not valid in many rural areas.

Trend projections consist of three steps: determining the rate of increase or decrease of a trend or activity during recent years, identifying the factors that may affect this rate and that can be quantified, and making a projection by extending the line in the direction and according to the rate of the past trend. Adjustments are made to the projected line in accordance with qualifying factors. This method, like demand analysis, is useful in urban settings. It is most valid for short-term predictions in a specific situation in which it can be assumed that tastes and other relevant factors remain constant or change only slightly.

Conventional planning standards for recreational facilities are set out in tables that indicate a recommended quantity or supply of various facilities per thousand population. These guides are useful in intensive-use urban recreational areas. They are not relevant, however, to rural areas if the data base for recommended supply levels is lacking and if the number of people served may be inadequate to support the activity.

PLANNING FOR HISTORIC PRESERVATION

Many rural towns have a common or plaza with a bandstand or monument in the center surrounded by a church, an historic hotel, stately old buildings, or shade trees. Town centers not only are attractive but also provide a focal point and activity center for the community. They are eminently worthy of protecting, for their beauty can quickly be destroyed by the introduction of incompatible land uses. An effective method of protecting a town center is to designate it as a special architectural zone or "sacred space." Use of the zone for purposes other than residential and municipal might require approval by the planning commission, which could also specify architectural and landscaping details for any changes made. This type of area zoning may be more readily adopted in rural areas where opposition to more comprehensive, traditional urban zoning is higher.

To protect and preserve other culturally important sites, an historic subcommittee should identify interesting old buildings, historic places, or landscapes and encourage the owners and the community to recognize their significance. Such actions as attaching a small plaque stating the date of construction of an old building add charm to a community and enhance civic pride.

CASE: MANTEO, NORTH CAROLINA

Manteo, a community on Roanoke Island on the Outer Banks of North Carolina, is the site of the Lost Colony established by Sir Walter Raleigh in 1584. It also is known for its experimental freed-slave colony during the Civil War and its long-established and innovative boatbuilding industry.[4]

In the early twentieth century, when a new bridge linked the Outer Banks to the rest of North Carolina and Virginia, tourism replaced boatbuilding and fishing as the primary economic resource. Over time, because it was five miles from the beach, tourists bypassed Manteo, and its relative importance in Dare County started to slide. By 1980 the community's waterfront was nearly dead; business had moved to the highway strip and the beach. Land values, the tax base, and community services shrank, and Manteo was losing its reason to be.

Four years before its 400th anniversary, Manteo took steps "to avoid both a tourist takeover and a junk culture."[5] The town board of commissioners hired a planning team to redesign the boardwalk as a waterfront park. The team soon determined that the problem was more serious than a deteriorated boardwalk. The result was a decision "to integrate the Quadricentennial Celebration and the boardwalk improvement project into one enduring community revitalization plan by developing low-keyed, historically-based tourist facilities which could house the 400th festivities but continue to be meaningful and attractive to tourists *and* residents after the celebration was over."[6]

The planning team set up a storefront office, interviewed hundreds of local people, and conducted detailed surveys that took the community's pulse. Community designers then developed a range of five choices, from doing nothing to building a "museumified Elizabethan theme park." Neither extreme was acceptable. The choice most attractive to local people was historically based tourist development in which townspeople could teach visitors about their past by demonstrating traditional shipbuilding, crafts, folk music, fishing, and boating.

The planning team conducted in-depth, door-to-door interviews to refine and clarify specific problems, community assets, and goals for development. The intent of the revitalization plan evolved through community workshops.

The goals were to upgrade the waterfront as a focus of economic development, maintain residential neighborhoods and a small-town atmosphere, minimize the impact of cars, encourage citizen participation, accommodate visitors without separating them from locals, and preserve the rural environment of Manteo.

Additional strategies such as putting all public utilities underground and preventing development in rural areas by restricting water and sewer extensions were adopted and codified in a land-use plan and coastal management plan. According to the planning team, "the goal-based land use plan was a powerful tool for preserving the rural lifestyle and landscape valued by local people because it legislated double-function facilities, guaranteeing that tourist development would not be segregated, and [it] restricted development [in] cherished land areas."[7]

An innovative and important concept articulated in the Manteo plan was the sacred structure. This concept resulted from the survey process, when people were asked first to identify places in town that most contributed to Manteo's uniqueness, then to measure their importance with a series of questions about tradeoffs. Randy Hester, the town's community designer, made the following report:

> A ranked and weighted list of significant places resulted. . . . One resident, upon seeing how many places ranked higher than the local churches and cemetery, dubbed the list the "sacred structures," and thereafter the list was called the Sacred Structures of Manteo. . . . The places included the marshes surrounding the town, Jule's Park, a drug store and soda fountain, the post office, churches, the Christmas Shop, front porches, the town launch, a statue of Sir Walter Raleigh, the Duchess Restaurant, the town hall, locally made unreadable street signs, the town cemetery, the Christmas tree in the gravel parking lot, park post lamps placed there in memory of loved ones, and two historic sites.[8]

Each component was mapped and a special zoning district created to protect it. Quantifying and formally adopting the protection of the sacred structures were the most innovative steps taken in Manteo. They effectively guaranteed that tourist facilities would be integrated with the local lifestyle: all new facilities had to be located amidst those special places, the sacred structures, valued by local people as essential to their community's rural character and sense of place.

The citizens of Manteo sought to maintain a balance between recovery and valued tradition. They wanted to avoid the extremes of not allowing tourists on the one hand, and on the other, allowing tourists to force them out through increased cost of living and incompatible life-styles. The planning

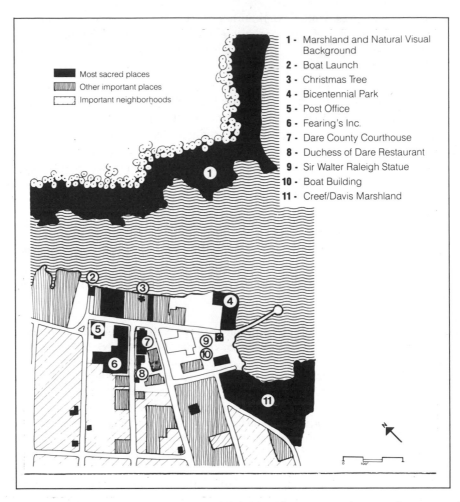

1 - Marshland and Natural Visual Background
2 - Boat Launch
3 - Christmas Tree
4 - Bicentennial Park
5 - Post Office
6 - Fearing's Inc.
7 - Dare County Courthouse
8 - Duchess of Dare Restaurant
9 - Sir Walter Raleigh Statue
10 - Boat Building
11 - Creef/Davis Marshland

Most sacred places
Other important places
Important neighborhoods

FIGURE 10.2. The Sacred Structures of Manteo. *The concept of a sacred structure emerged when people were asked to identify and then rank places that most contributed to Manteo's uniqueness. Each place was mapped and a special zoning district created to protect it against supplantation by tourist development.* (Adapted from map illustration provided courtesy of Randy Hestor, Manteo community designer.)

team concluded that Manteo, like other depressed rural towns, wanted to protect both its environment and its traditions. The solution in Manteo was to develop "a market where none previously existed by making capital investment attractive to outsiders while [at the same time] limiting the market to maintain enough control to preserve local life styles."[9]

CONCLUSION

Planning for scenic access, for recreation, and for the preservation of historic places and traditions are important components of a rural environmental plan. Asking people what they want and then working with them toward specific goals—tasks such as identifying scenic vistas, providing for recreation, and preserving historic sites—are some of the most enjoyable work of a plan. Although elements may be developed separately, when interrelated they reinforce each other.

The attractiveness of a rural place, its sense of scale, and its unique physical and cultural resources can be augmented by designating and maintaining rural byways, providing scenic turnouts, minimizing the impact of utility corridors, creating town commons and landscaped zones, establishing a tree nursery and planting plan, and reducing the cost and increasing the effectiveness of advertising and other signs. These actions, carried out by rural residents, enhance community pride and form the basis for economic revitalization.

11

Equity and Evaluation

PLANNING CAN BE criticized as elitist if it amounts to protecting and conserving a natural environment for a favored few. This charge has been valid in some instances, for example, where exclusive, expensive developments monopolize access to the public waters of a lake. Good planning increases the attractiveness of an area, which in turn increases property values. And increased property values lead to increased rents, placing an unfair burden on low-income residents. To prevent this sort of burden, a number of specific planning policies should be considered. Methods for positive social planning, social-impact analysis (SIA), and plan evaluation help to ensure that a community plan is designed to serve all citizens in an equitable manner.

POSITIVE SOCIAL PLANNING

Positive social planning is a collective reference to planning tactics that promote the welfare of all citizens, especially those of low to moderate incomes. Social planning elements that might be incorporated in a community plan include affordable housing, neighborhood integrity protection, public access to public waters, community parks and playgrounds, a public transportation system, and a bike and pedestrian trail system.

A requirement for affordable housing in a subdivision ordinance helps to offset the effect of much traditional planning, which has protected the property values of middle- and upper-income groups. The economic segregation caused by relegating all site-delivered, manufactured, or modular housing to MH zones or to trailer parks is inconsistent with the options for affordable housing now available. Less expensive but attractive and durable manufactured housing can be placed on foundations and then site-finished to be both affordable and compatible with custom-built homes.

To distribute the benefits of community planning more evenly, developers of more than four units of housing can be required to reserve a certain percentage of total area of land to be developed (say, 10 percent) for the construction of low-cost housing. Such areas, dispersed throughout the community, would be allowed development in greater (specified) density. The definition of low cost or affordable housing could be based on recent market criteria, such as "designed to sell for no more than 10 percent above the cost of the lowest-cost new houses sold in that jurisdiction during the past twelve months."

The provision for low-cost housing in a community plan can result in several benefits: implementation of this objective helps to provide affordable housing at no direct cost to the taxpayer; low-cost housing would not be concentrated in a single area, or future ghetto, but rather would be distributed throughout the community; and provision of affordable housing would allow a more equitable management of growth based on non-exclusionary, rational scheduling of capital improvements.

Neighborhood integrity protection is another method of providing equity for citizens within a planning jurisdiction. Sometimes regional development or highway construction threatens to disrupt or destroy well-established, viable neighborhoods. A new highway may be planned through a less affluent neighborhood or a small town, taking houses or cutting the community in two. Or a speculator may seek zoning variances to shift land use from residential to a more intensive use in order to increase income by increasing the value of benefited land. These procedures, practiced in many urbanizing regions, have frequently destroyed the integrity of residential neighborhoods.

In 1968 highway planners proposed that an access route for Burlington, Vermont's urban center be run through an established neighborhood of modest homes. The taking for right of way would have eliminated all the houses on one side of the street. A state representative who happened to live in the neighborhood led the opposition to the proposal. The neighborhood prevailed and the highway was relocated. This drama led a study team from the University of Vermont to a more careful review of the social unit of neighborhoods in the planning process. The team found that high-income neighborhoods were seldom the target of highway planners or efforts to rezone; it was the low-income neighborhoods that were especially susceptible. Threatened neighborhoods are well advised to organize neighborhood improvement or protection associations and get neighborhood integrity protection goals written into municipal or county plans. When such goals are stated in an adopted plan, it establishes legal standing and makes it much easier for a neighborhood association to protect its interests.

A few decades ago access to public waters, and to surrounding hills, woods, and pastures, was essentially free. This situation changed gradually as the population grew until many publicly owned resources were shut off from public access by the arrangement of private holdings. Public access is sometimes cut off as a result of the gradual change from rural to suburban land ownership. The process of redressing this imbalance and providing adequate access to public waters requires long-term planning. In rural communities the following steps can be taken: conduct an inventory of public access, develop public goals for access to public lands and waters with a survey, and develop a long-range plan to achieve public access in accordance with those goals and with the financial resources of the community.

Community parks and playgrounds are often omitted from plans for small towns and rural areas, being looked on as luxuries that come later in the development process. This policy should be reversed and high priority given to recreational and open-space areas serving everyone in a rural community. Once these areas are designated in the plan, land acquisition can be scheduled over time and community volunteers can see to development, utilizing small-scale and low-cost technologies from design and implementation to upkeep and maintenance.[1]

Public transportation systems are of great service to the elderly, the very young, and people with limited incomes. A low-cost, demand-responsive van or jitney system, one that fits the needs of underserved groups and other potential users, should be considered for the community. Federal subsidies and, in some areas, state funds and technical support are available for planning and implementing rural transit and paratransit systems.

Positive social planning also includes the designation of a bike and pedestrian trail system. Rural plans frequently ignore bicyclists and pedestrians. Rural communities can benefit from a system of combined pedestrian and bike paths that connect residents with schools, stores, post offices, parks, offices, work places, and public waterways. To establish a trail system interested residents must find or create a group with a keen interest in developing a trail system, study what other communities have done and what is possible locally, and participate in planning, getting the best proposal into the goal survey and ultimately into the adopted plan.

SOCIAL IMPACT ANALYSIS

SIA is a procedure that parallels benefit/cost analysis and environmental impact analysis. SIA, though, often yields negative rather than positive impacts. In conventional benefit/cost analysis economic impacts are often arranged to show benefits exceeding costs. Benefits tend to go to individuals or groups that are politically active in the promotion and implementation of a proposed project. Social impacts, by contrast, tend to be negative, that is, they describe adverse effects on people who are low-income or who have little political influence.

An SIA is a method of assessing the social effects of an existing plan or of evaluating the potential effects of a development proposal.[2] It may be conducted in four steps:

1. Identify types of impacts.
2. Specify the nature and severity of impacts and the number of people affected in each category.
3. Hold a review and discussion of perceived impacts.
4. Relate social impacts to the engineering, economic, and environmental impacts to provide the public and elected boards with a broader picture.

The first step is to draw up a list of the types of impacts (see fig. 11.1). This must be done simultaneously with the economic analysis, as the two analyses together comprise the broad spectrum of perceived impacts on all affected groups and interests. For example, in a proposed project to reduce flood damage by building a dam and detention reservoir, a downtown store owner would benefit if the store were thereby protected from flood damage. A rural village upstream from the dam, though, would be disadvantaged, both economically and socially, if the proposed reservoir required relocation of a road and increased the time and cost of travel to schools and to town.

The list of those affected, favorably or adversely, by a proposed project includes neighborhoods, villages, towns, school districts, and organized interest groups. Direct observation and interviews with people in an affected area will reveal what entities belong on the list. Many affected groups are represented by people who testify at advertised public hearings on proposed projects. Their testimony identifies the interest group and the nature and severity of the impact it expects to receive. Others adversely affected can be identified by comparing a proposed project with public land-use goals in adopted community or regional plans.

Many projects directly affect property values. An increase in land value is a windfall to the owner, especially if local tax assessment practices do not recognize the increased value. The same increase in property value may adversely affect renters who have to pay higher rent or move out. The significance of an increase or reduction in property value depends on the proportion of a person's total wealth represented by land ownership or the portion of income spent for rent. For low-income rural people, this may be a considerable amount.

The second step is to add to the list of possible social impacts a description of their nature, their severity, and the number of groups and people involved. Severity may be rated on a scale from 1 to 3, representing low to high impacts as shown in figure 11.1. A low-severity impact is a temporary or very

Action Proposed: _____			
Possible Social Impacts	*Nature of Impact (Describe)*	*Severity of Impact (1 to 3 High)*	*Number of People Affected*
1. Viability of village reduced	_____	_____	_____
2. Farmer's operations disrupted	_____	_____	_____
3. Town economic base reduced (farms eliminated, tax base eroded)	_____	_____	_____
4. Access reduced by road relocation	_____	_____	_____
5. School districts dissected or changed	_____	_____	_____
6. Neighborhoods disrupted	_____	_____	_____
7. Land values changed	_____	_____	_____
8. People displaced or for whom costs increased	_____	_____	_____
9. Public services reduced or costs increased	_____	_____	_____
10. Local businesses disrupted, costs increased	_____	_____	_____

FIGURE 11.1. Social Impact Analysis

limited inconvenience or one that easily can be repaired, compensated for, or adjusted. A medium-severe impact is one that seriously disrupts a group's activities or the pursuit of a group's goals. A severe impact is one that destroys a group's integrity, for instance by moving the group to another location or permanently disrupting its major functions. The purpose of this rating system is to permit public scrutiny and open discussion of various impacts.

The difference between economic and social impacts is this: economic impacts are visited on businesses, corporations, and land and capital owners and are measured in dollar value gains or losses of income or of property value; social impacts are economic effects on social groups such as families, neighborhoods, school districts, and small government units (see table 11.1). They are measured in numbers of people or numbers of groups affected and by the degree of severity of impact.

The third step is technical critique and public review. The identification and weighing of social impacts, which require judgment, may be biased by the researcher's values. To reduce this possibility, the report is subjected to professional criticism and to public review. Professionals include an qualified experts who do not have vested interests in the project under study. If the professional review raises questions, it will lead to further discussion of criteria or method or both, and the analysis will be refined. The findings of the analysis are also presented to the public through hearings, news releases, and

TABLE 11.1

Comparison of Environmental, Economic, and Social Impacts

	Type of Impact		
Aspect Compared	*Environmental*	*Economic*	*Social*
Affected group	General public	Landowners, businesses, economic interests, farmers	Social groups, neighborhoods, school districts, towns, villages
Unit of measure	Acres	Dollars	Numbers of people or social groups
Type of report	Descriptive analysis	Benefit/cost ratio or economic analysis	Descriptive analysis

editorials. The purpose is to inform and to receive comments from people affected by the project.

The fourth step is combining and weighing impacts. After the report and the technical and public reviews are completed, any adverse social impacts must be weighed against environmental impacts, economic impacts, and construction costs to determine if the project is in the public interest.

Combining and weighing impacts across this spectrum poses a special problem, because social impacts may be qualitative and not directly comparable to economic impacts. Fortunately there is a precedent for addressing this problem. Environmental impacts are frequently non-monetary and non-quantifiable in specific terms, but if all impacts are clearly identified and described they can be reviewed, evaluated, and incorporated into the political decision-making process. The decision process culminates in a vote on the proposed project by the appropriate government entity, that is, the town council or county commissioners. If this process is open, rigorous, and is free of dominance by lobbies or special interest groups, the decision that emerges will be in the public interest. Each person voting will compare social impact data with engineering costs and with environmental and economic impact analyses. While the decision will not please all participants, it will probably be acceptable to the public.

EVALUATING PLANS AND PLAN IMPLEMENTATION

Some rural areas or small towns already have a planning document, usually called a master plan or comprehensive plan. Many such plans were funded under the Housing and Home Finance Administration's planning program, originally authorized by the federal government under the Housing Act of 1954. The existence of "comprehensive" plans leads some citizens to think that local planning is complete. Unfortunately, this is not always true. Many community plans lie forgotten on the shelves of the village office or the county library, perhaps because they were developed without citizen participation. Evaluation of an existing plan determines whether or not it is being used regularly to guide public and private decisions.

Plans may not be recognized as bland or useless without standards by which to judge their effectiveness. Early in the development of REP, a University of Vermont research program assessed the planning process in rural communities by use of a rating system that evaluated six aspects of a number of adopted plans.[3] The rating system counts the number of recommendations in a plan, the number of bylaws adopted, the number of recommendations implemented, the number of variances granted, environmental content, and comprehensiveness, including social and economic components (see table 11.2).

The evaluation system for adopted plans can be used by state and regional planners, planning administrators, and students. The six aspects are evaluated, then the plan and the planning process are compared with several adopted plans in neighboring jurisdictions. Comparison should be emphasized here. There is no model or ideal plan to follow. The best plan is the one that rates highest by comparison with the plans of other jurisdictions in any county or region.

TABLE 11.2

Rating an Adopted Rural Community Plan

Step	Action
1	List all strong recommendations, i.e., those that include the words *recommend, propose, should, shall, will, must,* and *necessary.* Weak recommendations are those that include the words *may, could, might, should, encourage, suggest, hope, consider,* and *feasible.* Weak recommendations are not counted.
2	Count bylaw (or ordinance) adoption. Count 1 for each: zoning ordinance, subdivision regulation, official map, capital budget, and program. Adoption and use of all four is rated very good, one or less is very poor.
3	Count plan implementation actions. List specific recommendations implemented, in progress, and partially or not implemented at all. Evaluate recommendations implemented and the percentage implemented per year.
4	Count zoning variances. The number of variance requests compared with the number granted indicates how well zoning fits the needs of the community and how well the law enabling zoning is being followed.
5	Evaluate environmental content by counting recommendations for environmental actions and compare with plans in other rural jurisdictions.
6	Check the comprehensiveness of the plan by counting strong recommendations in each of six categories: (a) specific land use, (b) environmental protection and public access, (c) transportation, public utilities, and public facilities, (d) housing, (e) social and cultural resources, and (f) economic development.

STEP 1: COUNT PLAN RECOMMENDATIONS

The essence of a rural environmental plan is the list of strong recommenda-tions. Recommendations must be specific and capable of implementation if they are to achieve public goals. Without them, an inventory of present land use and a statement of goals do not make a plan. Hence the nature of rec-ommendations—their number, specificity, and comprehensiveness—are one indicator of the quality of rural plans. The first step in rating a plan is count-ing the number of strong recommendations. This was done for six Vermont communities as illustrated in table 11.3.

STEP 2: COUNT BYLAWS ADOPTED

State enabling legislation for planning usually allows rural jurisdictions to adopt four bylaws or ordinances for the implementation of adopted plans: a zoning ordinance, subdivision regulations, an official map, and a capital bud-get and program. Table 11.4 clearly distinguishes town A, which has adopted

TABLE 11.3

Plan Ratings for Six Chittenden County, Vermont, Municipalities

	Number of Strong Recommendations for Town (Date Adopted)					
	A	B	C	D	E	F
Subjects	(1974)	(1973)	(1974)	(1971)	(1970)	(1974)
Urban-type land uses	14	8	7	6	14	34
Natural areas	17	5	8	3	2	8
Transportation	7	1	—	—	1	15
Public utilities	5	—	3	—	1	10
Public facilities	14	3	8	1	—	14
Housing	3	—	—	—	—	6
Agricultural land	3	2	1	—	—	—
Other	1	1	3	—	—	9
Total strong recommendations	64	20	30	10	18	96
Total subjects covered	8	6	6	3	4	7

three required bylaws, from B, C, and D, which have adopted fewer bylaws. Town A is well on the road to planning. Towns C and D have hardly started.

STEP 3: COUNT PLAN IMPLEMENTATION ACTIONS

Plan implementation is also rated by counting the specific recommendations acted on each year. This measure quickly separates rural communities that show no intention of implementing their adopted plans from places seriously following their adopted plans. The method of evaluating land-use recommendations is to list proposals for change in the existing use of land resources. Specific proposals for future land use are implemented in one of two ways: funds are committed or equally definitive action is taken by town or county officials, or zoning regulations are adopted to make the proposed land use mandatory. This information is collected by interviews with public officials involved in the planning process. On the basis of these interviews each recommendation is classed in one of the following categories: not implemented—no action taken; implementation in progress—discussion stage only; partial implementation—some limited action; and recommendation implemented—funds committed, ordinance passed, or other definite action taken.

The number and percentage of recommendations implemented or partially implemented per year in six Vermont communities are shown in table 11.5.

TABLE 11.4

Adoption of Bylaws by Selected Chittenden County Towns

Bylaws (Ordinances)	Towns			
	A	B	C	D
Zoning ordinance	Yes	Yes	Yes	No
Subdivision regulation	Yes	Yes	No	No
Official map	No	No	No	No
Capital budget and program	Yes	No	No	No
Interim zoning	NA	NA	NA	Yes
Total	3	2	1	0
(evaluation)	(very good)	(good)	(poor)	(ineffective)

NOTE: NA = not applicable

We can see that towns A and C have high rates of implementation, while towns B and F have very low rates.

STEP 4: COUNT ZONING VARIANCES

A strong plan with a supporting zoning ordinance may be weakened if zoning variances are granted to all who apply without regard to the statutory requirements for variances. The purpose of a zoning board of adjustment, or for a planning committee functioning in that role, is to make allowance for error, hardship, and unique cases, not to let anyone with strong demands or political connections off the hook. Most state statutes that enable zoning are based on model legislation promulgated by the U.S. Department of Commerce. Vermont state law is representative. It authorizes zoning boards of adjustment to grant variances only under *all* of the following conditions, which must be specified in the board's decision:

TABLE 11.5

Implementation Recommendations Rating for Six Chittenden County Towns

	Town						
	A	B	C	D	E	F	Average
Number of years since plan adoption	1	2	2	1	2	5	NA
Specific land use recommendations	33	16	18	32	5	10	19
Not implemented	14	10	3	15	0	2	7
In progress	5	2	0	4	1	3	2.5
Partial implementation	6	3	3	6	1	0	3
Implemented	8	1	12	7	3	5	6
Recommendations implemented per year	8	0.5	12	7	1.5	1	5
Percentage implemented per year	25	3	33	22	30	10	20

NOTE: NA = not applicable.

1. That there are unique physical circumstances or conditions that prevent conformity with the zoning regulation.
2. That there is no possibility that the property can be developed in strict conformity with the provision of the zoning regulation.
3. That such unnecessary hardship was not created by the appellant.
4. That the variance, if authorized, will not alter the essential character of the neighborhood.
5. That the variance, if authorized, will represent the minimum variance that will afford relief and will represent the least modification possible of the zoning regulation and the plan.

In Vermont, and in most states with zoning based on the same model legislation, if these conditions are laid down, very few variances will be granted.

To evaluate zoning enforcement, it is necessary to count the number of variances granted each year since the zoning ordinance was adopted. If a relatively large number of variances were granted in proportion to the number of requests, the zoning bylaws are probably not being effectively enforced.

Table 11.6 compares the performance of six communities in Chittenden County, Vermont, as they enforced their adopted master plan. At the time of this analysis, town A (South Burlington) was not in the business of enforcing its plan but rather granted variances of questionable legality to nearly all

TABLE 11.6

Enforcement of Zoning Ordinances in Six Chittenden County Towns

| | Town | | | | | | |
| | (Date Zone Adopted) | | | | | | |
Number of	*A* (2/74)	*B* (6/74)	*C* (6/74)	*D* (2/72)	*E* (11/73)	*F* (12/73)	*Average*
Zone districts	13	10	8	9	6	8	9
Zone changes	2	0	2	1	0	0	1
Zone changes per year	1	0	2	1	0	0	1
Variances requested	78	8	15	13	22	55	32
Variances granted	75	4	12	2	16	26	22
Variances granted per year	53	4	12	.5	10	16	16

applicants. Town D (Shelbourne), on the other hand, was attempting to enforce its plan.

STEP 5: EVALUATE ENVIRONMENTAL CONTENT

This is done by counting the number of specific recommendations on matters of environmental concern. These are compared with the average number of such recommendations in other plans in the same region. Subjects analyzed may be taken from a checklist for this purpose (see fig. 11.2).

STEP 6: CHECK THE COMPREHENSIVENESS OF THE PLAN

The comprehensiveness of a plan can be checked by counting strong recommendations in each of the following categories: specific land use; environmental protection and public access; transportation, public utilities, and public facilities; housing; social and cultural resources; and economic development. Plans in any particular community, of course, will reflect the con-

Development Restrictions for		*Trail Systems Proposed for*	
Floodplains	——	Bicycles	——
Wetlands	——	Cross-country skiing	——
Stream banks	——	Hiking	——
Lakeshores	——	Walking	——
Higher elevations	——	Nature study	——
Steep slopes	——	*Public Access to Public Waters for*	
Poor soils	——	Fishing	——
Groundwater recharge areas	——	Swimming	——
Wildlife habitats	——	Canoeing or rafting	——
Prime agricultural land	——	Camping	——
Rural Quality Proposals for		Multiple-use	——
Scenic overlooks	——	*Miscellaneous*	
Beauty zones	——	Natural areas designated	——
Town common	——	Growth control plan	——
Tree plan	——	Clustering of development	——
Rural byways	——	Historic sites or landscapes	
Historical or architectural zone	——	identified	——
		Historic building recycling	——

FIGURE 11.2. Evaluation of the Environmental Content of a Comprehensive Plan

cerns and goals of its citizens. To ensure that concerns of all major interest groups are represented, a comprehensive plan should include recommendations for several social and economic components, such as an equitable, environmentally sustainable community economy; an inventory of job skills or crafts applicable to new income opportunities; the expansion of natural resource- or cultural resource–based tourism, increasing potential for small businesses or cottage industries; the creation or improvement of public transportation and other public facilities; and the provision for health care, emergency medical, senior citizen and child care, and other social services.

CONCLUSION

An effective rural environmental plan should benefit the majority of citizens it serves, including disadvantaged or low-income groups. Providing affordable housing, protecting neighborhood integrity, improving public access, and assessing social impacts are methods by which the plan seeks equity and inclusiveness.

A plan and its implementation can be evaluated by comparison with plans of other jurisdictions. This shows which plans are being used regularly to guide public and private decision-making. It also shows which plans, although adopted, are not being used effectively in guiding day-to-day community development decisions. A plan that puts forth strong recommendations that are then implemented at a regular rate is an effective guide for public and private decisions that will move the community toward its selected goals.

PART III

Guiding Rural Development

12

Guiding the Rural Economy

A RURAL ENVIRONMENTAL PLAN must incorporate information about the local economy and its regional setting. In any such plan economic development and protection of the natural environment should be mutually supportive goals. The words *economy* and *ecology* come from a Greek root meaning "house" or "home." Economy is, literally, "management of the home," and ecology is "knowledge of the home." The two go hand in hand, and management of each must be guided by knowledge.[1]

To guide the rural economy, to understand the implications of alternative economic policies, and to answer questions raised by landowners, local officials, potential investors, and tax-paying citizens, basic facts must be compiled and analyzed. Economic data should be collected and organized to show the community's sources of income, the local economy's relation to the regional economy, the total number of jobs available, and the possibilities for increasing economic activity. Economic data also provide a basis for policy decisions by local officials, such as whether to develop by exploiting the natural resource base of the surrounding area, by attracting outside capital to the local economy, or by self-help.

DEFINING THE LOCAL ECONOMY

A factual description of the local economy must precede any discussion of economic development. This information can be supplied through an economic profile of the community. Developing one sounds like a difficult task,

165

but at the local scale it is quite simple. A subcommittee designated to study the local economy produces an economic profile by following the procedures below.

ECONOMIC PROFILE

An economic profile for a town or rural area can be drawn by obtaining answers to the following questions:

1. How many economic production units are there (industries, businesses, home industries, services, ranches, and farms)?
2. How many people are employed by each of these production units?
3. What is the payroll of all businesses employing two or more people?
4. What percentage of local taxes are paid by industry, commerce, agriculture, tourism, and rural residences?
5. Where do residents make their household purchases?
6. Do residents exchange goods or services on a noncash basis? What types of goods or services are traded?
7. How many residents commute to other places to work? What locations and distances?
8. How many residents are seeking employment?
9. What type of economic development might be promoted to increase jobs and total income in the community?
   a. home businesses
   b. manufacturing
   c. agricultural cooperatives
   d. tourism, recreation
   e. shopping center
   f. residential development
   g. assembly industries
   h. processing industries (local materials or products)
   i. crafts
   j. none

Where can this information be obtained? Much of it is available at the state department of employment security, development, or planning, or at other state agencies that perform these services. While much statistical information is based on the decennial census, analysts in these agencies can make informed projections for subareas for use in planning. Additional information on community-level conditions can be obtained through interviews or by including one or two questions in the REP goals survey.

Who draws this economic profile? It is often put together by the local subcommittee on economic development, which may include several people interested in this subject or who have ready access to some of the information. One or more members might volunteer to go to the state capital or to the business bureau of the state university in search of data. It may also come from college students majoring in economics, economic geography, or rural planning as part of a class assignment. Most research universities maintain a data bank where statistical information on the state is collected and made available to the public.

ECONOMIC IMPACT ASSESSMENT

To make a decision in the public interest, local citizens and rural planners also need to know the benefits or costs to the public and the projected increases or decreases in the tax base that may result from various proposed actions. Economic choices affecting the use of land should be considered with reference to long-term effects on the tax base, the tax rate, and property values. This analysis indicates the incidence of potential impacts, whether impacts will be negative or positive, but it does not predict the exact effect on land values of specific land-use proposals. Table 12.1 illustrates the types of material relevant to an economic impact analysis. An analysis of economic impact can be made for any proposed land use, including tourist facilities, conservation zoning, a natural area, an intensive recreation facility, a trail system, a housing development, and a farmers' market. Experts who can help to make these estimates work for the local chamber of commerce, a regional development association, the state department of community development, and the state university, most often in the department of economics or resource economics.

LAND VALUES AND THE LAND MARKET

A review of recent land sales is one of the best indicators of the nature and intensity of land market trends. It also shows where land such as wetlands, coastal marshes, and agricultural land is vulnerable to changes in use. If carried out annually such a market study will identify and measure trends useful in understanding economic pressure for change in land use.

Location theory helps to explain the land market. This theory relates land use to distances and transportation costs from urban centers (see table 12.2).

Land value may be measured in market price per acre, return per acre, or dollar investment per acre.

A land market study is made as follows. First, go to the county land records office and tabulate, with acreage and price, all the land transfers that took place in the last calendar year. Unless there is a special reason for including them, houses and house lots can be excluded. Second, take this list to three people knowledgeable about land use in the area and ask them about the known or probable use of each tract by the purchaser. The list of uses might include farming, commercial farming, forestry, intensive land use (condominiums or a golf course, etc.), speculation, and residential. Third, summarize and interpret this data to obtain an overview of what has been going on recently in the rural area. Fourth, check results with a land economist at the state university to see how the local land market analysis compares with state and regional trends. The work of collecting data may be simplified by listing only larger parcels.

ECONOMIC ASSESSMENT OF NATURAL AREAS

Whenever a rural jurisdiction considers purchasing a natural area, the purchase should be subjected to economic analysis. First, classify the natural

TABLE 12.1

Economic Impact of New Industries or Businesses on the Tax Base in Small Rural Jurisdictions

Impact on	Effect on Tax Base	Possibility of analysis
Local tax receipts		
With tax moratorium	No increase	Can be estimated
With tax stabilization	Some increase	Can be estimated
With assessed tax payments	Increase	Can be estimated
General property values	Increase	Depends on size
Job opportunities	Increase	Can be estimated
Merchants' receipts	Increase	Depends on multiplier
		Can be calculated
Costs of public services	Increase	Can be calculated
School costs	Increase	Indeterminate
Number of people benefited directly	NA	Can be estimated

NOTE: NA = not applicable.

TABLE 12.2
Land-Use Intensity by Dollar Investment per Unit of Area

←— Most Intensive Use
Urban Center

Most Extensive Use —→
Rural and Open

————— Increasing Distance from Urban Center —————→

Urban Land	Rural Land	Extensive Recreational Land
High-rise Buildings[1]	Residences[1]	Watersheds[2]
Stores[1]	Orchards[1]	Hunting[1]
Factories[1]	Specialized Farms[1]	Extensive Parks[2]
Roads[2]	Mixed Farms[1]	Wilderness Areas[2]
Urban Parks[2]	Grazing[1]	Mountain Summit[2]
Utilities[3]	Forests[3]	
Residences[1]		
Golf Courses[3]		

NOTE: The uses listed above were selected from a great many possible uses to represent correlation of land-use intensity with distance from an urban center.

[1] Land allocated to use by market price.
[2] Land allocated to use by government planning and action.
[3] Land allocated to use by price and/or government.

area by type, for example, marsh, bog, or wetland, then rate its quality against that of other natural areas of the same category in the same region. Help in this can be obtained from the state natural resources department, ecologists, or the extension service at the state university. Second, conduct a survey to evaluate public support for a specific land use, for instance, nature study, research, bird observation, a wildlife reserve, and aquatic life generation. Third, develop a plan considering the public's interests, the suitability of available lands for various purposes, and the priorities expressed in the public attitude survey. Fourth, apply benefit-cost analysis when there is a narrow choice between alternatives, that is, compare the benefits and costs of the proposal with the benefits and costs of the next best alternative. Fifth, apply opportunity-cost analysis by asking whether project objectives could be attained by an alternative and cheaper acquisition, and whether the projected cost could be better spent to meet the stated public goals. Sixth, estimate increases or decreases in the tax base, including the appraised value of property and tax income resulting from public land acquisition. Finally, make the data public so that the community and elected decision-makers can take informed action.[2]

ECONOMIC DEVELOPMENT MODELS

The present economic development of rural areas can be explained and future development planned by reference to one or more of several prevailing models: resource determinism, industry attraction, self-reliance, and exurban development.

RESOURCE DETERMINISM

According to the model of resource determinism, rural economies grow when developable resources are discovered and exploited. Investment comes to such rural areas from urban centers. The resource (soil, minerals, hydroelectric power, scenery, forests, climate, etc.) is developed; the population in the rural area grows, sometimes rapidly; as extractive technologies or markets change, or as the resource is depleted, the local economy reverses and a decline begins. Dramatic examples of this process are the coal-mining towns of Appalachia, the copper- and uranium-mining towns of the Southwest, and the lumber towns of the Pacific Northwest.[3]

The rate of development is determined by the natural resource base, its distance to the nearest urban center, and the resource demands of nearby urban centers. The greater the quantity of the resource, or the closer it is to an urban center, the faster the area will develop. Rural areas far from urban centers, with few or poor resources or resources too expensive to extract and exploit, develop more slowly.[4] The economic history of many rural areas can be explained according to resource determinism. This theory can also explain an area's potential for growth and development.

INDUSTRY ATTRACTION

Advocates of the theory of industry attraction analyze the potential of a site to lure outside industry. They seek to attract industry to new locations through promotional efforts and subsidies such as tax relief or infrastructure provision, for example, industrial parks with utilities provided or designation of enterprise zones with various incentives. This strategy works well if planners and citizens in small communities pursue goals for economic development consistent with their resources, their location, and their ability to provide the infrastructure or other incentives. According to economic location theory, an urban-centered region with a population of at least 100,000 is the minimum necessary to attract a major industry. Small rural towns and rural counties have a special problem: to attract industry they must compete with urban centers that are better located and that have more financial, physical, and human resources.

Experience in Burlington, Vermont, a predominantly rural state, shows that rural counties or trade centers of only 50,000 are capable of attracting industry if they work together with neighboring communities in their labor shed and if they are assisted by a professional team in finding industries suitable to their resource base, regional labor pool, location and amenities. In the early 1950s many Vermont textile mills, attracted by cheaper labor, closed their doors and moved south. The Burlington area subsequently suffered a depression. In 1955 business leaders organized the Greater Burlington Industrial Corporation, devoted to finding an industrial replacement. They built an industrial park and succeeded in attracting an IBM plant, followed later by a General Electric plant, and several additional businesses.

Communities that decide to attract industries can form teams consisting of state development specialists, chamber of commerce members, and university economists. After establishing an economic development commission, they prepare an economic development plan. The plan identifies potential industrial sites and industries that might be attracted to those sites. The plan may also consider the designation of enterprise zones.

State and regional agencies specializing in industry location will assist rural communities that seek to attract industry. Potential industrial sites should be surveyed, and the town or county jurisdiction should adopt a capital improvement plan to provide the highway and rail spurs, sewers, power, and water support facilities necessary for industrial land use. To minimize noncompetitive transportation costs, a special effort should be made to attract industries that make a product of small volume but high value. Such industries can be located near a rural labor market and rural amenities.

SELF-RELIANCE

The self-reliance model of economic development is based on the theory that the abilities, organization, and vision of its residents are the foundation of a community's economic well-being. Experience with self-help projects, cooperatives, and other community-development organizations demonstrates that rural people can significantly improve their economic base and overall quality of life, even though they may have limited resources and a poor location according to the criteria of resource determinism and industry attraction. The most convincing evidence in support of self-reliance is the success of agricultural producer and consumer cooperatives throughout the United States and Canada. The cooperative movement, for example, brought electricity and telephone service to rural areas throughout the United States and provided markets for many farm products as well as farm supplies.

A case study presented in chapter 13 illustrates self-help strategies applicable to the political economy of the 1990s: an emphasis on human resources, local determination in the use of natural and other resources, internal savings and investment, and the introduction of structural changes to encourage local entrepreneurship. Advocates of the self-reliance strategy perceive that many rural communities are shifting their attention from attracting outside industry to building a business infrastructure from within, venture by venture, job by job, capitalizing on "whatever small benefit or advantage nature has granted them."[5]

EXURBAN DEVELOPMENT

The exurban model of economic development is based on a more recent phenomenon. As described in chapter 2, this widespread, postsuburban type of development followed the successive movements in environment, energy, and personal health that characterized the 1970s and 1980s. Exurban development is low density, independent of urban centers and contiguous urban services, and not based on rural agricultural resources. Exurban development is described by advocates as being rooted in an American tradition that places high value on small town and country living. Open space, recreational opportunities, natural resources, and the rural lifestyle attract a multitude of Americans from young adults with children to retirees on fixed incomes.[6] On the positive side, this movement brings to rural areas new residents who strongly support the rural values of low density, conservation, and participatory government. Together, newcomers and established residents can develop a rural environmental plan by determining local public goals and doing the kind of hands-on planning advocated by REP.

COMBINING STRATEGIES

Early in community planning two clusters of goals usually appear: environmental goals and economic development goals. Each set of goals requires a subcommittee to conduct planning. The economic development subcommittee may wish to consider the four models outlined above as well as the economic profile study to evaluate the situation of the community, where it is headed, and the economic choices it has. Towns where the natural resource base is depleted frequently find that their human resources have untapped potential, a discovery that turns many a pessimist into an optimistic activist. Towns lacking the advantages of location but blessed with scenery or skilled labor may decide to attract high-tech industries. Towns whose principle asset is rural atmosphere may discover that they too have several options: to increase tourism, develop crafts industries, or diversify the agricultural base by processing local products. Once these options are made explicit, residents can discuss the pros and cons and the benefits and costs of each, then select a strategy or mix of strategies to suit their community's level of development and their goals for the future.

Communities that need assistance in sorting out alternative economic directions can seek it from a number of state, regional, and private sources. Cooperative extension services at land grant colleges, for example, sponsor workshops, training, and technical assistance programs designed to help small towns assess their needs and resources. In addition, land grant colleges participate in regional or multistate rural development centers that collect and disseminate information to rural communities by way of conferences, leadership seminars, publications, videotapes, strategic management workshops, and similar activities. These centers, as well as a number of not-for-profit organizations, produce and distribute newsletters, business casebooks, and other materials aimed at building an economic infrastructure and creating new jobs in small rural communities.

PLANNING GROWTH MANAGEMENT

As noted in chapter 2, growth promotion has been a driving force in community planning in the United States since the period of canal building and railroad construction. This approach to development was logical when the population was increasing rapidly and frontiers were being settled. More recently, however, there has been increasing interest in guiding and controlling growth and in reducing the unintended effects of expansion. This change in attitude comes from an increasing awareness of the negative consequences of poorly managed growth, for example, traffic congestion, overbuilt shopping centers, poorly sited or inadequately served subdivisions, and strip development. To counter such trends, communities and states have made efforts to manage the rate and location of growth directly or to protect the environment, which has the indirect effect of reducing rate of growth.

CASE: RAMAPO, NEW YORK

The town of Ramapo, New York, played a pivotal role in the 1960s and 1970s as a model for the concept of growth management, or "phased growth." In the 1980s changing economic conditions caused adjustments in public policy in Ramapo that, although not as widely publicized, provide an example of flexibility as a strategy for community sustainability.

During the middle and late 1960s the township of Ramapo, an 89-square-mile area within the jurisdiction of Rockland County, New York, was experiencing the accelerated growth of many suburbs.[7] Between 1940 and 1969 the township's population increased by 285 percent. The opening of two freeways improved accessibility to New York City, about 25 miles away, making it increasingly attractive to newcomers. The trend toward urban sprawl outside a few incorporated villages brought in its wake the overloading of facilities such as sewers, drainage, roads, sidewalks, parks, and fire and police protection.

After making a number of inventories and studies, Ramapo developed and in 1969 adopted a new approach to regulating growth. Ramapo amended its zoning ordinance to create a new kind of special permit, "residential development use." Anyone wanting to use land for residential development could do so only with this permit, granted when standards were met for specific public services. These included a sewer system, storm drainage, parks or recreational areas, schools, roads, and firehouses. The ordinance set up a point system that assigned values to these services. A special permit required that a development satisfy fifteen development points. The town, for its part, pursued an overall development plan and a capital improvement program. If residential support services were missing, the Ramapo township planned to include them in its eighteen-year program of capital improvements; the first six years of improvements were specified in a capital budget.

The ordinance was taken to court by landowners who felt it destroyed the value and marketability of their property. In a split decision the court upheld Ramapo, saying, "Where it is clear that the existing physical and financial resources of the community are inadequate to furnish the essential services and facilities which a substantial increase in population requires, there is a rational basis for *phased growth,* and hence, the challenged ordinance is not violative of the federal and state constitutions."[8] The dissenting judges rejected the ordinance because they could not find specific authority for it in the state enabling legislation.

The court's findings strongly opposed the use of zoning for exclusionary purposes. Both majority and minority opinions found that exclusionary practices were not an issue. The court noted that the Ramapo plan included "provisions for low and moderate income housing on a large scale."

The goals of the town of Ramapo were clearly stated:

1. To economize on the costs of municipal facilities and services and carefully phase in residential development, efficiently providing public improvements
2. To establish and maintain municipal control over the eventual character of development
3. To establish and maintain a desirable degree of balance among the various uses of the land
4. To establish and maintain the essential quality of community services and facilities

The Ramapo plan was supported and reinforced throughout each stage of planning—the master plan, the official map, the zoning ordinance, subdivision regulations, the capital program, and complementary planning programs, ordinances, laws, and regulations. Two reasons for the court's decision in favor of the town were evidence that the adopted plan was being consistently implemented and was committed to building consistently according to a public adopted capital improvement program. Another reason was that the plan for controlled growth in Ramapo was established within a regional framework. One of the judges dissented, however, because of lack of complementary planning statewide and in other regions.

The Ramapo experience took another turn when economic conditions changed following a period of high interest rates in the late 1970s and a severe slowdown in the pressure for development in the early 1980s. The planning board, concerned that the requirements of their Fifteen-Point Program put Ramapo at a competitive disadvantage in a significantly reduced market, recommended to the town board in May 1983 that the portion of the local zoning law requiring residential development permits be repealed. The change was not intended to conflict with the objectives of environmental protection or the prudent management of capital improvements and phased growth. Rather, it was intended to reduce the appearance of complexity in the development review process and the loss of economic growth to neighboring communities. The environmental assessment accompanying the proposed amendment stated the following:

> Essentially, the [development] Plan recognized that the resources vital to the community's environmental, social and physical well-being were finite and therefore required respect and protection. The Plan also recognized, however, that growth and development were essential components of the Town's economic health. The Plan realized that these two goals, protection of resources and a strong economic base, although often conflicting, should not be mutually exclusive. As such, the intent of the Plan has always been to achieve and maintain a balance between the two.[9]

The planning board argued that the Fifteen-Point Program had outlived its usefulness, first, because the task of ensuring overall environmental performance had been taken over by the state through enactment of the New York State Environmental Conservation Law (ECL section 8–0101 et seq., McKinney, 1984). This act mandated compliance with a more thorough environmental review process and was administered statewide. Second, the technical skills of the local review staff and the sophistication of the planning, design, and engineering review process had improved to the point that community objectives could be met in a more streamlined, individualized review process.[10]

There are a number of lessons that can be learned from the Ramapo example. First, for a growth management plan to be acceptable, equitable, and capable of withstanding legal challenge, it should embody certain prerequisites: formal adoption of a master plan to accommodate growth; adoption by the legislative body of a zoning ordinance to implement the master plan;

fidelity to that master plan and ordinance through avoidance of spot zoning and the issuance of variances; establishment and adoption of an official map to implement the plan; adoption of comprehensive subdivision regulations; adoption of a succession of short-term capital-investment programs for public improvements; and finally, provision of low-cost housing to prove as well as to ensure that the plan is not exclusionary.

Ramapo also demonstrates that a growth managment plan must be flexible. Doctrinaire advocacy of unlimited growth or rigid opposition to all growth is inconsistent with community goals for long-term sustainability. A requirement of all growth should be to enhance the environment—not just to minimize degradation but to create a net improvement in the performance of the environment as a result of development. Real management of growth means being able to adjust to changing conditions, to allocate community resources fairly and prudently in periods of growth, and to streamline and simplify management in times of retrenchment without compromising environmental quality, rural character, or other community objectives.

ENVIRONMENTAL PROTECTION AS GROWTH MANAGEMENT

Equitable and enforceable growth management requires a consistent set of policies at the state level. This provides the basis for local jurisdictions to influence the quality, fairness and timing of growth in a manner that conserves and protects desired features of their environment. Since the environmental revolution of the 1960s and 1970s, several states have enacted environmental conservation legislation that has had the effect of reducing the rate of growth while guiding its location. Vermont, California, and Florida, among the first to pass this type of legislation, have been cited frequently as informative examples.

In 1970 the Vermont legislature enacted the Environmental Control Act or Act 250. The incident that sparked its enactment was a subdivision on a steep hill where the septic system effluent from higher lots ran down and polluted the water in wells on lower lots. The Vermont act introduced two new concepts: it provided for the development of a state land use plan, and it established regional commissions authorized to approve or disapprove all large developments with respect to ten environmental and planning criteria. After an intensive two-year effort the first part, the state land use plan, was dropped—there was too much opposition at public hearings. The environmental review process, however, was adopted and has worked well, virtually eliminating the poorly planned type of development that inspired the law's passage. It introduced environmental performance criteria comprehensible both to the public and to natural scientists in state environmental agencies. Two decades after its enactment evidence indicates that Act 250 has not reduced growth but rather significantly improved the quality of projects and reduced environmental damage.

An example of how Act 250 affects both growth and development quality is the case of Huntington, Vermont, a town with a population of 1,160. In 1988 a developer sought a permit to develop an eighteen-hole golf course in a hilly, scenic area called Sherman Hollow in the foothills of the Green Mountains, seventeen miles east of Burlington. Both the regional environmental commission and, upon appeal, the state environmental board refused the permit. The principal issue raised by residents of the area who opposed the development was that pesticides proposed for use on the golf course would pollute the surface and ground water that supplied them. The commission and then the board heard their argument, the counterargument of the developers, as well as expert testimony from the state environmental agency.

The EPA, it was argued during the hearings, recognized that much is still unknown about the environmental and health risks of the hundreds of pesticides on the market. Testimony was presented indicating that the effect of the proposed pesticides could not be determined. The developers' application was denied primarily on the basis of lack of information about the effect of pesticides on an environment with the specific soil and groundwater conditions of Sherman Hollow. This decision had three results: it stopped the development of the golf course for the present; it assured the public that no such growth would occur without specific knowledge about the probable effects of pesticides on water supplies; and the state environmental agency intensified its work on pesticide standards and pesticide review.[11]

On November 7, 1972, California voters approved a referendum called Proposition 20 that established a mechanism for guiding development along the state's coastline. Six regional coastal commissions and a superior state commission were set up. The regional commissions are made up of twelve to sixteen members. Some represent municipal and county governments; others are appointed by the governor, the senate rules committee, and the speaker of the state assembly. The state commission has six appointed members and six who represent regional commissions. These commissions were given the power first, to veto or modify all proposals for development along a thousand-yard-wide coastal strip, and second, to prepare and submit to the legislature a land use plan for conservation of the coastal zone, defined as the area three miles out to sea inland to the highest elevation of the nearest coastal mountain range.

The criteria the commissions use in evaluating development proposals are quite detailed and inclusive. In summary, a commission approves a permit only when it finds that a development would have no substantial adverse environmental effect and would maintain, restore, and enhance "the overall quality of the coastal zone environment, including, but not limited to, amenities." Pressure has been intense from both conservationists and developers, but in general the commissions have followed a middle path, allowing a substantial amount of development while denying most projects that would seriously harm the environment, radically change the density of existing neighborhoods, or commit large open tracts to development.[12]

The Florida Environmental Land and Water Management Act of 1972 was another innovative attempt to alter the direction of large-scale development to conserve natural resources. It established several regional planning councils to review and approve developments that had potential regional impact. It also authorized the governor and his cabinet to designate critical areas and to act as the appeal board for regional commissions. As much as 5 percent of the state, approximately 1.7 million acres, could be designated as critical under this law. In 1972 the voters also approved a $240 million bond issue for state acquisition of environmentally endangered lands.[13]

Thirteen years later the Florida legislature took another step in its attempt to manage growth by passing the Growth Management Act of 1985. This law requires that local governments (cities and counties) update their comprehensive plans for future growth and deny applications for development unless minimal public facilities are provided in seven categories: roads, water, sewage, storm-water drainage, mass transit, solid waste, and parks and recreation. According to the Florida law, all these services must meet predetermined standards "concurrently" with the developments that require them. Cities and counties must apply these growth regulations one year after comprehensive plans with growth-control provisions are submitted to the State Department of Community Affairs for review. Road standards are set by the State Department of Transportation, but other standards may vary, some jurisdictions choosing higher standards at higher cost and others lower standards at lower cost. The implementation of this law began in 1989 and will be monitored closely by planners and citizens in other communities interested in growth management.[14]

CONCLUSION

Economic development and environmental protection are mutually supportive public goals. Rural people usually give high priority to jobs, the protection of natural resources, and community well-being. Economic development planning, like watershed planning, should be conducted in a regional context, the planning goals of a rural community considered as part of a regional setting. This geographic configuration can be a county, a cluster of counties, a trade area, a river valley, or a labor shed (an area within which most workers live and commute to large employment centers).

Economic impacts along with environmental and social impacts should be considered in the decision-making process. A particular economic development strategy or mix of strategies is determined after analysis of both positive and negative aspects. In the case of a resource development strategy, the community is limited to consideration of those resources with which it is endowed and to their quality in comparison with the resources of competing areas. The community must examine sustainability through replenishment or replacement of resources. Industry attraction may require tax concessions or public infrastructure investment, which means significant local cost and which must be weighed against potential economic payoffs to the community.

A self-reliance approach to development may require a full cycle of planning, piloting, and replanning before residents enjoy its widespread benefits. Even then, economic impact may be limited to just one or two communities in a larger and impoverished region. Exurban development can add diversity and some service-support jobs to a rural community; however, care should be taken to ensure that sprawl or escalating property values do not destroy the very rural qualities that attracted the exurbanities or force out established members of the community, such as senior citizens on fixed incomes. Economic analysis should be used to evaluate options for generating jobs and income that will benefit all members of the rural community.

13 ⎯⎯⎯⎯⎯⎯⎯⎯⎯⎯⎯

Planning for Sustainable Development

PLANNING DOES NOT always start with a master plan for land use or resource conservation. Once community concerns are identified, the first step may be to deal with economic decline or crisis by planning for development. Because the Rural Environmental Planning process encompasses the entire ecosystem, it emphasizes economic development in balance with sustainable use of the land, the water, and the natural resource base and that enhances the human and cultural resources of a community. REP advocates adding economic value to natural resources where possible and creating a flourishing local economy where benefits flow equitably to the residents.

Many years ago this description of economic development would have been considered romantic or impractical. By the end of the 1980s, however, deterioration and underdevelopment of rural communities caused a reevaluation of development strategies that waste environments and do not equitably benefit rural residents.

In the 1980s some older resort communities began to assess the hidden costs of tourism. A *Denver Post* article of March 19, 1988, described the mounting problems of Vail and Aspen, Colorado. These communities suffered "increased crime, transient labor and fracturing . . . into haves and have nots. Workers paid low wages for changing beds and washing dishes can't afford to live in towns transformed from sleepy mountain villages into condo-and-commercial centers with inflated prices." While recreational resorts may have increased jobs in some rural areas, the jobs were often seasonal and low paying and usually did not provide career development for workers. Many better-paying jobs were filled by newcomers such as management personnel transferred in by the corporate owner. Some newcomers had sources of investment that enabled them to start new businesses and cash in on the growing economy. Long-term residents without access to resources often got stuck at the bottom of the economic ladder. Ironically, as these economics grew, the gap between the haves and the have-nots also grew.

This chapter looks more fully at one of the economic development models discussed in chapter 12, self-reliance, and extends it to incorporate certain changes that took place in the 1980s—changes in economic conditions, in federal and state agency budgets and staffing, and in opportunities and tactics for rural communities. Here we propose an alternative strategy: a holistic approach to economic development in which culture, ecology, and the inanimate components of an environment are regarded as mutually interdependent. This chapter describes the strategy to achieve this objective by identifying four elements that can guide the process and by presenting case examples that show the application of one or more of these elements in different geographic and cultural settings.

DEFINING SUSTAINABLE ECONOMIC DEVELOPMENT

A sustainable local economy is one that maintains mutually beneficial and equitable relationships internally, that is, within the community, and externally, with the larger society and economy. A healthy rural economy is able to change and renew itself through expansion and through spinoff activities based on existing resources and production. As the economy becomes more sustainable, investment funds increase along with local control of technology.

Communities weighing alternatives for economic development can learn from the experiences of other rural areas and regions that have experimented with traditional development approaches. Experience over the last four decades has led to a distinction between economic growth strategies and economic development strategies.

Economic growth is not the same as economic development. Economic growth may increase income while increasing the dependence of the economy on outside capital and technology; it may increase jobs without raising the level of income; it may utilize resources more efficiently while depleting or degrading them to the point where the local economy eventually begins to decline. Economic growth does not ensure a developing economy. A developing economy, on the other hand, is characterized by increased productivity and the creation and expansion of a more diverse mix of businesses and economic activities for both internal and external markets.

Paul Pryde describes the characteristics of a developed economy:

1. It has the capacity for continuing improvement and refinements in the way land, labor, capital and entrepreneurial ability are organized to produce a desired mix of goods and services for both external and internal markets.
2. These improvements and refinements as adopted by the local economy tend to reduce its vulnerability to sudden shifts in production technologies and in the market environment. Such an economy is, in other words, resilient, diverse and innovative.
3. It tends to be characterized by a high rate of job creation as well as an equitable distribution of income, goods and services.[1]

The building blocks for sustainable economic development in any community are its natural, human, and cultural resources. Careful management of these resources helps to increase local production of goods and services, replenish renewable resources, strengthen unique cultures, and broaden economic opportunity. The value of existing resources rises and goods and services expand. As the capacity to serve diversified local, regional, and export markets expands, so does the circulation of money.

There is no single blueprint for sustainable economic development. Strategies allow wide choices, including the recruitment of manufacturing and service firms, the extraction or harvesting of resources, and tourism. A given strategy is selected for its potential to conserve, enhance, or replenish resources (including cultural resources), increase self-reliance, and achieve economic equity. Many rural communities and regions that have suffered economic crisis or dislocation are becoming increasingly proactive in deciding their economic future. In 1988 the *Wall Street Journal* reported the following:

A radical change in thinking is beginning to ripple across much of rural America. Towns and counties that once based their hopes for prosperity—or survival—on roping in outside industries are beginning to see that the party's over.

Now, instead of looking outward, they are undertaking a long, painful struggle to develop their own industries, job by job. . . . If this effort is successful, the countryside eventually will have a more diverse economic landscape.[2]

Because each rural region is unique, development strategies differ. The distinctive attributes and comparative advantages of rural communities provide starting points for people to gain fresh perspective on the kinds of goods and services that could be produced to create unique economic roles for their own communities.

Rural communities have what most people value—a cleaner environment, scenic vistas, distinctive ethnic cultures and life-styles, folk arts and folkways—and herein lies the opportunity for rural residents to improve their economies. Exploiting the differences between rural and urban communities means applying rural standards to growth, land use, commercial zoning, and conservation. It also means applying rural standards to the selection of economic development strategies. For example, when a community adopts a plan advocating more beds for tourists, the plan may recommend the development of a network of bed and breakfasts rather than supporting the recruitment of a national motel chain. If recreational tourism is part of an adopted plan, one strategy could be to implement low-impact recreational development, leaving scenic and wild areas undisturbed rather than encouraging large-scale resorts and condominiums with their accompanying commercial centers.

Many rural communities and regions are the cultural wellsprings for various ethnic groups in the United States. Sustaining these cultures and their values is important to descendants who have moved elsewhere yet want to stay connected to their roots. Distinctive cultures are a rich national resource that can be preserved with development strategies blending the rest of traditional practices with modern production and marketing methods. Cultural diversity presents new economic opportunities in rural areas through the production and exporting of regional or ethnic foods, arts and crafts, and cultural events.

Creating an economic development strategy with the potential to conserve resources, increase local productivity, and equitably distribute the benefits is an art as well as a science. The science lies in inventorying basic building materials and designing the appropriate strategy. The art involves creatively incorporating the elements of sustainable economic development in the design. These elements are as follows:

1. *Emphasizing human development*. Development of human skills and talent fosters a competitive economy through the creation of new products, services, and production technologies.
2. *Expanding local control of resources*. The human community depends on sustainable use of land, water, and natural resources.
3. *Increasing internal investment capacity*. Residents need capital to underwrite business start-ups and expansions.
4. *Changing economic and social structures* to increase opportunity and

reduce dependency. An economy cannot develop with social and economic structures that prolong poverty and underemployment.

These four elements are not only key components in a development strategy, they are also an evaluation tool—a way to measure a proposed strategy or to assess an economy moving toward sustainability.

EMPHASIZING HUMAN DEVELOPMENT

For a community to direct its own economy and manage that economy's relationship to the larger economy, residents must acquire the skills not only of business management and marketing but also of collaborative planning and program development.

Acquiring collaborative planning and program development skills is not a short-term process. To begin with, economic development seminars, business creation workshops, university studio projects, and leadership training programs can be starting points to get the community's attention and attract local leaders. Sustaining and expanding community leadership requires following up these programs with practical, results-oriented projects. As projects demonstrate successes involving smaller problems, leadership and participation will grow to tackle larger problems that require more long-term solutions. Sustainable economic development depends on residents empowering themselves with the skills to control the development process. Similarly, developing people to generate increased and new economic activities is an equally long-term proposition.

Acquiring the skills of entrepreneurship, product design, marketing, and production technologies requires that employee training programs be redesigned and management and worker relationships restructured. Whether a business manufactures jewelry or packages tours, collaboration between managers and workers on product design, quality control, and marketing often results in new ideas that diversify the business or can be spun off to create a new business. According to Al Shapero, "more companies are generated out of small businesses than out of large ones. . . . Small companies beget more companies, and company formations trigger more company formations. There is often an epidemic quality about the process."[3]

New approaches to developing entrepreneurial skills go beyond traditional programs that teach the mechanics of a business plan. Some business development programs are experimenting with expanding such skills by getting new business owners in touch with more experienced entrepreneurs or by identifying mentors who can work one on one with an owner during the critical start-up and expansion stages. This results in fewer bankruptcies and better equips entrepreneurs to survive economic challenge and change.

Implementing sustainable development also involves local educational systems. While schools in some rural regions offer technical and vocational courses, students often leave the region for urban centers where job opportunities requiring their skills are available. Precisely because of the limited resources of many rural school systems, the opportunity exists for enriching educational programs with work-based experience or in-school enterprises. In some rural communities high schools are developing small businesses as part of the curriculum so that students graduate with practical experience in management and marketing. This helps to prepare students for real business opportunities in their communities. If training includes entrepreneurial skills, young people are prepared to advance in local businesses and to create new or spin-off companies.

The challenge of including less skilled or disadvantaged residents in an economic development strategy can sometimes be met with existing job training programs. However, to develop workers' capabilities beyond simple tasks, follow-up programs with incentives to acquire general-education degrees or to pursue postsecondary degrees will have to be put in place. Pay incentives, awards, and other forms of recognition are a part of such programs. Some businesses encourage workers to go on to technical school or community college by assisting with tuition.

Universities and government agencies may have experienced staff who can help to design innovative educational and training programs. As the following case shows, however, communities should also look to successful small business owners, cooperatives, worker-owned enterprises, and community development corporations for assistance in meeting human development needs and transferring skills.

CASE: GREENVILLE, MISSISSIPPI

South Street Square opened in December 1985 as a festival marketplace designed to accommodate twenty-four small businesses in retailing and services.[4] Located in a renovated YMCA facility, the incubator project offers space, security, and building maintenance for all tenant businesses. It also provides management assistance and training services in marketing, inventory control, publicity, and public information, and gives referrals to specialized professional services.

Greenville is located in the impoverished delta region of Mississippi, where public assistance payments serve as the major source of family income in fourteen of the surrounding fifteen counties. In 1967 residents of the area formed a multipurpose community development corporation, the Mississippi Action for Community Education (MACE). The corporation eventually attracted some twenty-six thousand members in the fifteen counties.

In 1983 the membership initiated planning for the incubator space in Greenville, which was to assist businesses owned by minority women willing to hire and train other low-income women. To identify potential owners and tenants, MACE sponsored a training and technical assistance program in the spring of 1985 for thirty-five enrollees, covering topics in business planning, accounting, and legal services. More than half of the initial trainees went on to receive individualized assistance when preparing loan applications and business packages.

A few months later MACE opened the South Street Square facility and, aided by private foundations, established a $150,000 loan fund for use as venture capital by the new tenants at the facility. Initial loans ranged from $7,500 to $20,000. The building itself had been renovated with grant funds from the Economic Development Administration of the U.S. Department of Commerce. Two years later businesses successfully operating at South Street Square included a clothing alteration shop, beauty salon, insurance company, collection service, fashion apparel store, and T-shirt shop, all of which had relocated from homes or other locations with limited space, services, or both. Nine new businesses operating at the square include a jewelry store, a formal-wear rental shop, a florist, two food stores, a bakery, an import shop, a hosiery store, and a specialty items shop.

While the incubator space and the loan fund were important to the formation of these businesses, ongoing education and training were critical to the success of the project. South Street demonstrates that the development of human capital is an essential component of successful enterprise creation and expansion.

EXPANDING LOCAL CONTROL OF RESOURCES

Some indigenous rural communities resist development of their scenic and natural resources unless traditional ceremonial, hunting, timbering, grazing, and fishing grounds can be maintained. By contrast, many newer rural communities were established for the sole purpose of mining, harvesting, or the recreational use of local resources. These communities resist conservation efforts if the result is a loss of jobs. In other communities where timbering, mining, or manufacturing has ravaged the environment, the challenge is to diversify the economy while working to contain environmental damage. The creation of new jobs through more environmentally sound businesses can defuse arguments that pit economic progress against conservation.

Strategies to expand local control of resources do not assume that such control automatically results in sustainable and conservation-minded usage. What is assumed, however, is that the local community has a vested interest in the environmentally sound development of existing resources. Planning must ensure that whoever wants to develop and whoever wants to conserve resources adopt shared goals recognizing constraints and opportunities in the environment.

Sound, objective knowledge of such constraints and opportunities must inform the process. If rural communities are to be the trustees of their resources, residents need to learn about environmental issues that can be complex. Sustainable development, which requires identification of the most sound and long-term productive use of available resources, should guarantee that this trusteeship is grounded in practical economics.

A sustainable economy is not likely to be achieved if decisions about resources are made outside the community without thought to their impact on its human or physical environment. Neither is a sustainable economy achievable if the community itself is unwilling to consider potential impacts, both on its own economic future and on that of the region, of activities harmful to the environment. A well-informed coalition of residents, public agencies, and private groups can often find enough in common with regard to resources to balance the objectives of conservation and development. Cooperation ensures effective stewardship of scenic, natural, and cultural resources.

Increased local control over the long term also means creating opportunities to add economic value to natural resources and agricultural products. An example is represented by the following sequence: logging, milling, furniture making, wood carving, sculpting. Each activity multiplies the value of the basic resource before it leaves the host community.

CASE: MARSHALL, MINNESOTA

Some 1,200 corn farmers in southwest Minnesota process more than 11 million bushels of corn yearly at their cooperative wet-milling plant, producing corn syrup, corn starch, corn oil, gluten feed for cattle and poultry, and ethanol fuel.[5] Even steep water (water in which the corn is soaked) is marketed as a growth medium for antibiotics. The wet-milling plant, opened in 1983, employs 100 workers, grosses up to $60 million annually in sales, and guarantees a market for southwest Minnesota corn growers far more profitable than the market that existed prior to the construction of the plant.

The idea for a wet-milling plant surfaced in spring 1980, when growers in the region decided they would respond to the plummeting price of corn by diversifying their range of locally produced corn products. They determined to increase the value of their corn by processing it right at home. Although initial interest was in the processing of corn for ethanol, a fuel additive, a core group of farmers took the advice of a staff person at the Minnesota Department of Economic Development and commissioned a feasibility study for the establishment of a more comprehensive wet-milling operation. The idea was to design and build a plant that would take corn soaked in water, then grind and separate it into its components for purifying and processing into starch, protein, fiber, corn oil, and ultimately ethanol as well. After a series of exploratory meetings in nine counties, the enthusiastic response convinced organizers to form a cooperative venture called the Minnesota Corn Processors (MCP).

Early in 1981 a temporary board of directors began recruiting other corn farmers from eighteen counties, asking each one to invest directly in the wet-milling project by contributing 5 cents per bushel on a minimum contract of 5,000 bushels. Through this effort some 2,100 farmers raised $900,000 in front-end money to fund the feasibility study and other co-op expenses. Armed with positive recommendations generated by the study, MCP obtained bank approval for a $38.5 million construction loan, 40 percent of which co-op members would have to raise as part of their equity share. A final campaign in June 1982 resulted in the raising of the equity pool. This, coupled with a tax financing package of $1.8 million, which the city of Marshall, Minnesota, provided as a business development incentive, made the project feasible. Funds from Marshall were ultimately used to prepare the site, build roads, and construct water and sewer lines. Ground was broken in July 1982.

For the next six years the wet-milling plant diversified its corn products and byproducts, which were processed locally and sold to major paper and feed companies across North America. In May 1988, with the market for their home-grown corn sufficiently diversified, MCP members expanded operations to produce ethanol fuel, capturing one more segment of an emerging market. The wet-milling plant enabled them to significantly increase their control over an agricultural resource by developing a range of value-added corn products. This reduced their dependence on and vulnerability to changes in the corn market.

INCREASING INTERNAL INVESTMENT

Capital to underwrite business start-ups and expansions is the third element in a sustainable development strategy. Acquiring or creating an internal pool of investment and credit funds for this purpose expands self-reliance and the ability to take appropriate risks with new technologies and ventures.

Few rural communities have enough capital to underwrite development. Rural banks may be available to the business owner with sufficient assets and experience, but many local banks lack the deposit base to make larger loans and are reluctant to take risks. However, banks are an economic resource in a community; if they are worked with they can gain experience in new fields of economic activity. One risk-sharing device is to attract large deposits from a public or private source to guarantee development loans or to lower the loan interest rate. The federal Community Reinvestment Act (CRA) requires all banks to make investments in their community without discrimination. Examining the CRA report of local banks can provide information on the degree to which they do invest in the rural community.

Banks, however, are not the only source for start-up or development monies. In the beginning stages business owners need "patient money." This is the kind of financing that the majority of small businesses are started with, for example, the personal assets and savings of entrepreneurs, their families, and friends. Patient money tailors investment payback to the growth of a business. If there are no financial resources allowing flexible terms, the prognosis for survival of a business is not good. Lack of patient money for less advantaged members of the community means business ownership is closed to them.

Since the demise of the War on Poverty programs of the 1960s and the systematic reduction of federal financial aid programs in the 1970s and 1980s, two new kinds of investment resources for economic development have emerged: alternative capital sources and development capital sources. These two resources represent different goals and require different support systems. Alternative capital sources, usually funded by public monies, make loans to businesses in the start-up phase and/or ventures considered risky because of innovative production and marketing technologies. Alternative capital sources often require the same collateral and terms as commercial capital sources and may require bank participation.

Technically innovative businesses are important to rural economies because such businesses diversify and expand the economic base. By 1989 twenty states had established alternative capital funds. The Iowa, Pennsylvania, and Texas funds combine bank participation with lowered interest rates and subsidized research. Alternative capital funds can be found in state economic development agencies, community development departments, economic development districts, or business development corporations.

For communities where low-income residents lack opportunity, capital or "patient money" is necessary to spur development. Development capital funds, usually from philanthropic sources, provide a flexible range of investment from small signature loans to long-term loans with low interest rates that may or may not be secured with collateral. Such creative lending practices as fitting terms to the cash flow of a start-up business and tailoring interest rates to its potential profit margin give low-income entrepreneurs the time to build their companies. Development lending does not usually succeed unless technical assistance and training are available through the start-up and expansion phases of a venture.

By 1989 over thirty community development loan funds in the United States had collectively lent millions of dollars and were experiencing relatively low default rates. While loan funds originally addressed housing needs in low-income and rural areas, since the early 1980s more funds have capitalized enterprise development in these areas.

Alternative and development investment funds do not replace commercial credit sources. Banks will usually lend to businesses with a good track record, adequate cash flow, and sufficient collateral. The purpose of both alternative and development investment funds is to help firms to establish a credit rating and track record, enabling them to approach banks for loans as they mature. These funds resemble the family savings account or pension fund. They act as a cushion during times of crisis. They can also leverage businesses that want to grow in new directions, and they can be sustained over the long term when earned interest expands the funds. Increasing a community's investment capabilities insures developing an equitable economy which fits local economic needs and conditions.

For the community that wants to develop a sustainable, self-reliant economy, an important step is to identify alternative and development lending sources and/or to create its own sources, either on a local or a regional basis A rural area of Massachusetts gives us an example of a community working with an existing bank to expand internal investment capacity and create greater self-sufficiency.

CASE: BERKSHIRE HILLS, MASSACHUSETTS

Located in Great Burrington, Massachusetts, the Self-Help Association for a Regional Economy (SHARE) was established in 1983 by community residents as a not-for-profit membership organization to recycle local dollars by earmarking 75 percent of local savings account deposits as collateral for business and community development loans.[6] In cooperation with a local bank, the SHARE credit fund supports loans to regionally based businesses in the southern Berkshire area. To obtain lower-interest loans from SHARE goods and services must be locally produced, using local materials, employing local people, and sold to a local market. Production methods and technologies must be environmentally sound, incorporating measures for energy conservation. One loan criterion is that SHARE gives priority to businesses that aim to fill an unmet local need and that foster self-sufficiency by producing basic necessities (food, shelter, energy) or providing essential social services (transportation, health care, job training, legal services).

The SHARE project is funded by ordinary citizens who open savings accounts designated for the SHARE credit fund. Members make up the loan committee, which can loan up to 75 percent of the deposit balances, an amount agreed to by the depositors, at interest rates of 10 to 13.5 percent to cover interest earnings (6 percent) and bank service fees. Borrowers must be SHARE members. The committee can make loans of up to $3,000 for two years or less. The bank in turn administers all loans at reduced overhead. As of 1989, the fund had seventy members with $25,000 on deposit and had issued fifteen loans to a variety of local projects, for example, a goat farm producing specialty cheese, a timber- and firewood-hauling business using draft horses, a knitting shop, a washer and dryer repair and reconditioning shop, and an enterprise that creates high-quality kites using low-cost fabrics. Together, these businesses had created forty-five new jobs by 1989.

Depositors are motivated to become SHARE members because they know their money will be directly invested in the community, making capital available to local entrepreneurs who might not qualify for start-up loans from the bank. This unique setup in turn enables the bank to service loans it could not issue without the normal requirements for collateral. On opening their accounts, depositors sign pledges authorizing SHARE to use their passbooks as collateral against loans that meet SHARE criteria. Depositors thus come to view their accounts as long-term investments in the community and the regional economy. As of the end of 1989, no loan backed by collateral from the SHARE credit fund had defaulted.

CHANGING ECONOMIC AND SOCIAL STRUCTURES

After conducting a survey of literature on economic development, the Kentucky Highlands Investment Corporation concluded the following:

> Economic development is growth in material productivity which involves change in the economic and social structure of a community. Economic growth and economic development are distinct. While neither is independent of social, political and cultural structures, economic growth can occur within existing structures and economic development requires changes in those structures.[7]

As sustainable development strategies reorient rural economies toward self-reliance, the structures of underdevelopment change. Dependence on outside capital, technology, and markets lessens with the expansion of interdependent ties with the larger economy, local entrepreneurial and technological skills, and local investment capital. Among the conclusions noted in the Kentucky Highlands Investment Corporation's report were these:

> The essential component of economic development is not production but *the capacity* to produce. . . . [8] Growth means more output and economic development implies both more output and changes in the technical and institutional arrangement by which produced.[9]
>   Under this view of development, no matter how great its output, a community or region where production facilities and technology are externally controlled is less developed than one in which production know-how is local in character.[10]

As an economy grows more self-reliant, conservation and the sustainable use of resources require shared decision-making among owners, users, and the local community. A developed economy distributes benefits more equitably because development strategies are designed to include the less advantaged. As those who have been left out of the economic mainstream become economically empowered, political relationships change. Because sustainable development strategies involve a community's educational, health care, and human services systems, the process of development creates closer ties among these systems and revitalizes the community as a whole. The following example demonstrates how a Navajo community brought about structural changes to improve local income and maintain cultural traditions.

CASE: NAVAJO INDIAN RESERVATION

The Ramah Navajo band, population 2,500 in 1980, resides in west-central New Mexico. For many generations this community relied on a traditional economy of livestock, dry land farming, weaving, and silversmith work.[11] The introduction of federally funded services and programs and the cash-based larger economy, however, eventually created a dependency on wage employment whenever jobs could be obtained. It also created chronic reliance on non-Indian traders on the reservation and pawn shops in surrounding towns. As a result, the community is afflicted with an 80 percent unemployment rate and an annual per capita income of $2,000 or less, with more than 70 percent of households receiving some form of public assistance.

Located in one of the most isolated areas of the Navajo Nation, Ramah's prospects for attracting outside industry is limited. In 1984 seventeen Navajo weavers, all women, founded the Ramah Navajo Weavers Association (RNWA) as a vehicle for improving family incomes and maintaining cultural traditions consistent with their land-based economy.

Unlike tribal enterprises or corporate-tribal joint ventures, RNWA utilized "bottom-up" development methods, that is, rebuilding the area economy through individuals. Using upright looms and drop spindles in the traditional manner, each weaver creates her own designs, spins her own yarn from the wool of locally raised sheep, and hand-dyes the yarn using dyes from sagebrush and other native plants. The woven textiles vary in size and shape from miniature placemats to full-size floor rugs. An RNWA standards committee approves the quality of all woven goods before they are offered for sale at Ramah or other outlets.

A major accomplishment of the RNWA has been the re-establishment of the Churro breed of Navajo sheep into weavers' flocks. Within the Navajo culture this breed is considered a sacred gift enabling good livelihoods. This and other agricultural projects have improved the quality of local wool and increased economic return to local growers and weavers. For example, members initiated a drip irrigation project to grow feed for an improved breed of sheep, a range management program to cut sheep losses from coyotes and other predators, a mechanized method of sheep shearing, and new procedures for wool grading and packaging to target the market.

By spring of 1991 the RNWA had forty-five members. They were trained not only in spinning and weaving but also in sheep and wool management and in cooperative business, product marketing, and leadership. Further plans called for the diversification of sheep and wool products: organic lamb, sheepskins, tanned hides, knitting yarn for outside sales, and other value-added byproducts. The Association has designed and is raising funds for a Hogan Center Home where spiritual, educational, and marketing activities can be housed. No longer dependent on trading posts, pawn shops, and other intermediaries, the Ramah Navajo weavers utilize community resources—sheep, land, and skills—to increase opportunity and ameliorate poverty.

CONCLUSION

Planning for sustainable economic development entails enhancing the environment, developing human and cultural resources, and nurturing self-reliant economic activity. These are steps toward an economy that will renew itself over time.

Four elements guide the path toward sustainable development: emphasizing human development, expanding local control of the use of resources, increasing internal investment, and changing economic and social structures to increase opportunity and reduce dependency. These four elements can be used to measure a proposed strategy or to assess the progress of an economy moving toward sustainability.

The case examples discussed in this chapter represent community-based development strategies in a variety of rural settings and among diverse cultural groups. Each strategy involved some type of participatory design and planning. A top priority was to create new economic activity to revitalize ailing rural economies. The next chapter presents a more complete case study of sustainable economic development. This detailed account of the *Ganados del Valle* organization in northern New Mexico presented in chapter 14 illustrates the full impact of the four fundamental elements that comprise sustainable economic development. [12]

14

Sustainable Development: Ganados del Valle Enterprises

THE MOUNTAIN VILLAGE of Los Ojos, New Mexico, is home to Ganados del Valle (Livestock Growers of the Valley), an economic development organization chartered in 1983 to revitalize the agricultural economy in northern Rio Arriba, one of the poorest counties in the United States. By 1991 the organization had created thirty-five new jobs, formed four businesses, organized agricultural support programs in co-op breeding, grazing, and financing, and established itself as a model for culturally beneficial and environmentally sound rural economic development. Specific Ganados enterprises included Tierra Wools (1983), a handspinning and weaving cooperative; Pastores Lamb (1988), a sheep growers' association marketing specialty and farm-flock lamb; the Rio Arriba Wool-Washing Plant (1989), a custom wool washing service for local and regionally grown wool; and the Los Ojos Feed and General Store (1990), a family business incubator marketing locally produced and handcrafted items (see fig. 14.1 for other project examples).

Located in north-central New Mexico, Río Arriba County is part of a six-county region that includes Taos, Mora, San Miguel, Santa Fe, and Sandoval. Two mountain ranges dominate the region: the San Juan Mountains, which frame the central and western portions of Río Arriba County; and the Sangre de Cristos, which separate Taos County from the high plateaus to the east. Characterized by high mountain peaks with alpine meadows and semi-arid mesas, the region has a wide range of elevations, temperatures, rainfall, and plant and animal life. The six counties total 20,311 square miles.[1] In 1988 their combined population was estimated at 237,200.[2] Río Arriba County by itself covers 5,856 square miles and had a population in 1988 of

196

32,600. By comparison, the area of Connecticut and Rhode Island combined is 5,927 square miles with a population of 4,226,000.

In the higher elevations small agricultural settlements are located primarily in irrigated valleys. Hispanic and Native Americans comprise a majority of the population. Some Native American communities have indigenous roots going back as far as A.D. 800 Spanish and Mexican settlers arrived in the early 1600s, favoring fertile areas along the Río Grande and narrow valleys and canyons in the mountains. An agropastoral economy based on horses, cattle, and the Churro sheep brought by Spanish-Mexican settlers made possible the settlement of isolated places by providing transportation, food, and fiber to these remote villages. The Churro is a long-wooled sheep which nearly became extinct. Its rich, colored fleece is prized by Hispanic and Navajo weavers. The settlers introduced sheep husbandry, wool processing, and weaving techniques to the Pueblo Indians, who subsequently conveyed these skills to the more remote Navajo and Hopi Indians. For over two hundred years Spanish-Mexican settlers of Mediterranean, Moorish, and Mexican-Indian background traversed the region, intermarrying with the indigenous people and creating a unique cultural ecology.[3]

In 1848, when the United States took over New Mexico and other southwestern territories under the Treaty of Guadalupe Hidalgo, Anglo property

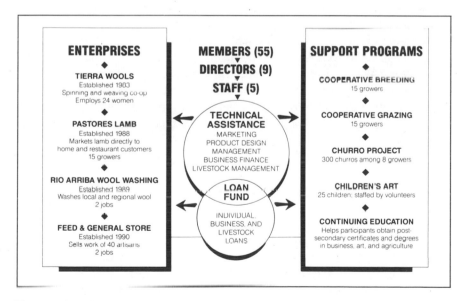

FIGURE 14.1. Ganados del Valle: Organizational Structure

law, contrary to the provisions of the treaty, was superimposed on the traditional pattern of cooperative land tenure. Such tenure had been required of the community land grants (*mercedes*) issued by Spain and later Mexico. Ultimately, the American concept of separately deeded property was enforced by court order and barbed-wire fencing. Spanish and Mexican law had designated large areas of land grant acreage to be held in common for pasture, timber, hunting, and other community uses. Settlers typically pooled their flocks and herds, having them graze high mountain meadows in the summer and lower river valleys in the winter. This system of sustainable grazing was disrupted as Anglo-Americans claimed and fenced off the common lands. Anglo-Americans also introduced commercial livestock production and export marketing, which forced traditional growers to discontinue the sheep husbandry methods that had evolved over two centuries in the fragile, semiarid, high mountain climate. With the loss of communal grazing lands, villagers were limited to small family plots on valley floors that became seriously overgrazed.

In the early 1930s severe winter storms coupled with a steep drop in wool prices wiped out most large-scale operations. When the huge flocks disappeared indigenous communities were left with an eroded landscape and a collapsed economy. As elsewhere in the country, these traditional communities had become linked to and dependent on a cash system. Ownership of livestock was often a liability instead of an asset as the high-elevation climate and loss of communal grazing lands required that feed be purchased six months out of the year. Many residents either left their villages or commuted long distances to jobs in more populated areas, a process that accelerated after World War II. Remaining ancestral land and water resources were underutilized or sold as villagers with little cash struggled for economic survival. Small-scale and subsistence-level sheep growing continued, however. Sheep, a cultural symbol as well as a food and fiber resource, buffered some families from abject poverty.

EVOLUTION OF A SUSTAINABLE DEVELOPMENT STRATEGY

The isolation of the region and its cultural ecology kept it from enjoying postwar economic growth and the federal interventions of the 1960s and 1970s that spurred development in other depressed rural areas of the United States. State and federal planners encouraged tourism in northern New Mexico, which had an abundance of scenic, recreational, and cultural resources.

However, in some villages where resort tourism competed for land and scarce water resources, residents who retained strong cultural ties to the land resisted and began searching for alternatives.

The Tierra Amarilla Land Grant in the upper portion of the Río Chama basin covers an area close to 1,000 square miles, ranging from fifteen miles over the Colorado border to the north to the Río Nutrias south of the village of Tierra Amarilla. The population of the Land Grant in 1980 was roughly nearly 3,000.

In 1980 the village of Chama applied for a section 111 planning grant from the FmHA. The Village Council retained the Design Planning and Assistance Center at the University of New Mexico to facilitate the planning process. A team of students and faculty from the center and citizen volunteers from the villages of the Chama Valley was formed. University personnel recommended that the REP approach, involving extensive community input, be used to develop a plan. Through surveys, community meetings, and mass mailings over a six-month period, comments and opinions were gathered and draft goals disseminated. Final goals were adopted and subsequently printed and distributed throughout the community in 1981. Among the goals expressed in the adopted plan were developing a community economy based on the use of local, natural, and cultural resources without ruining the environment or harming the people; increasing job and income opportunities for women and young people in the Chama/Tierra Amarilla Valley and evaluating the practicality of a locally based wool processing and weaving industry.[4]

At the conclusion of the planning process in 1981 the village of Chama, the project sponsor, was severely underfinanced and its officials could not envision a role for the village in implementing the plan. Regional and state economic development agencies did not take on the task of implementing the recommendations of the plan because the goals did not fit the state government's economic development strategy for the region, which favored tourism and the recruitment of light industry and high-tech firms. The state economic development agency, for example, supported the efforts of a private development corporation to create a downhill ski resort bordering on the headwaters of the Brazos River, which irrigates the southwestern portion of the valley. Many long-time residents concluded that this development would not be environmentally sound or culturally appropriate; if built, it would create primarily low-wage seasonal jobs. Moreover, it would not enhance the self-reliance and economic sustainability of the region as a whole.

Accordingly, a small group from the villages in the southern end of the valley decided to take steps more appropriate to their cultural ecology and the goal of economic sustainability. Their main concern was that a ski resort would raise land values and divert scarce water resources from agriculture to recreation. They reasoned that over time an increase in land value and water cost without a concomitant increase in income from the land would result in the transfer of ownership of land and water sources from local families to developers. There was also widespread concern that upstream development in the higher elevations would reduce access to irrigation water and increase water pollution, problems experienced by villages downstream from the Taos ski valley in neighboring Taos County.

While valley residents had previously succeeded in halting large-scale resort projects, they concluded that this was not enough; action had to be taken for appropriate and sustainable economic development. They defined this as development that would employ the cultural skills and resources of the region, expand business and professional opportunities for local people, provide year-round jobs, and respect the physical constraints of the environment. They began to work on the most urgent needs of local sheep growers: reducing the loss of sheep and lambs to predators, finding better markets for lamb, and obtaining higher prices for wool. If they were able to help solve these problems, and if people were willing to work cooperatively, an organization would be formed.

Through research they learned that livestock guard dogs to control predators were being tested throughout the country by the New England Farm Center in Amherst, Massachusetts. Further research identified a sheep growers' cooperative in the Pacific Northwest that marketed lambs from a four-state network through a national telephone auction. By the end of 1982 the villagers had accomplished two concrete objectives. First, the New England guard dog project placed two dogs with a 300-head flock and trained the owner to handle them. The first summer the dogs were used the flock's losses were cut from 45 percent to 12 percent. Second, the manager of the sheep growers' cooperative was invited to come and explain the telephone auction system. After inventorying area flocks the manager recommended that Chama Valley growers participate in his cooperator's next telephone auction. That year, participating growers received 7.5 cents more per pound for their lambs than was paid by local markets.

By March 1983 community residents expressed enough interest to form an organization. Eight people established Ganados del Valle as a private, not-for-profit economic development corporation. They chose not-for-profit status because it would enable them to attract funding and investment capital from philanthropic sources. In the early years funds for technical assistance, training, marketing, and loans were raised in small amounts from progressive foundations, churches, and concerned individuals.

The original board members set goals for the rest of the year and selected committees to work on each goal. The wool committee immediately began to look into alternative ways of utilizing local wool. A professional weaver and handspinner from Taos, Rachael Brown, was brought in to evaluate the quality of locally grown wool and to meet with residents to discuss handspinning and weaving. Brown determined that wool from the breed common to the area, Western Whiteface, would yield a lustrous handspun yarn that could be dyed striking colors and wholesaled on a test basis to yarn shops in the region. She also proposed that local weavers use the spinning wheel in place of the *malacate,* or hand spindle, used by traditional weavers in New Mexico. The spinning wheel had never been used in these remote villages, so Brown and the Ganados board of directors organized a demonstration in May 1983 at the old church in Los Ojos, an event that attracted people from all over the Chama Valley. Men and women, young and old, tried their hand at spinning. During the demonstration Brown noticed a room where six or seven looms had been set up around a woodburning stove. Inquiring further, she discovered that there was a handful of people whose hobby was the nearly extinct Rio Grande style of weaving. Their workmanship showed a great deal of promise, even though they used discount synthetic yarns in standard commercial colors. She suggested that as soon as the handspun yarn enterprise was under way, some of the weavers should be trained to produce a limited selection of products for wholesale; they might even pick up a little retail business from seasonal tourism. Retailing, Brown believed, would create financial reserves to support the handspinning business through lean periods.

In 1983 Brown was hired to come to Los Ojos once a week and hold classes covering professional production techniques, quality control, pricing, marketing, wholesaling, and retailing. A year later, at the completion of training, all weavers were skilled at selecting their own colors and patterns and each had contributed to a collaborative design. Business skills were also taught so that weavers would be able to read balance sheets, forecast cash flows, and plan annual production and marketing goals.

The number of residents, more women than men, interested in working on the weaving project grew. Soon the group was looking for a larger facility. An opportunity arose in summer 1983 to purchase an old adobe mercantile store that was going out of business. It was the only store left in the historic village of Los Ojos. Nervous board members took a deep breath and authorized the raising of funds for a downpayment on the 100-year-old 7,000-square-foot adobe building. The acquisition of this property was the turning point for the fledgling organization. Now it had a physical location and was credited with saving an historic property.

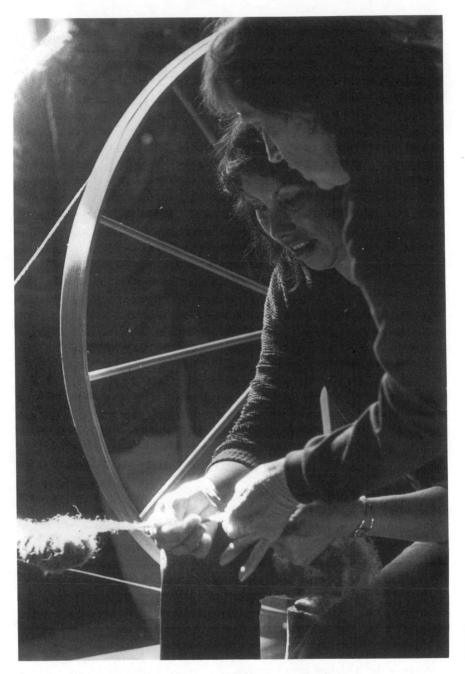

FIGURE 14.2. *Noted spinner and weaver Rachel Brown teaches Tierra Amarilla resident Maxine Garcia to use the spinning wheel during a 1983 demonstration and workshop.*

TIERRA WOOLS

The weavers and spinners who had been working with Brown chose the name Tierra Wools for this, the first business formed by Ganados del Valle. Tierra Wools opened for business in July 1983 as an unincorporated subsidiary controlled by the weavers. The new business was incubated under the corporate umbrella of Ganados del Valle during the start-up phase to secure grants and obtain technical assistance and further training. A loan from a revolving loan fund already established by Ganados del Valle financed start-up costs. Sales paid wages as well as production costs. Tierra Wools had its own checkbook and made its own business decisions, the Ganados board of directors merely seeing to certain legal technicalities.

By 1985 it was clear that the driving force behind Tierra Wools was weaving. It took two more years of steadily increasing sales with more efficient production and more effective promotion before some of the elements of its success were identified. The weavers came to realize that by revitalizing the centuries old Rio Grande weaving tradition and by using the wool from the valley, including the nearly extinct Churro sheep, they were addressing two overlapping market niches. One niche was cultural tourism, which attracts visitors looking for noncommercialized settings where they can share cultural experiences. The other niche is the growing national and international demand for natural fibers and high-quality handmade items. The quality handwoven work was offered for sale in an ordinary village setting where visitors could meet the artisans and observe wool being dyed, spun, and woven. By 1990 yearly sales for Tierra Wools were over $200,000, with twenty-four people working either part- or full-time.

GANADOS DEL VALLE REVOLVING LOAN FUND

The Ganados del Valle loan fund and support programs played a major role in bringing members skills and economic capacity along so that they could take advantage of emerging marketing opportunities. By 1989 the revolving loan fund had built community investment capacity to over $100,000 in cash. Two hundred sheep, moreover, had been acquired as part of the *partido,* or livestock shares program. Under this program ten to fifteen sheep were "invested" with a grower for six years. Each year the grower was required to return one lamb to the organization. These lambs in turn were reinvested with another grower or sold to fund a scholarship program. By the end of the sixth year the original borrower was required to return to the organization the same number of sheep originally invested, completing a full cycle of the shares program.

The revolving loan fund had been established in 1983 with a $5,000 grant and augmented the following year with additional grants totaling $25,000. In 1988 the organization received an $80,000 infusion of funds to assist with the purchase and start-up costs of a feed and general store. Over the years the loan fund has provided small cash loans to growers and weavers for equipment, for upgrading flocks, and to start new enterprises. These loans are made at a flat interest rate, usually a few points lower than local bank rates, and they are backed by full collateral. The loan repayment schedule fits the cash flow of the borrower, and the fund has the flexibility to set interest-only payments until a business is able to handle repayment of the principal. All interest earned is returned to augment the loan fund.

FIGURE 14.3. *Ganados farm manager Antonio Manzanares and sheep herder Martin Romero bring a cooperative band of sheep back from summer grazing in the W. H. Humphries wildlife area.*

RÍO ARRIBA WOOL WASHING PLANT

The availability of appropriate technology is as important for business start-ups as accessible capital. As the demand for wool grew with the expansion of Tierra Wools, so did the need for a more efficient method of washing it. When Tierra Wools was buying 500 pounds of wool a year from local growers and spinning it, the wool was washed in home washing machines. However, as production increased the co-op was buying over 2,000 pounds of wool a year. Not even several home washing machines were cost-effective. Large-scale commercial scourers, on the other hand, could not meet the needs of handcrafters who required wool washed in separate color lots.

Commercial scouring would also drain dollars from the community. Ganados del Valle thus began looking for a technology that would be more labor- than capital-intensive and that would be environmentally sound. Board members discussed the problem with Dr. Lyle McNeal, professor of animal sciences at Utah State University and director of the Navajo Churro sheep project. Professor McNeal had served as a consultant in animal husbandry to the Churro sheep-breeding project since the formative years of Ganados del Valle. He had also developed a prototype, intermediate-level wool washer for Churro wool at Utah State University. While the university washer was labor intensive and could handle 200 pounds of wool a day, it was not energy-efficient. Dr. McNeal allowed Ganados del Valle to use the prototype design and retrofit it in the interests of energy efficiency and commercial viability.

After reviewing technical resources for assistance in designing the retrofit, the organization assembled a design team of weavers, growers, a local machinist, and Dr. McNeal. They reasoned that a collaborative design was needed for a plant that could be maintained and perhaps later expanded with local expertise. In 1990, Río Arriba Wool Washing Services opened for business by training a plant operator who washed 1,000 pounds of local wool. In 1991 the plant hired an assistant for the operator and washed over 2,000 pounds. By 1992 a full marketing plan will be developed to attract Rocky Mountain and west coast consumers. The plant is one of the few intermediate-scale services in a four-state region for washing wool to handcrafters' specifications.

PASTORES LAMB

By 1988 Ganados del Valle support programs had begun to show results in larger and better lamb herds. Because sheep growers realize two-thirds of their income from lamb sales, better markets needed to be found for lamb. Taking note of the growing consumer demand for naturally grown, locally produced foods and regional specialty foods, Ganados del Valle hired a marketing specialist and test-marketed Churro lamb to Santa Fe restaurants and individual customers. At the same time, it applied to the USDA for certification approval of Churro lamb. The USDA granted it in 1989, meaning that customers who saw the certified Churro stamp on meat cuts knew the lamb was authentic. Growers chose the name Pastores (Shepherds) Lamb to market it, and in fall 1989 the cooperative offered fifty specialty lambs (Churro and Karakul) and one hundred and fifty farm-flock lambs (Columbia-Rambouillet Cross) to New Mexico restaurants and individuals. In 1990 Pastores Lamb received certification as an organic lamb grower and proceded to market 350 lambs, both Churro and Columbia Cross, to New Mexico customers. In both years, growers realized from 20 to 50 percent more income from marketing through Pastores Lamb.

PASTORES FEED AND GENERAL STORE

Ganados del Valle, meanwhile, purchased a second historic building in 1988, renovated it, and in 1990 opened Pastores Feed and General Store. This enterprise has two main goals: slowing the outflow of dollars from the local economy, and incubating family-based economic activity. By marketing livestock feeds, veterinary supplies, handmade gifts and foods, money circulates one more time through the local economy. Family-based enterprises, initially too small to warrant separate retail space, are encouraged to test-market homemade tortillas, baked goods, fresh eggs, jams, jellies, quilts, woodcarvings, and other folk and fine art work. Eventually, services such as horseshoeing, shearing, fencing, and saddle repair will be advertised through the general store. The mix of merchandise was designed for both local residents and visitors. The Ganados revolving loan fund provides seed money for the General Store, as well as small loans to artisans for the purchase of equipment and materials. It also provides technical assistance for product development, pricing, and packaging.

AGRICULTURAL SUPPORT PROGRAMS

Strengthening Hispanic ownership of land and water resources undergirds the sustainable economic development strategy of Ganados. Agricultural support programs help small growers overcome disadvantages of small economies of scale. For example, through the cooperative breeding program, members own expensive breeding rams in common. Growers pool their flocks during breeding season and select rams according to color and other characteristics. Members receive technical assistance from the Ganados marketing specialist in wool characteristics, genetic selection, flock health and nutrition. The cooperative grazing program allows members to pool their flocks under one shepherd and bring their sheep to high mountain pastures. Growers pay grazing leases of their respective flocks and share in the costs of the shepherd. By 1990 the Ganados del Valle membership had grown to fifty-five families. Nearly all members were directly involved in the projects, businesses, or marketing activities of the organization.

ELEMENTS FOR SUSTAINABLE DEVELOPMENT OF GANADOS DEL VALLE

While the Ganados del Valle experiment has not been without problems, in its seven years of operation it has benefited the local economy and work force. By focusing on human development, expanding local control of the use of resources, establishing a loan fund to increase internal investment capacity, and identifying appropriate technical and structural solutions, the Ganados model demonstrates how human and cultural resources can be utilized to build a sustainable economy.

EMPHASIZING HUMAN DEVELOPMENT

The basic components of development as set out by the organizing members of Ganados del Valle were the natural and agricultural resources of the area, and the local repository of cultural information and skills. The Ganados leadership designed training and support programs to integrate ancestral skills in sheep husbandry and wool crafting with modern techniques in business management and marketing.

Particular attention was paid to the selection of the technical assistance team. The organization sought consultants who were successful entrepreneurs in similar or related fields, understood the market the organization was addressing, would respect and build on cultural skills in collaborative teaching, and possessed the expertise or willingness to find technical solutions fitting the scale of operations and the resources available. In the first five years the successes of Ganados del Valle were due largely to its ability to locate consultants in weaving and animal husbandry who met these criteria. Funds were raised from philanthropic foundations to retain consultants on an annual basis. As members of Ganados del Valle gained skills, reliance on the technical team gradually decreased and was ultimately eliminated.

The Tierra Wools training program for weavers serves as a good example of the emphasis on human development. Rather than seeking a weaver with only artistic training, Ganados retained an expert skilled both in the art of weaving and in the practice of retailing. Tierra Wools was established from the outset as a business for the purpose of creating new jobs. It also sought to conserve cultural skills related to raising sheep and processing wool and to provide a source of off-season income to sheep growers and their families.

After a period of time, it became evident that Tierra Wools would itself have to train additional weavers to expand output and fill vacancies due to turnover. The Ganados del Valle planner, in collaboration with the Tierra Wools weaving consultant, developed a five-unit curriculum to train weavers. The program, taught by advanced weavers, covered basic wool crafting and entrepreneurial skills. By the fourth year advanced weavers were able to take on apprentices and have them produce marketable products within two months. Advanced weavers found that their skills deepened as a result of teaching, and many became articulate about their art. This improved their sales abilities.

Eighteen weavers of varying age and educational background have been through the curriculum. Because of its success, Ganados del Valle is negotiating with institutions of higher education to accredit a work-based program where Tierra Wools members will receive college credit for their own weaving course. Additional coursework would be offered in Los Ojos, enabling weavers and other community residents to apply these credits toward an associate of arts degree in business or fine arts.

LOCAL CONTROL OF RESOURCES

Prior to 1980 local sheep growers had no choice but to market their lambs outside the region. Each year lambs were sold "on the hoof," without bringing in the added value of separately marketed meat and wool. By establishing a local market for wool, as well as locally processing and crafting it, Ganados del Valle increased local decision-making about the use of this agricultural resource and brought increased income to the area. By 1989 the capacity to process lamb meat in the community and sell it directly to individuals and restaurants was being developed.

Local control of the use of resources also ensures that the area remains a cultural attraction. Ganados del Valle founders believe that the area's historic villages set in a mosaic of irrigated fields and pastures surrounded by high mountains and alpine meadows are an economic as well as a cultural resource. Throughout its history, Ganados del Valle has advocated that empowering a community to develop a sustainable economy must include local control over land and water uses. In 1986 members helped the county government to strengthen subdivision regulations aimed at conserving agricultural lands and water resources. They also wrote the section of the regulations which required subdividers to put in community water and sewage systems at a smaller density level than state law required. Residents countywide supported the requirement that environmental performance of subdivisions not threaten the valley's scenic resources and traditional agriculture.

Another effort to expand local control of the use of resources came in summer 1989 when Ganados del Valle sheep growers were confronted with a shortage of available grazing land. They engaged in direct action to feed their cooperative band of sheep and to demonstrate that livestock grazing can serve as a management tool to improve wildlife habitats. Because Ganados del Valle primarily serves small-scale landowners in the valley, the organization must secure long-term leases for summer grazing. Sheep growers cannot expand their flocks beyond subsistence level unless they are assured that larger flocks will be taken off home pastures and grazed on larger parcels with good summer forage. Long-term grazing leases assist flock owners in planning their expansions and projecting their sales and profits. Most traditional communal grazing lands of the Tierra Amarilla land grant are in the hands of the New Mexico Game and Fish Commission and private ranchers. Private ranchers have their own grazing needs or lease to cattle growers who can pay higher fees. Leasing grazing land from private owners has become doubly difficult, as larger ranches are now divided into smaller parcels or developed for recreation. Each summer since 1982 the Ganados del Valle flock manager has searched for private owners willing to lease for the longest term possible. Multi-year leases have not been available, leaving growers to the uncertainty of seasonal leasing.

The state of New Mexico controls over forty-four thousand acres of gamelands, managed primarily for hunting, in the northern mountain forests and meadows. Since 1982 Ganados del Valle had been involved in negotiations for use of this land in a grazing research project. The cooperative band of sheep would be utilized as a management tool to improve forage for game and to clear shrubs and weeds without the use of chemical defoliants. Ganados del Valle sought to apply wildlife forage-improving programs that had been used successfully with sheep and cattle in intensive, time-controlled grazing rotation in the Pacific Northwest as well as in South America and Africa.[5]

In 1989 Ganados del Valle received notice that its flock would have to leave the temporary grazing lands leased from the Jicarilla Apache before the end of the summer. The organization once again contacted the New Mexico Game and Fish with a request for emergency grazing and consideration of its standing proposal to demonstrate grazing as a management tool for wildlife habitat. Game and Fish declined. Growers had to choose between selling their flocks or taking direct action to bring attention to their plight. In August of 1989 members moved their sheep to the W. H. Humphries Wildlife area. This prompted the Governor of New Mexico to locate temporary acreage on a nearby state park for lease to the sheep growers for three more weeks, allowing their flocks to be moved out of the wildlife area. The Governor then organized a task force which included Ganados, environmental organizations, and related governmental agencies to design a research project to study the effects of controlled grazing on wildlife areas. When the task force failed, Ganados initiated mediation sessions with environmental groups, hoping to build alliances around the idea that wildlife conservation depends on rural communities building sustainable economies.[6]

INCREASING INTERNAL INVESTMENT

Ganados del Valle established its own revolving loan fund, initially with philanthropic contributions, to supply the seed capital for enterprises it planned to set up or assist. Initially, access to the revolving loan fund was limited to business activities associated with raising sheep and wool processing. This allowed the organization to augment the potential for payback at the same time it was developing markets for lamb and wool. The *partido,* or livestock shares program, also served as a mechanism to build internal investment. The placement of sheep with new growers increased area agricultural activity and enabled cooperators to participate in the breeding, production, and marketing activities of Ganados del Valle. The requirement to return the number of sheep equal to the total number originally lent ensured that this unique investment program would eventually become self-reliant.

By 1989 Ganados del Valle's revolving loan fund had grown from grants and returned interest to over $135,000. The number of sheep in the livestock shares program had grown from 150 to over 300. The program, however, got off to a slow start because of fluctuating markets for lamb and the lack of long-term summer grazing. The Pastores Lamb venture holds out promise of establishing a dependable regional market for specialty lamb, thus assisting in the growth of agricultural activity in the Valley.

CHANGING ECONOMIC AND SOCIAL STRUCTURES TO INCREASE OPPORTUNITY AND REDUCE DEPENDENCY

The organizers of Ganados del Valle believed that the commercial sheep industry had become excessively dependent on an export market that favored large-scale growers. Moreover, by 1980 the national sheep industry was in decline, bringing into question the wisdom of a development strategy based on growing and marketing lamb and wool. In the Chama Valley, however, sheep offered a unique opportunity for adding on value: lamb and wool were two diverse products to sell to local, regional, and national markets. Another reason for choosing this resource was that it was economically feasible for a greater number of families. Relatively little capital was needed to begin a flock, particularly if a family had access to a shares program. Work to increase the value of the wool, moreover, had been practiced for many generations in northern New Mexico villages.

Ganados del Valle introduced structural changes that responded to the specific problems of underdevelopment. First a broader market for lamb was found through a cooperative sheep producers' tele-auction in the Pacific Northwest. Second, lamb and wool markets were redirected and diversified by producers and processors using cooperatives and other economic organizations. Third, the reorganization of production technologies and the transfer of skills encouraged spinoff and the growth of related enterprises. Finally, changes were brought about in the roles and perceptions of residents regarding what they can do for themselves, what women can do in business, the economic value of small family farms, and traditional cultural activities.

When Ganados del Valle had first been organized, business development experts advised against retailing wool products in the isolated Chama Valley. Ganados del Valle agreed. Both turned out to be wrong. Neither the leadership of Ganados del Valle nor the business experts considered the increasing visitor traffic through the valley. Nor did they understand what visitors were interested in seeing or buying. Ganados del Valle members and the Tierra Wool weavers came to find that visitors appreciated the area precisely because of its undeveloped state and the fact that a unique culture resided in the old adobe villages near the headwaters of the Rio Chama.

The beautiful earth-toned Churro yarn and the retail products into which it was woven filled a market need that built the Tierra Wools enterprise and created thirty-five new jobs in Los Ojos. As demand for other Tierra Wools products grew, opportunities for new businesses opened up. The wool-washing plant, the feed store and the general store have created six additional new jobs and increased the incomes of over thirty-five families. The old one-way street economy, which had been draining resources, dollars, and talent from the community, has begun moving toward sustainable self-reliance by establishing interdependent ties with the regional economy.

CONCLUSION

There are many strategies for the economic development of rural areas. Each one brings both advantages and disadvantages. The applicability and results of each approach vary according to a community's unique situation, the characteristics of its resource base, its cultural values, its leadership, and other factors. Successful planning for an economy that is both sustainable and adaptable requires a clear understanding of the basic elements of self-reliance, as demonstrated in the Ganados del Valle case study. However, each community adopting a REP strategy must decide for itself which elements fit local conditions and opportunities for sustainable development.

15_____

The Legal Framework of Planning

BOTH THE RURAL ENVIRONMENTAL PLANNER and the citizens involved in planning in their community must have a working knowledge of the legal framework of planning. This is best obtained by a course of study on this subject, access to which may not be easy for many rural people. This chapter offers an introduction to such material. Its purpose is to inform rural residents of legal concepts and terms most likely to be encountered in planning their own community.

Lawyers and others involved in matters of law use special terms that have specific meanings and a long history of use and reference. The layman may have heard some of these terms but may not be quite sure what they mean. This chapter introduces and explains some basic legal concepts and related legal terms, then covers broader material such as state enabling legislation, the legal basis for planning and zoning, dedication, exactions, and the authority of planning commissions.

LEGAL CONCEPTS

An understanding of the following concepts can help rural citizens and their elected and appointed officials to make more effective use of lawyers and paralegal services when appropriate:

1. Five types of law
2. The legal concept of property

3. The bundle of rights concept
4. Partial rights in landed property
5. Easements
6. State enabling legislation: general and specific
7. Methods of public control over private land
8. Euclidean zoning
9. Compulsory dedication of land
10. Authority of planning commissions

FIVE TYPES OF LAW

The principal types of law are *constitutional* law, *statutory* law, *common* law, *judicial* law, and *administrative* law. Although each type enumerates a wide range of rights, including civil and human rights, this chapter will address only property rights and related property law. All property rights are ultimately vested in the sovereign authority of the state, which has a monopoly of force and so can enforce all rights and obligations within its borders. The sovereign state may delegate many of its rights to political subdivisions or to individuals. The delegation of authority may be expressed in constitutions, statutes, judicial decisions, or administrative decisions.

Constitutional law is embodied in the basic charter of the government. The charter enumerates the powers and responsibilities of the various branches of government and the rights of citizens, which the government is obliged to respect and protect. The federal constitution outlines the powers and duties of the various departments of the federal government, while state constitutions declare the powers of states and of their subdivisions.

Statutory laws are those established by the enactment of statutes, that is, by the legislature of the sovereign government. Both the federal and state legislatures enact laws by the authority granted them in their respective constitutions.

Common law comprises the body of legal principles and rules that derive their authority generally from precedents, that is, from usage and customs established over a long period of time or from the judgments and decrees of courts recognizing, confirming, and enforcing such usage. The term *common law* describes law that is not created by an act of legislature. In the United States, common law refers particularly to the ancient law of England. Common law usually covers areas of activity not covered by statutes or by constitutional law, but it may also cover other areas. Common law, for example, refers to judicial law established by the courts (sometimes including equity courts) in common law states. Common law states are those states that recognize common law in their constitutions. Additionally, statutory or judicial references to the old English common law may often be intended to include associated legislation. It should be stressed that common law is based on English tradition, as interpreted by courts in many sovereign states of the United States, not on the traditions of law, usage, and customs of other cultures within state jurisdictions.

Judicial law refers to law established by judicial decision. Constitutions, statutes, and common practice establish rules or actions of a general nature. Conflicts arise when there is disagreement or confusion concerning just how these laws should be applied in specific instances. The judge, in applying a law to a specific case, is interpreting the meaning of that law and hence "making law." Judicial law is practiced most often in subject matters governed by little or no legislation.

Administrative law, important in the field of property rights, refers to decisions of government administrators that have the force of law (unless they are overthrown by the courts). Any administrator of a government agency charged with responsibility for resources, such as water or land of which the government is proprietor, is called upon to make day-to-day and long-range decisions concerning the allocation and use of that resource within the relevant statutes. For situations not anticipated by basic statutes, or for subjects authorized by such statutes, administrative decisions constitute a significant body of law. An example of administrative law would be a water resource department classifying water quality by administrative procedure.

THE LEGAL CONCEPT OF PROPERTY

Property, considered like family and religion one of the basic institutions of human society, has been a subject of study from time immemorial. It constitutes an aggregation of performances and forbearances that organize large sectors of human activity. Throughout history, wars have been fought in attempts to alter the conditions of landownership or property.

The legal concept of property consists of an aggregate of certain rights that are guaranteed and protected by the government. According to *Black's Law Dictionary,* property is "the unrestricted and exclusive right to a thing; the right to dispose of a thing in every legal way, to possess it, to use it, and to exclude everyone else from interfering with it."

There are three attributes of property. Property must have an object and an owner, and it must be protected by a sovereign state. The object is any resource that by its nature permits ownership and control. The owner is an individual, a corporation, a group of people, or any unit of government. The sovereign state embodying the will of all participants, has through its monopoly on the use of force (police power) the ability to guarantee the rights of ownership. The rights of the sovereign state may be divided and delegated among political subdivisions. For instance, the right to acquire property or easements by eminent domain may be delegated to the state highway department or to municipalities for the purpose of creating public access to property or to public waters. Responsibility for protecting private property rights may be exercised at the local as well as the state level.

There are a number of different types of property: common, public, qualified, and real property. Common property sometimes refers to land owned by a municipality. A municipal park is common property. Property owned jointly by a husband and wife under the community property laws of some states is also common property.

Public property or *publici juris* refers to those things owned by the public, that is, all the people in the state or community. For example, the public road system is public property.

Qualified property applies to chattels, that is, moveable possessions as distinguished from real estate. Chattels by nature are not permanent but can exist at some times and not at others. An example would be wild animals that a person has caught and kept. The animals belong to that person only so long as he or she retains possession of them. Qualified property is used to indicate the claims in any ownership which a person has when others also have claims to that property. For example, the owner of mortgaged land is a qualified owner.

Real property refers to land and generally whatever is erected, growing upon, or otherwise permanently fixed to that land. Because of its importance in all planning, including rural planning, real property is the subject of the remainder of this chapter. Rights in real property may be applied to the surface of the land, its subsurface, or the air (space) above it.

The state may own property in the same way as an individual does, but there are other rights reserved to the sovereign state (unless it delegates them) that do not apply to private owners. They are the rights of eminent domain and of escheat. Eminent domain is the right or power of the state to reassert, either temporarily or permanently, its control over any portion of the land of the state to meet a public exigency and for the public good. Escheat signifies a reversion of property to the state when there is no individual competent to inherit it. The concept of escheat, like many legal concepts, goes far back in history. The state is deemed to occupy the place and hold the right of the feudal lord.

There are both direct and indirect rights in land. Direct rights are those that apply specifically to a parcel of land, such as a lease right, that is, a limited right to use, and a mortgage or equity right, which means the complete right to use or dispose of a property by the owner. Indirect rights refer to those rights of the government that may be used to control the use of land. Some of the government's indirect rights (or powers) are the power to tax, the power to spend for the common good and to regulate private activity for that purpose, the power to control interstate commerce, and the police power, that is, the right to do whatever is necessary to provide for the defense of the nation, the state, or other jurisdiction.

The owner of property is the person who has, or the agency of government that has, the right of disposition. A person may have only a small fraction of equity and may have leased the right of use, but if that person maintains the right of disposition, he or she is the owner of the property.

THE BUNDLE OF RIGHTS CONCEPT

To explain the legal concept of property, rights in land are often likened to fasces, the symbol of authority of Caesar's army (see fig. 15.1). The fasces is a bundle of sticks with an ax in the center. Each stick represents a land right while the ax represents the supreme authority of the state. The bundle of sticks may be divided into three smaller bundles: the right to use, the right to lease, and the right to dispose of. These three rights may be further subdivided. The right to use includes the rights to cultivate, to improve, to harvest growth, to not use, and in some cases, to use up or to destroy. The right to lease includes the right to lease to anyone the owner chooses under any of a great number of possible arrangements. The right to dispose of includes the right to sell all or part of the property or the interests therein, to bequeath it, to mortgage it, and to establish a trust.

PARTIAL RIGHTS IN LANDED PROPERTY

Fee simple ownership represents the largest number of rights concentrated in the hands of an individual. Fee simple means the possession of all rights save those reserved to the state. There are a number of partial rights in land that have various applications and are important for understanding landed property.

Deed conditions are special provisions in land title deeds that place limits or conditions on the use of land by the owner. Deed conditions must be consistent with social policy. For example, conditions that discriminate against ethnic groups cannot be placed on a subdivision. When certain rights

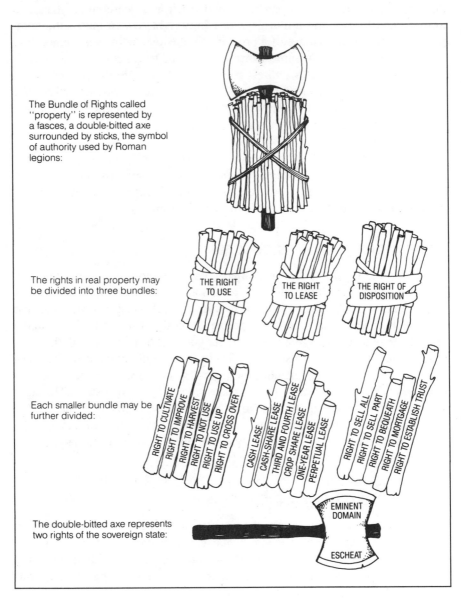

The Bundle of Rights called "property" is represented by a fasces, a double-bitted axe surrounded by sticks, the symbol of authority used by Roman legions:

The rights in real property may be divided into three bundles:

THE RIGHT TO USE

THE RIGHT TO LEASE

THE RIGHT OF DISPOSITION

Each smaller bundle may be further divided:

RIGHT TO CULTIVATE
RIGHT TO IMPROVE
RIGHT TO HARVEST
RIGHT TO NOT USE
RIGHT TO USE UP
RIGHT TO CROSS OVER

CASH LEASE
CASH-SHARE LEASE
THIRD AND FOURTH LEASE
CROP SHARE LEASE
ONE-YEAR LEASE
PERPETUAL LEASE

RIGHT TO SELL ALL
RIGHT TO SELL PART
RIGHT TO BEQUEATH
RIGHT TO MORTGAGE
RIGHT TO ESTABLISH TRUST

The double-bitted axe represents two rights of the sovereign state:

EMINENT DOMAIN

ESCHEAT

FIGURE 15.1. The Bundle of Rights Concept of Property I

are reserved, these conditions are called deed reservations. Examples are deeds to building lots that require a certain size and type and setback for any dwelling to be erected. Deed conditions are usually accompanied by reverter clauses that provide for the forfeiture of property whenever restrictive conditions are broken.

A life estate is the possession and enjoyment of property during the lifetime of a person. At the end of that lifetime the property reverts to someone designated as the receiver of the estate. A life estate can be created by a trust document in a contractual arrangement.

A lease is a relationship created by contract that gives a tenant the right to possess and use property held or owned by a landlord or leasor. The tenant has a leasehold estate. The landlord retains a reversion interest. A mortgage, on the other hand, represents an encumberance on landed property by a borrower to a lender as security for the payment of a debt.

Land or purchase contract arrangements are used in some areas as a means for buyers with little capital to acquire rights to property. The buyer of a land contract gradually builds up equity in the property to the point where he or she converts the contract into a mortgage or, if all payments are made, assumes complete ownership. As long as the buyer continues to operate under a land contract, the title of property remains with the holder of the contract.

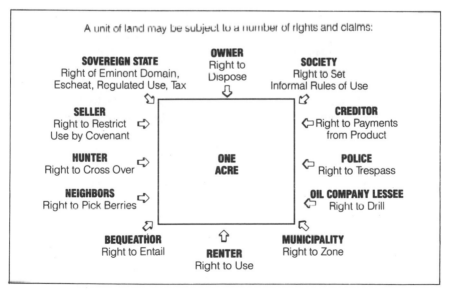

FIGURE 15.2. The Bundle of Rights Concept of Property II

A lien is the right of certain classes of creditors to sell a debtor's property to satisfy some debt or charge.

EASEMENTS

Easements are very important to land-use planning. An easement is an agreement, usually permanent, that transfers one or more of a landowner's property rights to another party. The concept of easement is based on the legal concept that property ownership consists of a bundle of rights. The right to cross another's land, for example, has often been transferred through easements for access roads, irrigation ditches, or power lines. Easements can also be used as a means of protecting fish and game habitats and scenic areas and of creating public recreational facilities.

Both state and federal agencies have used easements to improve fish and game habitats and to acquire public hunting and fishing rights. For example, waterfowl hunting rights may be acquired along with the right to preserve wetland habitats for migration and to protect waterfowl areas from draining or filling. Public fishing rights are often acquired through stream bank easement along with the right to improve fish habitat using stream channel and stream bank devices.

Highway scenic easements are perhaps the best known and most successful use of the easement in land use planning. These easements often include prohibitions against timber cutting, billboards, and dumping, as well as restrictions on adjacent commercial establishments and residences. Highway scenic easements usually apply to areas covering the field of view from the highway.

A review of successful easement programs identifies six conditions that must be met for a program to be successful. First, an effective public relations campaign should be undertaken to make the program understandable and meaningful to landowners (and also to the courts). Second, there should be a provision for equitable compensation. As a rule of thumb, the value of the easement should equal the prior value of property minus the value resulting from the burden of easement. Third, landowners should understand exactly which rights are being transferred and which are being retained (many easement violations result from misunderstanding). Fourth, the terms of easements must be enforced. Fifth, notice must be provided of easement restrictions so that any new owner is aware of the assumed obligations. Sixth, easements should be permanent because renegotiation can be costly and because temporary easements sometimes negate the advantage of lower property taxes.

A number of benefits may accrue when these criteria are met: easement is often cheaper than fee simple purchase; the landowner performs maintenance unless otherwise stipulated; the land stays on the tax rolls; the landowner pays lower taxes; easements, being permanent, are not subject to amendment or variance; the landowner may get free title review; the landowner may get flank protection from neighbors who sell out; and conservation easements can cause land values to increase.

STATE ENABLING LEGISLATION

Careful study of state statutes relating to the powers, rights, and limits of local jurisdictions and citizens will pay substantial dividends in improving the ability of concerned citizens and rural planners to guide the community planning process. The examples and methods given in the following sections are common to and applicable in most jurisdictions of the United States.

The authority of town and county governments to act is granted by the state government. This authority, called enabling legislation, may be of two kinds, general and specific. In the establishment of municipal jurisdictions town officials are given general authority to do whatever in their judgment is in the interest of public health and general welfare. This blanket authority, which actually covers a wide range of activities in the public interest, including planning and zoning, is widely known as the police power.

Specific enabling legislation consists of state laws that grant subordinate jurisdictions special authority to perform specified functions. Specific enabling legislation is desirable because it removes the doubts that often arise when actions are taken on the basis of general enabling authority. For example, the conduct of planning and zoning is greatly facilitated by specific legislation authorizing the various steps in the planning and zoning process.

In 1928 the U.S. Department of Commerce published a standard city planning enabling act as a guide to planning. This act was quickly and widely copied by a great many states. Today most states retain some form of enabling legislation copied from that original Department of Commerce act. Sections 6 and 7, taken from that act and quoted below, demonstrate the extensive authority given to planning commissions:

United States Department of Commerce:
A Standard City Planning Enabling Act (1928)

Sec. 6. General Powers and Duties. It shall be the function and duty of the commission to make and adopt a master plan for the physical development of the municipality, including any areas outside of its boundaries which, in the commission's judgment, bear relation to the planning of such municipality. Such plan, with the accompanying maps, plats, charts, and descriptive matter, shall show the commission's recommendations for the development of said territory, including among other things, the general location, character, and extent of streets, viaducts, subways, bridges, waterways, water fronts, boulevards, parkways, playgrounds, squares, parks, aviation fields, and other public ways, grounds and open spaces, the general location of public buildings and other public property, and the general location and extent of public utilities and terminals, whether publicly or privately owned or operated, for water, light, sanitation, transportation, communication, power, and other purposes; also the removal, relocation, widening, narrowing, vacating, abandonment, change of use or extension of any of the foregoing ways, grounds, open spaces, buildings, property, utilities, or terminals; as well as a zoning plan for the control of the height, area, bulk, location, and use of buildings and premises. As the work of making the whole master plan progresses, the commission may, from time to time, adopt and publish a part or parts thereof, any such part to cover one or more major sections or divisions of the municipality, or one or more of the aforesaid or other functional matters to be included in the plan. The commission may, from time to time, amend, extend, or add to the plan.

Sec. 7. Purposes in View. In the preparation of such plan, the commission shall make careful and comprehensive surveys and studies of present conditions and future growth of the municipality and with due regard to its relation to neighboring territory. The plan shall be made with the general purpose of guiding and accomplishing a coordinated, adjusted, and harmonious development of the municipality and its environs which will, in accordance with present and future needs, best promote health, safety, morals, order, convenience, prosperity, and general welfare, as well as efficiency and economy in the process of development; including among other things, adequate provision for traffic, the promotion of safety from fire and other dangers, adequate provision for light and air, the promotion of the healthful and convenient distribution of population, the promotion of good civic design and arrangement, wise and efficient expenditure of public funds, and the adequate provision of public utilities and other public requirements.

PUBLIC CONTROLS OVER PRIVATE LAND

A common misconception is that the only method available for public control of private land is by purchase in fee simple or by zoning. It also is popularly held that purchase is too expensive and that zoning is of doubtful efficacy. In fact, there are many methods of public control over private property. The following list of techniques is a good basis for discussion of the appropriate method for each land-use recommendation. Some techniques are more applicable than others in specific situations. For example, designation may be the best method for protecting natural areas, conservation zones are effective for protecting wetlands, compulsory dedication can be applied to school sites, tax stabilization agreements may be used to keep land in agriculture, and federal licensing authority provides fishing and canoeing access to streams. Here are the various methods of exercising public control over private land:

Exercise of police power
1. Zoning (Euclidean, historic, and conservation)
2. Compulsory dedication
3. Subdivision regulations
4. Building codes
5. Health regulations
6. Antinuisance ordinances
7. Adopted master plan
8. Critical control policy
9. Growth control policy
10. Sewer and construction moratorium
Taxation
11. Preferential taxation
12. Tax stabilization agreements
13. Forest or other special resource tax law
Regulation
14. Development permit system
15. Land sales regulation legislation
Acquisition of rights
16. Purchase in fee
17. Purchase and lease-back
18. Lease
19. Gift
20. Condemnation (exercise of eminent domain)
21. Easements
Other
22. Nonpublic land trust agreements in which the public is a third-party beneficiary
23. Common law
24. Subsidies
25. Designation

26. Emergency powers
27. Site plan review
28. Federal or state licensing authority

EUCLIDEAN ZONING

The most common type of zoning in the United States is Euclidean zoning.
It takes its name from the Supreme Court case *Euclid, Ohio v. the Ambler
Realty Company*. This precedent-setting decision supporting the legality of
zoning as practiced throughout the country was handed down in 1926. The
Euclid v. Ambler case established zoning as a proper exercise of the police
power, provided that state enabling authority exists, that zoning is not arbitrary or unreasonable, and that it supports public health, safety, morals, and
welfare. By the end of 1928 zoning enabling laws had been enacted by forty-
seven states. The finding and opinion in the Euclid case are presented later
in this chapter.

COMPULSORY DEDICATION OF LAND

One of the most important planning tools is the requirement for compulsory
dedication of land through the development process. Because of lack of fa-
miliarity this tool is little used in rural areas.

Throughout the history of the United States it has been considered the
developer's responsibility to furnish the land needed for streets and for public
areas such as the town common, squares, parks, and public building sites.
This was true in early colonial towns built in both the English and the Spanish traditions and later, in towns developed by railroad-backed land speculators. The practice was not merely a matter of custom. It was required first by
royal charters, and then by charters granted by early state legislatures. In
addition to statutory requirements, courts imposed a common law requirement that an owner dividing a parcel of land make adequate provision for
access from existing streets to any interior lots. Whenever a developer is
called upon to dedicate land, the facilities provided in this manner become a
part of a package that the lot purchaser receives. Their cost is normally re-
flected in the price of the lot. Without minimum support facilities paid for at
least in part by others, including streets, schools, and fire protection, there
would be very little market for lots at all. Many developers find that providing extras such as parks and school sites results in a larger return on their
investment.

Two Supreme Court decisions of 1987, known as the Nollan and First

English cases, emphasize the need for care in defining the timing of and the requirements for land dedication of easements serving community goals. These cases, discussed later in this chapter, more fully define conditions limiting exactions and just compensation for takings.

THE AUTHORITY OF PLANNING COMMISSIONS

The legal authority of small-town planning commissions and rural residents, without the assistance of community planners and without legal counsel, is often challenged, bluffed, or threatened. For example, if a parcel of land would be affected by a proposed zone change that the owner regards as undesirable, the owner, or a person representing the owner, may tell the planning commission that it does not have the authority to take such action or may threaten to sue it. Though the charge may be unfounded, it can still be effective if the planning commission is unclear about its prerogatives.

Statutes in most states list the specific actions planning commissions are authorized to take. The key to good planning is just and equitable application of these statutes. For example, in Vermont the actions available to planning commissions are specifically authorized by statute. Planning commissions there, as in most states, are able to:

1. Promote public health
2. Promote public safety
3. Promote public morals
4. Promote prosperity
5. Promote comfort
6. Promote convenience
7. Promote efficiency
8. Promote economy
9. Promote general welfare
10. Eliminate present land development problems
11. Provide space for forests
12. Provide space for agriculture
13. Provide space for residences
14. Provide space for recreation
15. Provide space for commerce
16. Provide space for industry
17. Provide space for public facilities
18. Provide space for semipublic facilities
19. Protect forests

20. Protect soils
21. Protect birds (that is, other natural resources)
22. Preserve open space
23. Provide a sound economic base
24. Protect historic features
25. Enhance the Vermont scenery
26. Distribute population
27. Provide jobs
28. Guard against overcrowding
29. Prevent traffic congestion
30. Prevent loss of peace
31. Prevent loss of quiet
32. Prevent loss of privacy
33. Reduce noise
34. Reduce air pollution
35. Reduce water pollution
36. Provide for transportation
37. Facilitate provision of water
38. Provide for sewerage treatment
39. Facilitate provision of schools
40. Facilitate provision of parks
41. Regulate growth
42. Encourage the most desirable use of land
43. Minimize the adverse impact of one land use on another

Vermont statutes authorize planning commissions to take any "reason-able" action to protect the public interest, if they have public support, that is, if public support outweighs public opposition. *Reasonable* is a commonly used legal term meaning what the majority of people would call reasonable if the question were raised in a court of law, and if people qualified as re-spected members of the community were asked to give their opinion. Public interest is that which benefits public health, safety, and welfare in the judg-ment of an elected council or their representatives.

Public support is not a legal requirement but rather a social or political condition. For example, it might be reasonable and in the public interest for the planning commission to propose the fluoridation of water. However, if a large, vocal group of townspeople opposes fluoridation it might be unwise politically for the planning commission to require it. Not only would it be unsuccessful, it would also erode if not destroy the credibility and usefulness of the planning commission. In fact, town officials are more likely to be guided or restrained by political or social considerations and pressures than by legal requirements.

While planning commissions in most jurisdictions are authorized to work for and promote specific public actions, unless authority has been specifically delegated by the elected board, their actions are only recommendations to that board or to the council. Elected administrators may either approve or disapprove them.

The Supreme Court of the United States is the final arbiter in interpreting the meaning and application of laws in this country. Because of their importance to the application of laws related particularly to planning and zoning in rural areas, three cases argued before the Supreme Court, one in 1926 and two in 1987, are discussed here.

CASE: *EUCLID V. AMBLER REALTY COMPANY*

This case, argued before the Supreme Court in 1926, concerned a zoning ordinance in Euclid, Ohio. Now called Euclidean zoning, it described traditional zoning categories utilized by many local governments. The entire area of Euclid, Ohio, was divided by the zoning ordinance into six classes of use districts. The six use districts were classified with respect to the type of buildings that could be erected within their limits and to possible construction densities. The ordinance also included a seventh class of use that was prohibited altogether.[1]

The ordinance was challenged by the Ambler Realty Company on the grounds that it violated section 1 of the Fourteenth Amendment to the Federal Constitution. The realty company charged that the ordinance deprived it of liberty and property without due process of law, denied it equal protection under the law, and offended against certain provisions of the constitution of the state of Ohio. Ambler Realty claimed that the ordinance attempted to restrict and control the lawful uses of its land, which amounted to a confiscatory taking by destroying a great part of its value. As such, it violated the constitutional proscription against uncompensated takings.

The U.S. Supreme Court resolved the case by raising and addressing two questions. One was the general use of police power in zoning, the other the specific question involved in the case at hand. The court found that decisions by state courts were numerous and conflicting, but those that supported the use of police power in zoning greatly outnumbered those that denied it altogether. It also discovered a tendency to increasingly broaden the approved use for which police power restrictions may be imposed. The court agreed that there is an important and fine dividing line between the use of police power in the public interest and confiscating the land without adequate justification or compensation.

The opinion stated that before a zoning ordinance could be declared unconstitutional, its provisions had to be shown to be clearly arbitrary and unreasonable and to have no substantial relation to public health, safety, morals, or general welfare. The court held that the ordinance's general scope and dominant conditions constituted a valid exercise of authority.

CASE: *NOLLAN V. CALIFORNIA COASTAL COMMISSION*

The Nollan decision of 1987 involved the issue of whether a property exaction, in this case a compulsory land dedication in the form of an access-easement requirement imposed by the California Coastal Commission, violated the Fifth Amendment's taking clause.[2] The Nollans, property owners, applied for a coastal development permit to replace their bungalow with a larger single-family house. The Coastal Commission, by an enabling statute, recommended that the permit be granted subject to an exaction that the Nollans allow the public an easement to the beach.[3] The public purpose served by the exaction was to protect the public's "visual and psychological access to the beach."[4] The Nollans objected, claiming that the exaction violated the Fifth Amendment's prohibition against taking private property for public use without just compensation.

The Supreme Court held that the Coastal Commission's exaction requirement did indeed violate the Fifth Amendment. In doing so, the court enunciated a new constitutional test for exactions: an exaction had to "substantially advance a legitimate public purpose" if the permit condition served the same public purpose that justified the denial of the permit.[5] This requirement (as described by the dissent) involved a two-step analysis.[6] First, would the condition imposed violate the Fifth Amendment? Second, if so, would requiring it in the form of an exaction alter the outcome? Under this analysis, the court found that if the commission had required the Nollans to convey the beach easement, it would constitute a taking.[7] Next, the court stated that the public purpose underlying the exaction requirement failed to further the end advanced as the justification for the prohibition.[8]

The ramifications of this finding require a more careful look at exactions for planning actions in all jurisdictions, including rural communities and counties. Exactions had been described, prior to the Nollan case, as the new "hero" and the "hottest issue" in land-use planning.[9] Nearly 88 percent of the nation's municipalities employ some form of exaction.[10] There are four basic types: compulsory land dedication, compulsory physical improvement, cash payment in lieu of land dedication, and impact fees. Each type of exaction is used as a police power tool to require developers to contribute to infrastructure as a condition of plat or permit approval.[11]

CASE: *FIRST ENGLISH EVANGELICAL LUTHERAN CHURCH OF GLENDALE V. THE COUNTY OF LOS ANGELES*

Further definition of the appropriate powers and limits of exactions was provided by the Supreme Court in this 1987 case.[12] It addressed the concern of temporary taking and defined the remedy for regulatory taking, in this case as compensation. The First Evangelical Lutheran Church of Glendale, California, purchased 21 acres in the Los Angeles National Forest, 12 acres of which were flat land along the banks of Mill Creek.[13] This property, known as Lutherglen, was used by the church as a retreat center for handicapped children. In 1978, after a fire deforested 3,600 acres upstream, serious flooding destroyed the buildings at Lutherglen. In 1979 Los Angeles adopted an ordinance forbidding reconstruction of the buildings within an interim flood protection area along Mill Creek. Lutherglen was located within this protected area.

The church instituted a suit alleging that the ordinance violated the Fifth Amendment's taking clause. The Supreme Court addressed not the issue of whether a taking occurred but only the question of what remedy was available to a plaintiff alleging a regulatory taking. The court found that the remedy for a temporary regulatory taking of property is compensation, not merely invalidation or recision of the regulation or ordinance.[14] Moreover, the court indicated that compensation may extend to a "much earlier" date, when interference with the use of property started.[15]

CONCLUSION

The conduct of REP requires a general knowledge of planning law. It is more reasonable and efficient for a citizen or rural planner to gain at least a functional understanding of planning law than to expect a lawyer to learn about planning rural communities. A rural citizen's or planner's need to understand planning law is similar to an individual's need to understand medicine. Everyone need not be a doctor, but the more first aid and health science a person knows, the more that person can help in a crisis and the better equipped that person is to call on a specialist at the appropriate time.

The law is intended to be a common tool and guide enacted by and for laypersons, not an arcane system accessible only through the intercession of specialists. Experts are called in when there are questions of law that laypersons cannot answer. If a rural environmental planner, an interested citizen, or a planning commissioner is familiar with state enabling statutes and with significant federal legislation and key court cases, the local planning process will proceed more smoothly. The planner or citizen with a working knowledge of planning law will know how to distinguish a legal question from a planning question.

State statutes are bound into volumes, carefully indexed, and regularly updated and summarized; they are available in public libraries, state universities, and many community colleges. In small communities or remote areas without a public library, information on specific statutes or laws pertaining to a general area of concern can be requested through local agencies such as the town council or county commission.[16]

Notes

CHAPTER 1

1. "Community Development Plan for the Village of Chama and Surrounding Area" (Albuquerque: Design and Planning Assistance Center, University of New Mexico, 1980).
2. "Village of San Ysidro de los Dolores, Sandoval County, New Mexico: A Handbook of Issues, Opinions, Choices for the Future" (Albuquerque: Rural Planning Studio, Community and Regional Planning Program, University of New Mexico, June 1985).
3. "Proposal for a Quality Environment" (Essex, Vermont: Essex Planning Commission, 1972).
4. Interviews with Ann Harroun, Vermont state legislator, and Noah Thompson, former chair of the Essex Town Planning Commission, July 1989.

CHAPTER 2

1. Linda S. Cordell, *Prehistory of the Southwest* (Orlando, Florida: Academic Press, 1984), p. 190.
2. Ibid., pp. 222–23.
3. Ibid., p. 246.
4. Among others, see William Lumpkins, "Reflections on Chacoan Architecture," in David Grant Noble, ed., *New Light on Chaco Canyon* (Santa Fe: School of American Research Press, 1984), p. 20.
5. Ordinance 35, cited and translated in Dora P. Crouch, Daniel J. Garr, and Axel I. Mundigo, *Spanish City Planning in North America* (Cambridge, Massachusetts: MIT Press, 1982), p. 8.

231

6. Crouch, Garr, and Mundigo, *Spanish City Planning*, p. 67.
7. John Friedmann and Clyde Weaver, *Territory and Function: The Evolution of Regional Planning* (Berkeley: University of California Press, 1979), p. 30.
8. Ibid., p. 31.
9. Benton MacKaye, *The New Exploration: A Philosophy of Regional Planning, 1928*, cited in Friedmann and Weaver, *Territory and Function*, p. 32.
10. Lewis Mumford, *The Culture of Cities, 1938*, cited in Friedmann and Weaver, *Territory and Function*, p. 33.
11. Howard Odum, *American Social Problems, 1939*, revised 1947, cited in Friedmann and Weaver, *Territory and Function*, p. 37.
12. Howard Odum, "Regional Quality and Balance of America," in H. W. Odum and K. Jocher, eds., *In Search of the Regional Balance of America*, cited in Friedmann and Weaver, *Territory and Function*, p. 38.
13. Friedmann and Weaver, *Territory and Function*, p. 89.
14. During the period from 1965 to 1989, the Universities of Vermont and New Mexico sponsored over thirty REP projects. For more information, see addresses noted in Preface, REP Exchange.
15. See early Reagan reports such as *Better Country: A Strategy for Rural Development in the 1980s*, 1983, and *Rural Communities and the American Farm: A Partnership for Progress*, 1984 (Washington, D.C.: USDA, Office of Rural Development Policy).
16. Donald K. Larson, "Will Employment Growth Benefit All Households? A Case Study in Nine Non-Metro Kentucky Counties," *Rural Development Research Report* 55 (Washington, D.C.: USDA Economic Research Service, January 1986).
17. For a recent state case study see R. D. Sloan, "The Colorado 'Urban and Rural Enterprise Zone Act' of 1986: Legislative Passage and Administrative Implementation," *The Western Governmental Researcher*, vol. 3, no. 1 (summer 1987): pp. 39–48. Also, contact the Department of Housing and Urban Development in Washington, D.C., for updates and comparative data across the states.
18. See in particular the reports produced by the Rural Development Policy Project, Institute of Urban and Regional Development, University of California, Berkeley: Edward J. Blakely, Ted K. Bradshaw, Phil Shapira, and Nancey Leigh-Preston, "New Challenges for Rural Development," *Working Paper Four Hundred* (January 1983), and Edward J. Blakely and Ted K. Bradshaw, "Rural America: The Community Development Frontier," *Research in Rural Sociology and Development* vol. 2 (1985): pp. 3–29.
19. Frederic O. Sargent, "An Economic Model of Rural-Agricultural Sectors," *Growth and Equity in Agricultural Development* (Proceedings of the Eighteenth International Conference of Agricultural Economists, Jakarta, Indonesia, 1982, published in 1983).
20. Joseph Doherty, "The Out-of-Towners," *Planning* (November 1987): p. 10.
21. John Herbers, "Take Me Home, Country Roads," *Planning* (November 1987): p. 4.

22. Ibid., p. 5.

23. Ibid., pp. 5–6.

24. Edward T. Ward, "Rural and Small Town Planning in a New Era," unpublished paper presented at the American Collegiate Schools of Planning Conference, Los Angeles, California, November 1987.

25. Ibid., p. 4 and 7.

CHAPTER 3

1. John Dewey, *Experience and Nature,* cited in John Friedmann, *Planning in the Public Domain: From Knowledge to Action* (Princeton: Princeton University Press, 1987), p. 189.

2. For a discussion of the permit system as a substitute for zoning, see Frederic O. Sargent and Blaine P. Sargent, *Rural Water Planning* (South Burlington, Vermont: Vervana Press, 1979), p. 50.

CHAPTER 4

1. Frederic O. Sargent, "Public Goals and the Planning Process" (University of Vermont, Agricultural Experiment Station, 1971).

2. Rick Saunders, "A Quality Environment Plan for Henniker, New Hampshire, 1975," masters thesis, Department of Resource Economics, University of Vermont, Burlington.

3. "Village of San Ysidro de los Dolores, Sandoval County, New Mexico: A Handbook of Issues, Opinions, Choices for the Future" (Albuquerque: Summary publication of student research projects in Rural Planning Studio, Community and Regional Planning Program, School of Architecture and Planning, University of New Mexico, June 1985).

CHAPTER 5

1. Frederic O. Sargent, "The Resource Allocation Process: A Distinguishing Characteristic of Land Economics," *Land Economics* vol. 40, no. 3 (August 1964).

2. See Miguel A. Altieri, *Agroecology: The Scientific Basis of Alternative Agriculture* (Berkeley: Division of Biological Control, University of California, 1983); William Lockeretz, *Sustaining Agriculture near Cities* (Ankeny, Iowa: Soil and Water Conservation Society, 1987); and Bill Mollison, *Permaculture: A Designers' Manual* (Tyalgum, Australia: Tagari Publications, 1988).

3. James H. Mann, "Information-Education Approach to Improve Water Supply Quality," masters thesis, University of Vermont, 1974.

4. David Lujan, "Natural Resource Needs Assessment Report" (Albuquerque, New Mexico: Tonantzin Land Institute, 1988).

5. "Community Development Plan for Chama and Surrounding Area" (Albuquerque: Design and Planning Assistance Center, University of New Mexico, 1980).

CHAPTER 6

1. Frederic O. Sargent and Justin H. Brande, "Classifying and Evaluating Natural Areas for Planning Purposes," *Journal of Soil and Water Conservation,* vol. 31, no. 8 (June 1976): pp. 113–16.
2. For more information on methods to ensure scientific objectivity and to insulate against challenge by alternative scientific opinion, see John Clark's landmark work, *The Sanibel Report: Formulation of a Comprehensive Plan Based on Natural Systems* (Washington, D.C.: Conservation Foundation, 1976), summarized in Judith de Neufville, ed., *Land Use Policy Debate in the United States* (New York: Plenum Press, 1981).
3. New England Natural Areas Project, Vermont Natural Resources Council, Montpelier, Vermont, 1971.
4. Duane D. Barber and Donald A. Bourdon, "Proposed Quality Environment Plan for Ferrisburg Vermont" (Department of Resource Economics, University of Vermont, 1972).
5. Frederic O. Sargent, "Camels Hump Park: A Proposal to Keep a Promise to a Mountain" (Resources Research Center, University of Vermont, October 1967).

CHAPTER 7

1. South Dakota Codified Laws, Section 47–9A-3 (1974).
2. Techniques adapted and updated from Frederic O. Sargent, "Alternative Methods for Keeping Land in Agriculture," *Journal of the Northeastern Agricultural Economics Council,* vol. 2, no. 2 (October 1973).
3. Robert D. Yaro, Randall G. Arendt, Harry L. Dotson, and Elizabeth A. Brabec, *Dealing with Change in the Connecticut River Valley: A Design Manual for Conservation and Development* (Cambridge, Massachusetts: Lincoln Institute of Land Policy, 1988), p. 169.
4. For additional information on and examples of the application of transferable development rights, see Linda A. Malone, "The Future of Transferable Development Rights in the Supreme Court," *Kentucky Law Journal* 73 (1985): pp. 759–93, and Myre L. Duncan, "Toward a Theory of Broad-Based Planning for the Preservation of Agricultural Land," *Natural Resources Journal* 24 (January 1984): pp. 121–29.
5. "Tax Stabilization Contracts" (Montpelier, Vermont: Vermont Tax Department, 1972).
6. James G. Ahl and Gordon Bachman, *Land Economics,* vol. 54, no. 2 (May 1973).
7. See *Growing Our Own Jobs: A Small Town Guide to Creating Jobs through Agricultural Diversification* (Washington, D.C.: National Association of Towns and Townships, 1988).
8. Robert E. Coughlin and John C. Keene, eds., "The Protection of Farmland: A

Reference Guidebook for State and Local Governments" (Amherst, Massachusetts: Regional Science Research Institute, 1981), pp. 281–84.

9. Example from Anita P. Miller, "Keeping Them on the Farm in New Mexico: Innovative Ideas for the Preservation of Agricultural Land" (Albuquerque: Potter and Kelly Law Firm, March 1987).

10. Ibid.

11. "Town of Mesilla Master Plan Update" (Mesilla, New Mexico, November 18, 1987).

12. Letter from Ken White, town of Mesilla planner, to Dr. William Stevens, secretary of the New Mexico Department of Agriculture, February 23, 1987.

13. Ibid.

14. Ibid.

CHAPTER 8

1. See *Water in the West*, vol. 1, *What Indian Water Means to the West;* vol. 2, *Water for the Energy Market;* and vol. 3, *Western Water Flows to the Cities* (Santa Fe: Western Network, 1988).

2. This system of indices was developed by Philip Berke and Frederic O. Sargent of the University of Vermont.

3. This section was adapted from F. O. Sargent and Frank J. Zayac, "Index of Lake Basin Land Use for Land Use Planning Purposes," *Water Resources Bulletin* 13 (1977): pp. 365–72.

4. Peter Warshall, *Septic Tank Practices* (Garden City, New York: Anchor Press, 1979).

5. Sargent and Zayac, "Lake Basin Land Use."

6. Robert Ward, "The Granite Lake Study: A Water-Related Land Use Plan" (Concord, New Hampshire: New Hampshire Office of State Planning in Cooperation with the Granite Lake Association, July 1972).

7. Don Meals, "Seymour Lake Watershed Plan," masters thesis, University of Vermont, Department of Resource Economics, 1977.

8. Sanilogical Sewage Treatment Plants, Sanilogical Corporation, Denver, Colorado.

9. Solar Aquaculture Wastewater Treatment Plant, Hercules, California.

10. Sim Van der Ryn, *The Toilet Papers* (Santa Barbara, California: Capra Press, 1978).

CHAPTER 9

1. Frederic O. Sargent, "A Critique of Floodplain Planning in the Connecticut River Basin," *Journal of the Northeastern Agricultural Economics Council,* vol. 4, no. 1 (1975).

2. David F. Lamont, "A Plan for the Winooski River," masters thesis, University of Vermont, Burlington, 1978.

3. Project sponsors at the University of New Mexico were the Natural Resources

Center, the Southwest Hispanic Research Institute, and the Native American Studies Center.

4. "The Course of Upper Rio Grande Waters: A Declaration of Concerns" (Albuquerque: The Upper Rio Grande Working Group, University of New Mexico, 1985).

5. "Upper Rio Grande Waters: Strategies" (Albuquerque: proceedings of a conference on traditional water use, University of New Mexico, 1987).

CHAPTER 10

1. "Shelburne, Vermont, Quality Environment Plan" (University of Vermont: Department of Resource Economics, 1973).

2. Frederic O. Sargent, "A Scenery Classification System," *Journal of Soil and Water Conservation*, vol. 21, no. 1 (1966).

3. Frederic O. Sargent, "New Approaches to Rural Recreation Planning," *Journal of the Northeastern Agricultural Economics Council*, vol. 5, no. 1 (1976).

4. Credit goes to Randolph T. Hester, Jr., and Marcia J. McNally, "Protecting Rural Landscapes and Lifestyles from Tourism" (University of California at Berkeley: Department of Landscape Architecture, September 1983).

5. Randolph T. Hester and Marcia J. McNally, "Manteo, North Carolina, Avoids the Perils of Boom-or-Bust Tourism," *Small Town*, vol. 14, no. 3 (1983): p. 4.

6. Hester and McNally, "Protecting Rural Landscapes," p. 3.

7. Ibid., p. 6.

8. Randolph T. Hester, "Subconscious Landscapes of the Heart," *Places*, vol. 2, no. 3 (1985): pp. 13–14.

9. Hester and McNally, "Protecting Rural Landscapes," p. 13.

CHAPTER 11

1. See Mark Francis et al., *Community Open Spaces; Greening Neighborhoods through Community Action and Land Conservation* (Washington, D.C.: Island Press, 1984).

2. Frederic O. Sargent, "Social Impact Analysis for Water Resource Projects" (University of Vermont: Agricultural Experiment Station, research report no. 42, January 1985).

3. Adapted from Frederic O. Sargent, "Town Plan Analysis System," *Journal of the Northeastern Agricultural Economics Council*, vol. 4, no. 2 (October 1975).

CHAPTER 12

1. *The Oxford English Dictionary*, 2d ed. (London: Oxford University Press, 1989).

2. Frederic O. Sargent, "A Resource Economist Views a Natural Area," *Journal of Soil and Water Conservation*, vol. 24, no. 1 (1969): pp. 8–11.

3. Frederic O. Sargent, "Growth and Decline of Rural Towns: A Proposed Model" (University of Vermont: Agricultural Experiment Station, research report no. 17, 1982).

4. Frederic O. Sargent and Blaine P. Sargent, *Rural Water Planning* (South Burlington, Vermont: Vervana Press, 1979), p. 182.

5. See "Depressed Rural Towns Develop Jobs from within as Industrial Lures Fail," *Wall Street Journal*, August 4, 1988.

6. See John Herbers, "Take Me Home, Country Roads," *Planning* (November 1987).

7. See *Golden v. Planning Board of the Town of Ramapo*, Court of Appeals of New York, 1972, 30 N.Y. 2d 359, 285 N.E. 2d 291.

8. Ibid.

9. From "Environmental Assessment: Proposed Amendment to Zoning Local Law, Town of Ramapo, New York, May 6, 1983," p. 1.

10. Personal correspondence with Joan Weissman, deputy administrative assistant to boards and commissions, town of Ramapo, Suffern, New York, July 1989.

11. Matthew Witten, "State Ruling Prompts Golf Course Debate," *Vermont Business Magazine* (January 1989); and interview with Kristin Juergens, Sherman Hollow Association, February 10, 1989.

12. Robert Healy, *Land Use and The States* (Baltimore: Johns Hopkins Press, 1976), pp. 64–102.

13. Ibid., pp. 103–38.

14. Articles by George Hatch, Talahassee bureau, and Craig Pittman, staff writer, Sarasota, Florida, *Herald-Tribune*, March 5, 1989.

CHAPTER 13

1. Paul L. Pryde, "Human Capacity and Local Development Enterprise," in *Expanding the Opportunity to Produce: Revitalizing the American Economy through New Enterprise Development*, Robert Friedman and William Schweke, eds. (Baltimore: The Corporation for Enterprise Development, 1981), p. 523.

2. *Wall Street Journal*, August 4, 1988.

3. Al Shapero, "Entrepreneurship," *Proceedings of the Community Economic Development Strategies Conference* (Iowa State University: North Central Regional Center for Rural Development, 1983), p. 132.

4. An earlier version of this case example appeared in Sara K. Gould and Jing Lyman, "A Working Guide to Women's Self-Employment" (Washington, D.C.: The Corporation for Enterprise Development, February 1987).

5. An earlier version of this case example appeared in *Growing Our Own Jobs: A Small Town Guide to Creating Jobs through Agricultural Diversification* (Washington, D.C.: National Association of Towns and Townships, 1988).

6. An earlier version of this case example appeared in Shanna Ratner and Peter Ide, "Strategies for Community Economic Development through Natural Resource Use in Northern New York" (Ithaca: Cornell University, Agricultural Experiment Station, A. E. res. 85-10, May 1985).

7. Kentucky Highlands Investment Corporation survey, cited in Pryde, "Human Capacity," p. 522.
8. Han Singer, cited in Pryde, "Human Capacity," p. 522.
9. Charles Kindelberger, cited in Pryde, "Human Capacity," p. 522.
10. Pryde, "Human Capacity," p. 522–23.
11. An earlier version of this case example appeared in Yin-May Lee, *The Workbook* vol. 14, no. 1 (Albuquerque: Southwest Research and Information Center, January/March 1989). Yin-May Lee is a member of the Ramah Navajo Weavers Association.
12. Mention should be made that one of the REP co-authors, María Varela, helped to found Ganados del Valle and the subsequent projects described in the case study.

CHAPTER 14

1. U.S. Department of Commerce, Bureau of the Census, *Number of Inhabitants: United States Summary, 1980.*
2. U.S. Department of Commerce, Bureau of the Census, *County Population Estimates, July 1988,* series P-26, no. 884 (August 1989).
3. John R. Van Ness, "Hispanic Land Grants: Ecology and Subsistence in the Uplands of Northern New Mexico and Southern Colorado," in Charles L. Briggs and John R. Van Ness, eds., *Land, Water, and Culture: New Perspectives on Hispanic Land Grants* (Albuquerque: University of New Mexico Press, 1987).
4. "Community Development Plan for the Village of Chama and Surrounding Area" (Albuquerque: University of New Mexico, Design and Planning Assistance Center, 1980).
5. For the experiment in Oregon, see editorial in the *Albuquerque Tribune,* June 6, 1989. For reports on time-controlled uses of rangelands in South America, Africa, and elsewhere, see Allan Savory, *Holistic Resource Management* (Washington, D.C.: Island Press, 1988).
6. Donald Dale Jackson, "Around Los Ojos, Sheep and Land Are Fighting Words," *Smithsonian* (April 1991), pp. 37–47.

CHAPTER 15

1. See Arnold W. Reitze, Jr., "Environmental Planning: Law of Land and Resources," *North American International* (1974).
2. *Nollan v. the California Coastal Commission,* 107 S. Ct. at 3141 (1987).
3. Id. at 3142.
4. Id. at 3143.
5. Id. at 3151.
6. In his dissent, Justice Blackmun expounded on the majority "nexus" requirement, stating that land-use problems cannot be advanced by the majorities' "eye for an eye mentality . . . which imposes a rigid, close nexus between

benefits and burdens created by development and a condition imposed pursuant to a state's police power" (id. at 3162).

7. *Loretto v. Teleprompter Manhattan CATV Corporation,* 458 U.S. 419 (1982).

8. *Nollan,* at 3142.

9. Richard F. Babcock, ed., *Law and Contemporary Problems* (Durham, North Carolina: School of Law, Duke University), vol. 50 (Winter 1987), Foreword p. 1.

10. Robert K. Best, "New Constitutional Standards for Land Use Regulation; Portents of Nollan and First English Church," *Proceedings of the Institute on Planning, Zoning and Eminent Domain* (New York: Matthew Bender, 1988), 6.1/.25.

11. See generally Smith, "From Subdivision Improvement Requirements to Community Benefit Assessments and Linkage Payments: A Brief History of Land Development Exactions" 50, *Law and Contemporary Problems* 5–6 (1987): *The Constitutionality of Subdivision Control Exactions: The Quest For A Rationale* 52 Cornell L.Q. 871 (1967).

12. Best, at 10.

13. *First English Evangelical Lutheran Church of Glendale v. the County of Los Angeles,* 107 S. Ct. 2378, 2381 (1987).

14. Id. at 2389.

15. Id. at 2389.

16. Review of and input into this chapter by Susan L. McMichael of the University of New Mexico's School of Law are much appreciated.

Additional Readings

CHAPTER 1

Bradshaw, Ted K., and Edward J. Blakeley. *Rural Communities in Advanced Industrial Society.* New York: Praeger, 1979.

Browne, William P., and Don F. Hadwiger, eds. *Rural Policy Problems: Changing Dimensions.* Lexington, Massachusetts: D.C. Heath, 1982.

Carlson, John E., Marie L. Lassey, and William R. Lassey. *Rural Society and Environment in America.* New York: McGraw-Hill, 1981.

Getzels, Judith, and Charles Thurow, eds. *Rural and Small Town Planning.* Chicago: Planners Press, American Planning Association, 1979.

Lapping, Mark B., Thomas L. Daniels, and John W. Keller. *Rural Planning and Development in the United States.* New York: Guilford Press, 1989.

Lassey, William R. *Planning in Rural Environments.* New York: McGraw-Hill, 1977.

CHAPTER 2

Benevolo, Leonardo. *The Origins of Modern Town Planning.* London: Routledge and Kegan Paul, 1967.

Howard, Ebenezer. *Garden Cities.* Cambridge: M.I.T. Press, 1965. First published as *Tomorrow: A Peaceful Path to Real Reform.* London: S. Sonnenschein, 1898.

McHarg, Ian. *Design with Nature.* Garden City, New York: Doubleday/Natural History Press, 1969.

Lapping, Mark B., Thomas L. Daniels, and John W. Keller. *Rural Planning and Development in the United States.* New York: Guilford Press, 1989.

Longacre, William A., ed. *Reconstructing Prehistoric Pueblo Societies.* Albuquerque: University of New Mexico Press, 1970.

241

Van Ness, John R., and Christine M. Van Ness, eds. "Spanish and Mexican Land Grants in New Mexico and Colorado." Special issue of *Journal of the West* (July 1980).

CHAPTER 3

Daniels, Thomas L., and John W. Keller, with Mark B. Lapping. *The Small Town Planning Handbook*. Chicago: Planners Press, American Planning Association, 1988.
Swanson, Bert E., Richard A. Cohen, and Edith P. Swanson. *Small Towns and Small Towners: A Framework for Survival and Growth*. Beverly Hills: Sage Publishers, 1979.

CHAPTER 4

Daniels, Thomas L., and John W. Keller, with Mark B. Lapping. *The Small Town Planning Handbook*. Chicago: Planners Press, American Planning Association, 1988.

CHAPTER 5

Agriculture, Food and Human Values (previously *Agriculture and Human Values*). Quarterly publication, College of Agriculture, University of Florida, Gainesville.
Ekins, Paul, ed. *The Living Economy: A New Economics in the Making*. New York: Routledge and Kegan Paul, 1986.
Kneese, Allen V., and F. Lee Brown. *The Southwest under Stress: Natural Resource Development Issues in a Regional Setting*. Baltimore: John Hopkins Press for Resources for the Future, 1981.
New Directions in Rural Preservation. Preservation Planning series no. 45. Heritage Conservation and Recreation Service. U.S. Department of Interior. Washington, D.C.: U.S. Government Printing Office.
Robinson, Gordon. *The Forest and the Trees: A Guide to Excellent Forestry*. Washington, D.C.: Island Press, 1988.
Savory, Allan. *Holistic Resource Management*. Washington, D.C.: Island Press, 1988.
Star, Jeffrey and John Estes. *Geographic Information Systems: An Introduction*. Englewood Cliffs, New Jersey: Prentice Hall, 1990.

CHAPTER 7

AgAccess: Agricultural Source Book. Davis, California.
Altieri, Miguel A. *Agroecology: The Scientific Basis of Alternative Agriculture*. Berkeley: Division of Biological Control, University of California, 1983.
The Community Land Trust Handbook. Emmaus, Pennsylvania: Rodale Press, The Institute for Community Economics, 1982.

Healy, Robert G., and James L. Short. *The Market for Rural Land: Trends, Issues, Policies.* Washington, D.C.: Conservation Foundation, 1981.

Lockeretz, William. *Sustaining Agriculture near Cities.* Ankeny, Iowa: Soil and Water Conservation Society, 1987.

Mollison, Bill. *Permaculture: A Designers' Manual.* Tyalgum, Australia: Tagari Publications, 1988.

Steiner, Frederick. *Ecological Planning for Farmlands Preservation.* Chicago: Planners Press, American Planning Association, 1981.

CHAPTER 8

Getches, David H. *Water Law in a Nutshell.* St. Paul, Minnesota: West Publishing, 1984.

Sargent, Frederic O., and Blaine P. Sargent, *Rural Water Planning.* South Burlington, Vermont: Vervana Press, 1979.

Sheaffer, John R., and Leonard A. Stevens. *Future Water: An Exciting Solution to America's Most Serious Resource Crisis.* New York: William Morrow, 1983.

Worster, Donald. *Rivers of Empire: Water, Aridity and the Growth of the American West.* New York: Pantheon Books, 1985.

CHAPTER 9

Briggs, Charles L., and John R. Van Ness, eds. *Land, Water and Culture: New Perspectives on Hispanic Land Grants.* Albuquerque: University of New Mexico Press, 1987.

Brown, F. Lee, and Helen M. Ingram. *Water and Poverty in the Southwest.* Tucson: University of Arizona Press, 1987.

DuMars, Charles T., Marilyn O'Leary, and Albert E. Utton. *Pueblo Indian Water Rights: Struggle for a Precious Resource.* Tucson: University of Arizona Press, 1984.

Smith, Zachary A., ed. *Water and the Future of the Southwest.* Albuquerque: University of New Mexico Press, 1989.

Yaro, Robert D., Randall G. Arendt, Harry L. Dodson, and Elizabeth A. Brabec. *Dealing with Change in the Connecticut River Valley: A Design Manual for Conservation and Development.* Cambridge, Massachusetts: Lincoln Institute of Land Policy, 1988.

CHAPTER 10

Alderson, William T., and Shirley Payne Low. *Interpretation of Historic Sites.* Nashville, Tennessee: American Association for State and Local History, 1976.

Barker, James F., Michael J. Buono, and Henry P. Hildebrandt. *The Small Town Designbook.* Mississippi State University: School of Architecture, Mississippi State University, 1981.

Francis, Mark, Lisa Cashdan, and Lynn Paxson. *Community Open Spaces: Green*

Neighborhoods through Community Action and Land Conservation. Washington, D.C.: Island Press, 1984.

Hester, Randolph T., Jr. "Landstyles and Lifescapes: 12 Steps to Community Development." *Landscape Architecture* (January 1985).

"Historic Preservation in Small Communities." *Small Town,* vol. 5, no. 9 (March 1975).

Long, Patrick T., Lawrence Allen, Richard R. Perdue, and Scott Kieselbach. "Recreation Systems Development in Rural Communities: A Planning Process." *American Planning Association Journal* (summer 1988): pp. 373–76.

Morrison, Charles C. "The Plan for the Future of the Lake George Park." Albany: New York State Department of Environmental Conservation, 1987.

"Preparing an Historic Preservation Ordinance." Planning advisory service report 374. Chicago: American Planning Association, 1982.

Ziegler, Arthur P., and Walter C. Kidney. *Historic Preservation in Small Towns.* Nashville, Tennessee: American Association for State and Local History, 1980.

CHAPTER 11

Fuerst, J. S., ed. *Public Housing in Europe and America.* New York: John Wiley, 1974.

Johnson, Wayne H., ed. *Rural Human Services: A Book of Readings.* Itasca, Illinois: F. E. Peacock, 1980.

Midgley, James, and David Piachaud, eds. *The Fields and Methods of Social Planning.* New York: St. Martin's Press, 1984.

CHAPTER 12

Brower, David J., C. Carroway, T. Pollard, and C. L. Propst. *Managing Development in Small Towns.* Chicago: Planners Press, American Planning Association, 1985.

Cole, Barbara A. *Business Opportunities Casebook.* Snowmass, Colorado: Rocky Mountain Institute, 1988.

Ekins, Paul. *The Living Economy: A New Economics in the Making.* New York: Routledge and Kegan Paul, 1986.

Henderson, Hazel. *The Politics of the Solar Age: Alternatives to Economics.* New York: Doubleday, 1981.

Malizia, Emil E. "Economic Development in Smaller Cities and Rural Areas." *American Planning Association Journal* (Autumn 1986): pp. 489–99.

Rural Economic Development in the 1980's: Preparing for the Future. Washington, D.C.: USDA, Economic Research Service, 1987.

Salant, Priscilla. *A Community Researcher's Guide to Rural Data.* Washington, D.C.: Island Press, 1990.

Woodruff, Archibald M., ed. *The Farm and the City: Rivals or Allies?* Englewood Cliffs, New Jersey: Prentice-Hall, 1980.

Zimmerman, Erich W. *World Resources and Industries*. New York: Harper and Brothers, 1933 and 1951.

CHAPTER 13

Galtung, Johan, Peter O'Brien, and Roy Preiswerk, eds. *Self-Reliance: A Strategy for Development*. London: Bogle-L'Ouverture, 1980.

Ekins, Paul. *The Living Economy: A New Economics in the Making*. London: Routledge and Kegan Paul, 1986.

Henderson, Hazel. *The Politics of the Solar Age: Alternatives to Economics*. Garden City, New York: Anchor Press, Doubleday, 1981.

Osborne, David. *Laboratories of Democracy*. Boston: Harvard Business School Press, 1988.

Van Dresser, Peter. *A Landscape for Humans: A Case Study of the Potentials for Ecologically Guided Development in an Uplands Region*. Albuquerque, New Mexico: Biotechnic Press, 1972.

CHAPTER 15

Best, Robert K. "New Constitutional Standards for Land Use Regulation: Portents of Nolan and First English Church." Southwest Legal Foundation, *Proceedings of the Institute on Planning, Zoning and Eminent Domain*, 1988, 6.1–.25. New York: Matthew Bender, 1988.

Bryant, R. W. G. *Land, Private Property, Public Control*. Montreal: Harvest House, 1972.

Landau, Norman J., and Paul D. Rheingold. *The Environmental Law Handbook*. New York: Ballantine/Friends of the Earth, 1971.

Moss, Elaine, ed. *Land Use Controls in the United States: A Handbook on the Legal Rights of Citizens*. New York: Dial Press, 1977.

Rose, Jerome G. *Legal Foundations of Land Use Planning*. New Brunswick: Center for Urban Policy Research, Rutgers, The State University of New Jersey, 1979.

Wright, Robert R., and Susan Webber. *Land Use in a Nutshell*. St. Paul: West Publishing, 1978.

About the Authors

FREDERIC O. SARGENT studied at the universities of Mexico, Paris, and Wisconsin, earning a Ph.D. in land economics at the latter. He taught at the universities of Colorado State, Texas A. & M., Guelph, Ontario, and Vermont. At Vermont he was Chairman of the Department of Resource Economics, director of the University Resources Research Center, and head of the masters program in Rural Planning. He has published four books on rural planning and has supervised development of thirty land-use plans. He has served on planning commissions in Fort Collins, Colorado; Guelph, Ontario; and South Burlington, Vermont. Professor Sargent is now a planning consultant specializing in lake watershed planning.

PAUL LUSK, AICP, Associate Professor in Architecture and Planning at the University of New Mexico, teaches courses in site, environmental, water- and energy-conservative design and graduate professional practice studios in rural environmental planning, community, and urban design. He has twenty-eight years professional experience in neighborhood, village, pueblo, city, and comprehensive regional planning in New Mexico, Massachusetts, and Pennsylvania. For the past twenty years he has conducted independent research in small-scale, intensive farming, animal and aquaculture production, wildlife habitat enhancement, and environmentally sustainable community development.

JOSÉ A. RIVERA is Associate Professor of Public Administration at the University of New Mexico where he teaches seminars on Rural Community Development, Social Policy and Planning, and The Practice of Policy Development. He also serves as the Associate Director for Latin American Programs and teaches rural development courses to graduate students from Central and South America. Formerly he was

Executive Director of the Home Education Livelihood Program, Inc., a statewide community development corporation in New Mexico. In addition to his teaching assignment at the university, he presently serves as the Director of the Southwest Hispanic Research Institute, an interdisciplinary research unit.

MARÍA VARELA is a rural planner and community organizer who has, since 1963, worked with African-American, Mexican-American, and Native-American rural communities organizing toward economic, political, and social empowerment. She is also an Adjunct Professor of Community and Regional Planning in the School of Architecture and Planning at the University of New Mexico. In 1990 she was the recipient of a MacArthur Foundation Fellowship for her life's work, including her participation in the founding of Ganados del Valle, a private not-for-profit economic development corporation in northern New Mexico featured as a case study in this book.

Index

ALSO AVAILABLE
FROM ISLAND PRESS

Ancient Forests of the Pacific Northwest
By Elliott A. Norse

Balancing on the Brink of Extinction: The Endangered Species Act and Lessons for the Future
Edited by Kathryn A. Kohm

Better Trout Habitat: A Guide to Stream Restoration and Management
By Christopher J. Hunter

Beyond 40 Percent: Record-Setting Recycling and Composting Programs
The Institute for Local Self-Reliance

The Challenge of Global Warming
Edited by Dean Edwin Abrahamson

Coastal Alert: Ecosystems, Energy, and Offshore Oil Drilling
By Dwight Holing

The Complete Guide to Environmental Careers
The CEIP Fund

Economics of Protected Areas
By John A. Dixon and Paul B. Sherman

Environmental Agenda for the Future
Edited by Robert Cahn

Environmental Disputes: Community Involvement in Conflict Resolution
By James F. Crowfoot and Julia M. Wondolleck

Forests and Forestry in China: Changing Patterns of Resource Development
By S. D. Richardson

The Global Citizen
By Donella Meadows

Hazardous Waste from Small Quantity Generators
By Seymour I. Schwartz and Wendy B. Pratt

Holistic Resource Management Workbook
By Allan Savory

In Praise of Nature
Edited and with essays by Stephanie Mills

The Living Ocean: Understanding and Protecting Marine Biodiversity
By Boyce Thorne-Miller and John G. Catena

Natural Resources for the 21st Century
Edited by R. Neil Sampson and Dwight Hair

The New York Environment Book
By Eric A. Goldstein and Mark A. Izeman

For a complete catalog of Island Press publications, please write:
Island Press, Box 7, Covelo, CA 95428, or call: 1–800–828–1302